JOURNALISM
FOR THE
21st CENTURY

JOURNALISM
FOR THE
21st CENTURY

Online Information,
Electronic Databases,
and the News

TOM KOCH

PRAEGER

New York
Westport, Connecticut
London

For
John Schidlovsky
and
Lenore Magida,
colleagues
who became
friends

Library of Congress Cataloging-in-Publication Data

Koch, Tom.
    Journalism for the 21st century : online information, electronic
databases, and the news / Tom Koch.
        p.   cm.
    Includes bibliographical references and index.
    ISBN 0-275-93820-4 (alk. paper)
    1. Electronic news gathering.   2. Data bases.   3. Information
storage and retrieval systems—Newspapers.   I. Title.   II. Title:
Journalism for the twenty-first century.
    PN4784.E53K63   1991b
    070.1′9—dc20   90-47332

British Library Cataloguing in Publication Data is available.

A hardcover edition of *Journalism for the 21st Century* is available from the
Greenwood Press imprint of Greenwood Publishing Group, Inc. (ISBN 0-313-27750-8)

Library of Congress Catalog Card Number: 90-47332
ISBN: 0-275-93820-4

First published in 1991

Praeger Publishers, One Madison Avenue, New York, NY   10010
An imprint of Greenwood Publishing Group, Inc.

Printed in the United States of America

The paper used in this book complies with the
Permanent Paper Standard issued by the National
Information Standards Organization (Z39.48-1984).

10 9 8 7 6 5 4 3 2 1

The function of the press in society is to inform, but its role is to make money.

A.J. Liebling, *The Press*

The problem of journalism in America proceeds from a simple but inescapable bind: journalists are rarely, if ever, in a position to establish the truth about an issue for themselves, and they are therefore almost entirely dependent on self-interested "sources" for the version of reality that they report.

Edward Jay Epstein, *Between Fact and Fiction: The Problem of Journalism*

The true inquiry is the developed truth, whose scattered parts are assembled in the result.

Karl Marx, then a reporter for Horace Greeley

The key question of ethics is the relation between the individual's own preferences or interests or valuations and his obligations as a member of various groups or communities.

Joseph Leighton, *The Individual and the Social Order*

We misunderstand the limited nature of news, the illimitable complexity of society; we overestimate our own endurance, public spirit, and all-around competence.

Walter Lippmann, *Public Opinion*

Contents

Illustrations

Acknowledgments

This is a book about public information, about how it is gathered and then presented. Specifically, it is about the news and the effect that electronic databases and online libraries will have on its content. The whole is the work of a professional journalist and sometime academic and thus attempts to walk the rather thin, high wire that separates texts into the categories of, first, practical or "useful" and, second, historical, academic, and analytic. This work follows upon and builds from an earlier book, *The News as Myth: Fact and Context in Journalism*, which described in detail specific problems in contemporary newswriting without attention to the "why," the historical factors that created the problems of fact and context which are critical to the failure of contemporary journalism.

That failure of perspective was impressed upon me at the University of Hawaii, where I was invited to lecture on the issues raised by *The News as Myth*. In a seminar organized by the Department of Geography, both journalists and geographers asked two critical questions for which I had no real answer. While accepting my argument, they wanted to know the origins of the problems outlined and the degree to which new technologies—those based on modern computer links—might adequately redress what most agreed was a powerful imbalance between public author and official source.

This book is my attempt to answer those questions while providing a practical guide to the evolving technologies currently available to all—journalist, writer, corporate employee, advocate, and private citizen—seeking information beyond the ephemeral quote or isolated news brief on virtually any issue.

I certainly would be remiss if I did not acknowledge my gratitude to the participants in that Hawaii seminar, and especially to University of Hawaii geographer Mark Ridgley, who organized the session for me. That he is a friend does not mitigate my debts to him, both for that opportunity and for the time he devoted to criticizing early drafts of this work while instructing me in the basics of information theory.

I am similarly indebted to Ohio State University's Hugh Carter Donahue, whose assistance was invaluable in the early stages of research. His support was the more remarkable because it was given with the cheerful admission that he was neither versed in nor particularly interested in the new technologies of electronic information storage. It is the rare individual who offers help to another from no other motive than the shared spirit of intellectual inquiry.

A number of working journalists also provided me with the benefit of their experiences. Reporters and editors from Toronto, Ontario, to Honolulu, Hawaii, took time from uniformly hectic schedules to talk about the degree to which these new technologies had or had not affected their work and lives. I am especially indebted to Canadian newsman John Daly, of BCTV in Vancouver, B.C. He provided both a sounding board for the arguments developed here and assignments that not only became case studies for this book but also constituted deeply appreciated material support.

Finally, the support and encouragement of the Greenwood Publishing Group requires mention. Greenwood vice-president James Sabin provided encouragement, advice, and a contract as well as allowing me the pleasure of working again with production editor Catherine Lyons.

Grateful as I am to all these people, the responsibility for any errors this book may contain is reserved, of course, for myself alone.

Introduction

This is a book about the news, the way it is written and the forms it takes. Its subject is online information services and how they will affect the narrative form of the individual news story as well as the general context of daily and weekly journalism. The central argument in this text is that the marriage of computers and online libraries creates a radically new technology that will fundamentally alter the relations between writer and news subject. News is used here as a symbol and, at times, a metaphor for the more complex topic of public information, its content and its diffusion. Daily and weekly news reports, disseminated in print and by broadcast are, after all, modern society's primary venue for public information. News is the essential source by which citizens acquire the data they need to make personal and communal choices. Thus, to the extent that an informed electorate is the keystone of a democratic system, any study of contemporary, periodic journalism's perceived strengths or inherent deficiencies will strike directly at the essential structure of North American society, politics, and culture.

What is of interest here is the degree to which contemporary news, and therefore public information in general, is limited by its traditional sources of information and restricted by historical definitions of data and narrative form. The issue is not one of "bad" reportage or "great" writing.

Newswriting is a narrative form with its own rules and assumptions, which guide and limit the work of even the most gifted journalists. Therefore, the examples included in this text were chosen in part because they are representative, neither appreciably better nor demonstrably worse than the majority of largely ephemeral stories that make up the television news hour, metro page, or forty-five-second radio spot.

To the extent that this book can be used as a training manual, it is for the "hacks," "flacks," or "advocates" seeking to place a position or report within the public context. Hack is not used here as a pejorative but to describe those who write using a specific, precisely defined narrative form on the command of editors who choose the subject, dictate its treatment, and decide the story's ultimate length. Flacks are public relations writers whose purpose is to gain the widest possible dissemination for their employer's position and the best possible public exposure for that employer's product. Advocates are those who work for nonprofit, special interest groups and whose aim is to gain public exposure for specific positions or arguments.

All three, working together, make the general media a public forum and are successful to the degree their work appears in newspapers, newsmagazines, or broadcast formats. But separate from issues of production and publication are values brought to the writing of a news story by the reporter, editor, or researcher whose job it is to translate the information provided by flacks, advocates, and other news subjects into newspaper copy, tape, or film suitable for publication or broadcast. These institutional and instrumental goals, which include "objectivity" and "completeness," are reevaluated here within the context of the effect of electronic databases on news as a system of information diffusion and their resulting effect on the media's institutionalized, social role.

People have suggested for years that, in the words of one reporter in the early 1980s, "data bases are going to revolutionize newspaper work"[1] or that "computer-assisted journalism is the new future of this business."[2] "Databases" are electronically stored libraries of journals, reports, newspapers, newsletters, and reference material that can be searched with incredible specificity by a personal computer linked to the database through a modem. Computer-assisted journalism is a more general term describing the use of a wide variety of software—spreadsheets, word processors, data management programs, telecommunications systems, and electronic databases—on a computer terminal. Journalism textbooks currently make a bow to the vague promise of the new technology's revolutionary potential with brief descriptions of the joys of online searching and its potential benefits for reporters and editors.[3] Despite these hopes, none have so far demonstrated how or in what way online databases are to "revolutionize" journalistic output. Although trade and academic publications have carried articles describing the potential importance of online information sources for a number of years, as recently as 1988 astute researchers noted that "as yet, however, little is known about specific benefits and problems which systematically result from using electronic databases for reporting. While trade press articles have followed the trends, their data are largely anecdotal in nature."[4]

"THE SAME OLD JOURNALISM"

One reason for this lack of systematic consideration of the effects of electronic databases on the news may be the widely held but largely unexamined assumption that computer-based research is "just" research, whose effect on the context of the news is and will be minimal. As Philip Meyer, a University of North Carolina journalism professor, put it: "It's the same old journalism but with better tools."[5] The future of the business, in this view, is its past, and any editorial revolution will be not fundamental but incremental, one of efficiency and not of narrative structure. Computers will help organize information and bring data to the reporter, public relations official, or independent researcher, but it is assumed that changes in the medium of research will have no fundamental effect on a story's narrative structure or the writer's point of view. The promised "revolution" is thus immediately reduced to an increase in researcher efficiency that requires no necessary change in the resulting text itself. Thus the majority of articles that have appeared in journalistic publications have offered largely anecdotal examples of how one or another newspaper,[6] reporter,[7] or free-lancer[8] used one or more electronic resources to complete a traditionally defined project or journalistic assignment. Absent from any discussion has been an analysis of the effect of this technology on the structure of the news story itself or the fundamental changes it may bring to the relation between writer, interviewer, or reporter and his or her specific subject. Any critical examination of the potential effect of online information technology must begin with a critical paradigm that presents a context in which their effect in these two areas—the structure of the story as information and the relation between writer and subject—can be understood.

The lack of such a perspective may be why, despite the promises and fanfare, most news and general information providers do not regularly subscribe to electronic libraries and, even when they are used, why intelligent and efficient employment remains relatively rare. A 1987 study of Michigan newspapers[9] found, for example, that 96 percent of those surveyed did not subscribe to any online information service. Reasons given were doubt about both the efficiency and necessity of the technology, reservations concerning the expense of online searching, and, finally, a lack of expertise in the use of online databases on the part of journalists. Even when online information resources are available, they are often not used or are used badly. A 1986 study of newspapers with online access found that few editorial writers used these resources because of a perceived lack of time to do "research" and, perhaps more importantly, unfamiliarity on the part of writers with the technology itself. Only on those newspapers where trained researchers were hired to assist newspeople with online searchs did editorial writers avail themselves of electronic information resources with any frequency.[10] Members of allied fields, including academic journalism, small public relations firms, and advocacy groups focusing on specific issues, are assumed to hold similar reservations, although no studies detailing use in their areas have been found.

Those who do use electronic information services, not surprisingly, tend to be those corporations that can afford to spend a great deal of money for online research and to hire librarians or data specialists to perform online searches for general staff members. Thus the use of online resources has been concentrated in major newspapers,[11] large corporations,[12] and government agencies.[13] If these are only expensive conveniences, one would expect their use to be dominated by large and wealthy corporations that can afford the perhaps useful but structurally unnecessary service. One study of newspaper use of computer databases described the mean circulation of users as 358,798 readers with a median circulation of 283,845 readers.[14] In this user category, acceptance of online technologies has been both extensive and expensive. In 1987, for example, the *Washington Post* newspaper spent more than thirty thousand dollars a month on computerized information[15] and, as early as 1983, a *Washington Post* reporter used one thousand dollars of computer time in one month to research a book on U.S. foreign policy in the Persian Gulf.[16]

Smaller organizations have tended to shy away from electronic research when faced with the promise of similarly enormous bills and no compelling argument for their use in turning out "the same old journalism." Indeed, one suspects that the glowing reports of some who advocate the use of online electronic resources may have been a deterrent to others concerned about budgets. For example, it is all very well for former *Washington Post* reporter Scott Armstrong, now the executive director of the National Security Archives, to extoll the virtues of online resources and their efficiency. He praised the economies achieved through spending thirteen hundred dollars on a computer search that quickly yielded a wealth of data and leads which would have taken a team of reporters months to duplicate by traditional methods.[17] But first an organization has to be able to budget thirteen hundred dollars for a computer search and then must have the staff and other resources to follow those electronically generated leads through the process of interview and editorial review to a publishable conclusion. The majority of newspapers, businesses, and advocacy groups lack the staff to pursue a months-long investigation and cannot—or do not believe they can—afford search bills of more than one thousand dollars for a single story.[18]

Another argument, based on published reports of electronic database use, is that the results obtained are often not only expensive but also inconclusive or trivial. In 1983, when Storer Broadcasting Company's San Diego station KCST-TV signed up on *Nexis* database, employees ran up almost five thousand dollars worth of charges in the first month.[19] No Pulitzer or critical exposé resulted from that research. The bill represented, instead, experimentation by staff members—the costly "learning curve" of a new technology. At most newspapers, magazines, broadcast stations, and firms where I've been employed, a five thousand dollar research bill (excluding library overhead, librarian training costs and monthly service charges for the service itself) for anything but the guaranteed date of Judgment Day (and the promise of advance interviews with both Archangel Gabriel and Saint Peter) would have been unthinkable. Finally, where databases have been used extensively, the results often have been trivial and expensive simultaneously. For most editors, reporters, writers, and researchers, the potential benefits are not outweighed by the cost of online searches (and the time required to learn their use), and "the same old journalism" is done the same old way by most writers and reporters today. Although one can, as Tom McNichol suggests, write a nice story about individuals who have bequeathed their heads for us in theatrical productions of Hamlet by asking a database to find all published stories including the words *skull* and *Hamlet*, most editors for whom I've worked would balk at the resulting research bill.[20] To spend twelve hundred dollars, as did *National Journal* writer Burt Soloman, to discover that Henry Kissinger was quoted 10,187 times in 1987 would be seen as a needless expense by most local TV and radio news managers.[21] One suspects most city editors would also hesitate to approve that large a bill for so trivial a featured "fact."

valuation is not value-free, and to understand the role of electronic information in the news, the assumptions of public information and its disseminating organs must also be addressed.

News is simultaneously a public service, protected in the United States by the Fourth Amendment to the Constitution, a highly profitable business, a public trust, and a complex of individuals working for pay at specific trades (photographers, press operators, editors, reporters, editorialists, etc.). It promises, in theory, "objectivity," "fairness," "completeness," "skepticism," and at least minimal completeness in its treatment of any single event or issue. None of these goals can, at present, be quantified with any precision. Simultaneously, news as a business must pay investors a satisfactory return and employees a salary while satisfying the demands of advertisers whose financial support is necessary for any newspaper, magazine, or broadcast station's continuance. A.J. Liebling summed up the tensions nicely when he stated that "The function of the press in society is to inform, but its role is to make money."[30] Thus news presents a complex of conflicting and often ill-defined objectives within a context of social expectations unrelated to very specific financial goals and needs.

Tensions between the role and the function of the news are set in sharp relief when the issue of a new technology is introduced. The potential benefits these electronic databases offer are weighed by news managers against the apparent costs of the database system's introduction and use. Issues of cost and efficiency are discussed here within the context of the more complex issue of the relation between a new technology and information diffusion. For one to understand the effect of these electronic resources upon news writing, it is not enough simply to demonstrate that information can be obtained or that it can be obtained more efficiently with these tools. In relation to the form and content of the news, the critical issue these electronic resources raise is the degree to which they enhance or impede what might be called the "minimal completeness and objectivity" criterion by which newspeople judge their own performance. This work attempts to advance a theoretical position

Finally, there has been a concern that use of these resources will take too much time and, in the slash and burn of dead-line journalism, may slow down newswriters who, by definition, need to be fast. As one managing editor told Fredric F. Endres: "A key question beyond the depth of research these services offer is whether reporters will have the time and inclination to use them. I also wonder whether access to that much information won't slow down the news-gathering process and bury the reporter in data."[22]

Lack of use thus seems to be based on legitimate concerns in which cost is weighed against potential benefits. Most writers, reporters, and public relations professionals do not use these databases because they are perceived as too expensive and, even when they are available, many will not use them because they don't know how. Further, since their main advantage is one of efficiency and they are not perceived as necessarily affecting narrative content, many professionals prefer to do their research by traditional methods without the added cost of electronic searching. If journalism is "now" and "facts," the story need not be "buried" in reams of background data which electronic sources are presumed to provide.

These practical reservations are further complicated by the rapid growth of both available data bases, each of which provides more or less specialized information in a single area, and data vendors who package and sell those bibliographic resources to the public. A single database like *Disclosure*, for example, which provides information from Securities and Exchange Commission filings by public corporations, is offered by a number of vendors including Dow Jones News Retrieval, CompuServe, Dialog, and BRS. In addition, each retail-level vendor typically has a unique pricing structure, an idiosyncratic search language, and an individual series of user commands that the dedicated neophyte interested in using the service must learn. It is therefore not surprising that only the most affluent, who can afford to hire specialists—and the extremely dedicated—have made extensive use of these resources.

One aim of this book is to demonstrate how online resources can be used efficiently and inexpensively by generalists lacking the financial resources of a large corporation like the *Washington Post*. A combination of intelligent search techniques, the judicious choice of data vendors, and a precise understanding of the ways in which online research can transform a story, can yield inexpensive and yet extremely powerful research within the budget of most freelancers and almost all organizations. One of the most effective searches described in this book cost $6.50, including telephone connect charges. The most expensive and comprehensive online search, one of thirty-five newspapers for specific stories published over a three-year period, cost approximately ninety dollars.[23]

PRACTICAL AND THEORETICAL

The practical issues of online use are presented here within the context of both the parameters of contemporary journalism and the means by which these technologies address its limits. Ultimately, the success or failure of this text will rest on its ability to demonstrate the degree to which the use of electronic information services can and will create a radically new journalism in which the resulting report, news story, or press release is free from traditionally accepted editorial limits. Technology affects not only the means of production and the efficiency by which the physical product is created, but also its very content. The relation between a new technology and existing modes of production, while important, is treated here as a secondary issue and considered only to the extent that it affects the diffusion of online research technologies.

The news managers' mundane concerns regarding the potential cost benefits of these technologies are largely subsumed in the broader discussion and through the text's practical examples, which advance the general, theoretical position. Two separate chapters, one describing search technologies and the other, a review of database organization, may be the most "practical" from the perspective of the

neophyte or journeyman news and public inform
Certainly, a single practical guide for public
writers interested in tailoring general, online s
niques to public information writing would be us
extent that this book functions as such a guide
growing library of texts that tailor information ab
resources to the needs of individuals in specific fi
rently available are specialty books describing the
of specific database vendors, like Dow Jones New
and CompuServe.[24] Other texts currently available
the use of electronic information resources at the
specific subjects or trades, including financial ana
business,[26] academics and life-science research.
available and of use primarily to information broker
research librarians[29] are bibliographies—publishe
tronically or traditionally—of available online data
ies.

While this book can, one hopes, join its technica
descriptive predecessors in its promise of the practical,
as both an organizational complex (the newspaper, n
magazine, TV news hour, etc.) and as a specific typ
narrative requires a somewhat different treatment.
need not ask, for example, about the nature of data emplo
or the social goals informing the work of investment brok
to demonstrate how, using online financial libraries, t
might best track the performance of an individual sto
Business performance is evaluated on the basis of high
specific data (price-earning ratios, stock price performanc
yields, etc.). How that information is retrieved, either onlin
or from the newspaper's financial page, does not change th
methods of analysis to which the resulting data are sub
jected. But the news story is based on a much broader and
less exact complex of information including, to name only the
most major categories: academic studies, government reports, official statements, Congressional debates, legal decisions, press releases, and individual news reports from local,
regional, and national reporters around the world. Unlike a
stock exchange's opening and closing quotes, this range of
data—to be of any use—needs to be examined, sifted, and
focused for use in an interview or final story. That process of

that argues there are or will be compelling differences between the "same old journalism" and stories that exploit the potential of electronic, online research. These differences go far beyond the added efficiencies and flexibilities that, one one level, online information certainly offer. The practical examples employed in this text attempt to demonstrate the degree to which computer-assisted information resources result in, for newswriters, a significantly altered narrative form and, more generally, a new relation between public information writers and their subjects. This new form allows daily newswriters, perhaps for the first time, to approach the standards of completeness and "objectivity" that many have long asserted.

The central thesis argued here is that online data technologies empower writers and reporters by providing them with information equal to or greater than that possessed by the public or private official they are assigned to interview. The effects of this empowerment, it is suggested, will eventually redefine the form of the news in specific and of public information in general. In short, this book argues that intelligent use of these online resources is not the "same old journalism" (or public relations or position paper) but has the potential to fundamentally alter the rules of the public information game.

It will be shown that another benefit of the use of electronic information resources is increased flexibility for newswriters and editors. The boundaries of specific and separate "beats" tend to disappear when reporters switch from traditional to electronically backgrounded reportage. It allows generally trained writers or researchers to cross with impunity between topical boundaries previously the exclusive domain of "specialists." The medical writer soon finds that issues of financial cost—to corporations, society, or the individual—is a salient concern when a new surgical technique or piece of equipment is touted, while the business writer researching a specific corporation finds, in the electronic files, stories on the political and social effects of that company's products and practices. For the employer, this greater flexibility translates into improved productivity as reporters are empowered to cover with increased criticality progressively broader classes of events. For hacks, flacks, and advocates, this means their work is no longer necessarily bounded by individual "beats" or "specialties" but that any can write and work wherever an assignment or personal conviction may lead. Contemporary journalistic definitions and generally accepted editorial assumptions impose severe constraints on the writers of individual stories that, it is argued here, have resulted in limits on both the range of stories published and the degree to which pertinent, if officially unpopular, information can be presented. Computer information systems are changing those boundaries by broadening immeasurably the range of subjects and issues which can be covered intelligently and critically—by a single individual.

TECHNOLOGY

There is a wide literature on the effect of new technology upon old industries. This literature is especially relevant to the historic relation between printing and information technologies. Marshall McLuhan's arguments, popular in the 1960s, were based on the assumption that information technology radically changed cultural imperatives.[31] More recently and, perhaps, more successfully, others have demonstrated the clear relations between socioeconomic patterns and the growth of public information as both a technology and a socioeconomic tradition.[32] To the degree that this book is successful in demonstrating that new online technologies create a radically new relation between author and subject, it also enters the ongoing literature examining the relation between technology and subject in the arena of public information.

The operative assumption is that new technologies, defined here as online or electronic databases, will force a reevaluation of the relation between "official" expert and passive reporter or publicist while breaking down within news or public information agencies those bailiwicks of individual expertise—"beats"—that have traditionally defined and limited the topical responsibilities of individual writers. Thus it is argued that the acceptance and appropriate application of these technologies will occasion change not only in the relation between writers and subjects, but simultaneously among newspeople who, in the past, were divided by their respective responsibilities for a specific, topical specialty rather than united in their ability to focus on a story or issue.

In short, it is the intention of this book to examine the relation between the content of public information and the potential effect of new technologies on the degree and type of information available in the public forum through a structural analysis of contemporary news in specific and public information in general. The resulting analysis uses concrete, casebook examples to demonstrate the degree to which news information—and by extension the information presented by other groups—can be changed through the efficient and cost-effective application of online bibliographic resources accessed by personal computers.

NOTES

1. Tim Miller, "Information, Please, and *Fast*," *Washington Journalism Review* 5:7 (September 1983), 51.

2. Tim Miller, "The Data-Base Revolution,"*Columbia Journalism Review* 26:3 (September/October 1988), 35. Over the last two decades, the words *data base* have gone from full separation, through hyphenation to conjunction as a single word. *On line (on-line, online)* has gone through a similar transformation. Except in titles or direct quotes, this book follows current usage by excluding hyphen or spacing between the originally separated words.

3. Brian S. Brooks et al., *News Reporting and Writing,* 3d ed. (New York: St. Martin's Press, 1988), 142-49. Much of what this textbook describes is information management with the computer and not online resources.

4. Thomas Jacobson and John Ullmann, "Commercial Databases and Reporting: Opinions of Newspaper Journalists and Librarians," *Newspaper Research Journal* 10:2, (Winter 1989), 16.

5. Miller, "Data-Base Revolution," 36.

6. Margaret Genovese, "*Sun-Times* Gets Scoops at Press of Some Buttons," *Presstime* 3:10 (August 1981), 25-26.

7. C. David Rambo, "Database Searches," *Presstime* 9:3 (March 1987), 10-12, is an example, as are most of Tim Miller's pieces.

8. Ken Haswell, "Extend Your Reach Electronically," *Quill* 76:2 (February 1988), 40. This is an example of anecdotal reportage on electronic resources by a newsperson who interviewed editors and reporters about one or another aspect of online service. Extolling the virtues of computer-assisted reportage has become something of a specialty for some free-lancers.

9. Stan Soffin et al., "Online Databases and Newspapers: An Assessment of Utilization and Attitudes." Paper presented at the Association for Education in Journalism and Mass Communication, San Antonio, Texas, ERIC no. ED-286178, August 1987.

10. John Kerr and Walter E. Niebauer, Jr., "A Baseline Study of the Use of Outsize Databases: Fulltext Retrieval Systems by Newspaper Editorial Page Writers." Paper presented to Newspaper Division, Association for Education in Journalism and Mass Communication, Norman, Oklahoma, ERIC no. ED-27765, August 1986.

11. Tom McNichol, "Databases: Reeling in Scoops with High Tech," *Washington Journalism Review* 9:6 (July/August 1987), 28. "Because of the high cost of data banks, their growth traditionally has been limited to large metropolitan dailies."

12. Dow Jones Information Service provides a service tailored to corporate information needs; WestLaw provides information services for legal firms, etc.

13. Many privately owned services currently offered to the public online began as government services first, which were contracted out and then commercialized. *Disclosure*, for example, is the public, electronic outgrowth of Securites and Exchange Commission filings and reports. The U.S. Health Care Financing Administration publishes a *National Health Standards and Quality Information Database* (NHSQUIC), currently available for a fee on BRS computer service. There are scores of government agencies and documents whose

data, once stored electronically, have become accessible to the public through online technologies.

14. Jacobson and Ullman, "Commercial Databases," 18. Further, the single most popular database was Vu/Text, which puts newspaper morgues into an electronically accessible format. The degree to which those using these "electronic resources" were, in fact, only using their own newspaper clipping files in an electronic form is unclear from the study.

15. McNichol, "Databases." According to one report, in the mid-1980s the *Washington Post* spent in excess of $20,000 a month on Nexis searches alone, plus an additional $10,000 a month on other data banks."

16. Miller, "Information Please," 52.

17. Miller, "Data-Base Revolution."

18. Another survey completed in 1987 found that one-third of the newspapers using electronic databases spent between $1,000 and $10,000 a year on those services. The rest were divided between newspapers spending between $10,000 and $20,000 a year, and those spending up to $30,000 a year for electronic research. There are few who spend more than that amount. See Rambo, "Database Searches," 10.

19. Miller, "Information, Please," 53.

20. Tim Miller, "The Database as Reportorial Resource," *Editor and Publisher* 117:17 (April 28, 1984), 70. The cost is an estimate assuming a global news search on Nexis with full text and excluding the monthly subscription charge of $50 the service levies on its customers.

21. It is important to remember that the average U.S. newspaper has a circulation of well under one hundred thousand readers.

22. Fredric F. Endres, "Daily Newspaper Utilization of Computer Data Bases," *Newspaper Research Journal* 7:1 (Fall 1985), 34.

23. In 1988 the author received an access grant from Vu/Text Information Services and conducted the search under that grant. Had I been charged, the $80 fee quoted here would have resulted from the combination of line connect charges and those incurred through time spent on the database itself.

24. See, for example, Alfred Glossbrenner, *Alfred Glossbrenner's Master Guide to CompuServe* (New York: St. Martin's Press, 1987). He has also written an intelligent introductory guide to online services: Alfred Glossbrenner, *How to Look It Up Online* (New York: St. Martin's Press, 1987), as well as an excellent introduction to general telecommunications issues: Alfred Glossbrenner, *The Complete Handbook of Personal Computer Communications* (New York: St. Martin's Press, 1985).

25. Financial Sourcebooks Staff, *Online Sources: A Step-by-Step Guide to Access and Using Business and Financial Databases* (New York: Financial Sourcebooks, 1988).

26. John F. Wosik, *The Electronic Business Information Sourcebook* (New York: John F. Wiley and Sons, 1987).

27. Cuadra-Elser Staff, *Online Databases in the Medical and Life Sciences* (Santa Monica, Cal.: Cuadra Publications, 1987). Those seeking further examples of detailed and specialized books and bibliographies are referred to the current *Books in Print*. In the 1988-89 edition there were forty-three listings with "Online" as the first word in the title.

28. Information brokers are individuals who specialize in online research as a freelance business. The Online Connection in Gainesville, Florida, run by Maureen Corcoran, is one such service.

29. There is currently for librarians a newsletter specializing in online resources. Its masthead proclaims it "a monthly rag with library hardware and software opinions found nowhere else." Edited by Eric S. Anderson, it is: *Wired Librarian's Newsletter*, 20 Congress Ave., Sioux City, Iowa, 51104.

30. Quoted in J. Herbert Altschull, *From Milton to McLuhan: The Ideas behind American Journalism* (White Plains, N.Y.: Longman, 1990), 262.

31. Although certainly best known as a visionary heralding the rapid arrival of an electronically-based "global village," it is McLuhan's early work on the relation of technology—especially print-based technology—to public information which is most important here. See Marshall McLuhan, *The Gutenberg Galaxy: The Making of Typographic Man* (Toronto: University of Toronto Press, 1962).

32. See, for example, Alvin Kernan, *Printing Technology, Letters, and Samuel Johnson,* (Princeton: Princeton University Press, 1988). Kernan's work and perspective will be referred to repeatedly in this book, especially in Chapters 2 and 5.

JOURNALISM
FOR THE
21st CENTURY

1

The News:
Myths and Realities

What is the function of contemporary news and what is the role of those who write for these public and commercial forums? In general we can say that news stories present a consistent and rational system, an abstracted interpretation derived from the chaos of a given moment and filtered through the stages of fixed, editorial necessity. The organization of the news is not ordained by reality, nor necessarily a complete description of it, but instead is artificially and fully mediated by the culture it supports. News is, in a real sense, the means by which society chooses its own reflection and, simultaneously, a culture's bulwark against the chaos of the world's events. As a socially constructed reality, news, like other institutions (law, cinema, cuisine, medicine, etc.), has a history of development that manifests a pattern of adjustment and change closely linked to events in the technological and cultural history of its community. It is, in short, a system whose rules are at least partly based on one or more modes of production within the greater society's more general pattern of historical change.

What is unclear is the degree to which this social construct currently fulfills its generally defined contract with society as a whole. Advocates (some might say apologists) of the modern press insist it functions as a watchdog of officialdom, providing a communal voice for the electorate it is designed to serve. In theory, the news is a public trust, and its professional class performs a service benefiting not simply employers or stockholders but society as a whole. "The first article of the Bill of Rights was placed there as a pledge of safety to the people," James Reston argued years ago in a position still popular among journalism instructors. "He [the news professional] does not owe that primary allegiance to the owner of his newspaper, or to his managing editor or to his government, or to the sources of his information; he owes it to the people."[1]

This notion of news as service, as a service by members of the Fourth Estate to the greater social weal, is a constant theme voiced time and again by those who write about the media. Journalists and editors are presumed to put personal and economic considerations aside so that citizens can receive full and complete information on the political and social events that will affect their lives. For democracy to have meaning, its members must be able to act responsibly, and their ability to do so depends, in turn, on the availability of accurate and reasonably complete information, which will come, at least in theory, from the public sphere's principal disseminators of information—news reporters, periodical writers, public relations officials, and a concerned citizenry given voice through the media.

Lee Sigelman has described this function of the news in a supposedly free society as an "institutional myth"[2] in which public service by journalists and their parent corporations is defined by the presentation of information untainted by self-interest or bias. Its corollary is an "instrumental myth" which, in turn, defines the canon of journalism as the promise of complete, "objective," and unbiased descriptions of culturally or socially significant events.[3] Jeff Greenfield of ABC News combined both the instrumental and institutional when he said, on *Nightline*, that: "It is the job of our free press to probe the workings of our criminal justice system, to probe international affairs, to track new developments in the field of commerce, and to pursue all such stories guided only by our own independent sense of what does and does not matter."[4]

To perform its institutional function—the dissemination of public information, news must present data on any reportorial event judiciously, without favoring any specific element of society in its description of events of community interest. To serve adequately, it must present information without bias or else the news becomes propaganda and the social service becomes promotion for one or more individual elements of society. Journalists tend to speak of "goals" or "standards" and not "myths," but, important differences in nomenclature aside, generally recognize both instrumental and institutional objectives. Functionally, of course, the goal of newspeople is also to make money from their job so they can pay the bills while earning the social esteem that accrues to those employed in a socially responsible position. Their employers' first requirement is to turn a profit sufficient to pay everyone's salaries (including their own) and to generate a rate of economic return for investors, including, typically, themselves.

In this century, those commentators writing about the success or failure of journalism within the context of either its institutional or instrumental goals have balanced the concept of social trust or unbiased information against the fact that the dissemination of public information is primarily an economic enterprise in a capitalist society. The issue has been seen by some as the tension between a postindustrial society's means of information production and the social role that public information in theory is required to serve. Joseph Pulitzer juxtaposed journalism's twin functions—public good and corporate profit—when he attempted to describe in 1904 what excellence meant in the field:

> What is a journalist? Not any business manager or publisher, or even proprietor. . . . He is not thinking of his wages, or of the profits of his owners. He is there to watch over the safety and the welfare of the people who trust him. . . . The editor . . . must be known as one who would resign rather than sacrifice his principles to any business interest. It would be well if the editor of every newspaper were also its proprietor, but every editor can be at least the proprietor of himself. If he cannot keep the paper from degrading itself, he can refuse to be a party to the degradation.[5]

For many of the media's critics, news has become simply a business and not the public service Pulitzer believed it to be. Were every editor and reporter to resign before his or her news organ sacrificed a populist perspective, the media would virtually vanish overnight. Reporters and editors should "watch over the safety and the welfare of the people [readers and viewers] who trust them" but, instead, allow that aim to be devalued by the policies of the news corporation that employs them. Journalists have, in theory, a public trust. But at the same time their livelihood depends on the economic viability of both their individual media outlets and of the individual station, newspaper, or magazine's controlling parent corporation. News professionals thus must balance a functional goal of self-interest with professional values of service if they are to work and to eat. Reporters serve editors who answer to publishers whose goal is not simply or even primarily public information but first and foremost the maintenance of a profitable business. Writing about TV news coverage following the 1988 presidential election, Mark Crispin Miller, for example, said of TV reporters that they "serve commercial television. Their aim is to boost ratings: They always tell the people what they think the people are already thinking."[6]

But if TV reporters serve commercial television, then print newspeople serve commercial publication, aiming to build circulation. Newspeople, whatever their medium, want readers, viewers, or listeners whose numbers translate into advertisers or sponsors. Thus, one one level, reporters and editors must protect their constituency through the information they provide because, in Charles Kuralt's words, "This is not just good journalism, it's good for the country. This kind of country can't work unless people have a reliable way of finding out what's going on."[7] But at the same time news professionals are wage earners or hourly employees whose livelihood and social position depend on an employer's sufferance and financial continuance, which, in turn, are dependent on the sale of advertising space sufficient to assure at least minimum profitability for the media corporation.

Any discussion of modern journalism must therefore accept as its context a tension between at least two competing goals in the production and dissemination of organized news. A media corporation's institutional, social rationale may be the presentation of "all the news that's fit to print," but at the same time its corporate goal must be to sell enough advertising to allow for a return on investment. A journalist's professional aim is, at least in theory, to improve society through as complete a description as possible ("without fear or favor") of contemporary events. But at the same time, reporters and editors want and need to earn money sufficient to sustain their own lives and, if possible, to support agreeable life-styles. News corporations may wish to perform a public service through the information their individual organs present but they are first and foremost economic entities whose focus is on the financial successes of the corporate group at large.

Illustration 1 summarizes the tensions among institutional, instrumental, and general, functional goals, both for journalists and for the organizations that employ them. Functional goals, while defined here economically, include a positive social valuation. Thus news employment allows the reporter both to pay the rent and to enjoy the status of being a "journalist" in a society whose mythology emphasizes the necessary, honorable nature of the job, which in addition is assumed to be both exciting and personally rewarding. Money earned by media corporations also provides its editors, publishers, and corporation executives with presumably gratifying social credibility at local, regional and national levels of political and social intercourse. Although apparently simplistic, the relation among these elements can be used, as Chapter 2 will demonstrate, in a general paradigm that makes clear the effect of information technologies, electronic and traditional, on the information presented in individual stories.

Further complicating the ideal of journalistic service and the implementation of its instrumental myth is the issue of who is a credible source to be interviewed or quoted and how the parameters of a story are to be defined. For news to be "objective," it must treat all sources equally. To serve as an unbiased source of information, media outlets must be able consistently to describe events not as one or another special interest group wants them to be portrayed but, rather, in some way distanced from those partial, limited

Illustration 1.1
Myths and Goals

	Institutional A	Instrumental B	Functional C
Reporter -1-	To serve through providing information	By presenting unbiased coverage	Earn money to pay expenses; maintain social position.
Publication: -2-	All the news that's fit to print (or broadcast)	Earn enough to pay staff to produce the show or publication	Achieve adequate return on profit for investors and for employee salaries.

interpretations. But news as it is defined today is typically generated by officials—governmental, academic, or corporate—whose leaders are uncritically quoted by all media outlets. In 1986, for example, Carlin Romano noted that "the percentage of news that directly arises from press releases and public relations—estimated at more than 50 percent in 1930—is probably higher now."[8] This daily avalanche of reports, "media opportunities," official statements, and "news releases" generated for corporations, government agencies, and special interest groups by public relations specialists defines, in a real way, the information that is daily presented in supposedly impartial media.

The conflicting priorities of journalists, their employers, and of the corporate or government officials who are the subjects of news reports, all can be subsumed under the distance between the ideal of an unfettered, questioning free press and the reality of news production, which typically cedes the ability to control the dissemination of information to officials (corporate, appointed, and elected), inside and outside the media, about their actions and activities. The tension between the myth of an unfettered press and the fact of pervasive, official domination of news reports is the dark continent of contemporary news, a disputed terrain between warring camps either critical or apologetic of contemporary North American journalism. Both groups see news as, in theory, a public trust, but the former believe that trust is fulfilled while the latter insist that the news has been debased by those who would yield to the temptation Pulitzer described: the abdication of social principle to financial or business interests.

In its examination of the effect of online databases on public information, this work acknowledges the tension between financial and social goals as a starting point, a first context in the overlapping patterns of judgments and necessity that define the news in postindustrial society generally and North America specifically. Using Sigelman's myths as a general yardstick to measure the success of contemporary news, this work accepts that the means by which public information is disseminated through modern society is a result of a series of economic, social, and historical filters, which give contemporary reportage its shape and feel. This is true whatever the medium of publication or broadcast. Because they function in a single society with specific economic and social imperatives, news employees at all levels—whatever the medium of their individual reports—share a series of narrative forms, professional standards, and an editorial perspective based on cultural values and a single, shared journalistic tradition.

This study enters the debate of contemporary journalism's efficacy by examining a central but rarely considered assumption of news production. Almost without exception, those who have commented on, criticized, worked in, or studied contemporary journalism have assumed that the media are at heart a fundamentally print-oriented system of public information and that their successes (or failures) could be discussed within the context of or as an outgrowth of the printing revolution that began during the eighteenth century.[9] During that period, the very idea of mass-produced, public journals carrying information on contemporary events for the general citizen first became not only financially viable and socially accepted but, as importantly, technically feasible. At the same time, the ideal of information as objective and unbiased, of "facts" that did not require the endorsement of crown or clergy, grew out of the printing revolution's production of public reference works, a category of literature that included Samuel Johnson's dictionary and Diderot's encyclopedia.[10]

Concurrent with these changes (which through the eighteenth and the nineteenth centuries led to modern concepts and forms of "news"), the idea and ideal of the professional writer or journalist developed to assure a constant flow of articles would be available to fill the newspapers, magazines, and books that publishers ordered and their printers produced.[11] The tensions among the ideals of the author ("journalist" or "writer"), the expectations of a publisher, and the financial necessities of both have been a constant of the market place since the days of Samuel Johnson.

It was Johnson who wrote the first reports on a legislative debate, and first made his living grinding out reams of copy for early magazines, who wrote commentaries and authored books for the general population.[12] He did all this on deadline and for pay, taking some pride in the fact that his living was made not only as a "writer" but as a Grub Street writer, a hack who wrote on demand and for financial compensation. As Alvin Kernan states authoritatively: "No great writer before Johnson, it can be argued with considerable assurance, either made or fully accepted that he made his living from the sale of his writing to the bookseller and through him to the public to the extent that Johnson did."[13] At that time the bookseller was also the publisher of magazines and newspapers; the daily news periodical had yet to be conceived. The point is that it was with Johnson that individuals first conceived of writing for the public as a sustaining craft or trade, and, during his lifetime, that writers first entered self-consciously into the now common, professional contract of trading a wage for the printed word. The ramifications of that change—which itself followed upon a series of economic, social, and technological transformations—created the context in which contemporary journals and periodicals are published or broadcast today.

The very assumption of a literate electorate informed by the labor of news professionals was a result of both the increasing availability of faster printing presses and a mercantile system that assured publishers would have paper stock and ink with which an article could be printed. With these technologies, and the economic system that assured the materials to utilize them effectively, the ideal took root of a public press free of official patronage or bias and able to present necessary information to the increasingly literate electorate. The U.S. Constitution's First Amendment, prohibiting Congress from passing any laws limiting the freedom of the press, is testimony to a nineteenth-century recognition of the then newly conceived importance of an unrestrained, popular news media, one available to any who had the money to publish or who could convince others that what they had written could be profitably reproduced.

This book, whose subject is the role of a fundamentally new information technology in the dissemination of public information, accepts that historically most researchers have considered the news primarily within the context of a mode of production with social, political and economic ramifications. Although that posture and the analysis that follows from it are not minimized here, I argue that it is just as important that the media (print, television, and radio) have been since Johnson's day a system of information accumulation that is in essence orally based. Contemporary journalism remains basically a relay system for orally transmitted information disseminated in the form of printed material. Thus news is "not what happens, but what someone says has happened or will happen."[14] To the extent that contemporary journalism fails to present unbiased facts in the general service of public information, that failure can be understood only in terms of both the media's systems of information production and of data retrieval. It is this fundamental but rarely discussed aspect of contemporary journalism, its historical and still primary function as a means of oral transmission, that online computer technologies will change.

To understand the potential effects of a new information technology on the structure of public information, it is necessary first to consider the contemporary social functions of modern news organizations as well as the functional roles of those who work for them. Together these form the general context resulting from the operative technologies and cultural patterns in which, after all, the new will find root. The functions and roles of media organizations and professionals are economic, social, and technological. Accepting Sigelman's twin myths as a conceptualization of the ideal role and social objectives of the news, we must first examine the effects of this complex of social factors on public information. Technology—current and future—exists within the social, economic, and historical complex of a greater social system. To examine any aspect requires at least a general review of the whole.

THE NEWS: CORPORATE CONTEXT

Newspapers

There is a financial imperative and a corporate context determining the viability of the media. "News organizations earn their keep by producing stories that attract audiences, and thus advertisers."[15] It is easy to forget in discussions of news bias and news legitimacy that contemporary media are first and foremost businesses whose primary, corporate goal is to earn a profit for investors and owners. Newspapers, periodicals, and TV and radio networks exist as public corporations whose purpose—currently called the "bottom line"—is, first, to make money through the sale of advertising (measured in column inches by periodicals and newspapers but in minutes or seconds of time by broadcasters) and, second, through sale of the physical publication itself.[16] Advertising, which subsidizes the media in return for either print space or broadcast time that is then filled to the advertiser's specifications, is what makes news corporations prosper.

As Noam Chomsky points out and others have emphasized, corporate advertising subsidizes the news periodical and allows it to be sold at a fraction of the real costs of production.[17] V.O. Key observed, "Newspaper publishers are essentially people who sell white space on newsprint to advertisers."[18] A daily newspaper or weekly magazine can have increasing subscription and street sales while losing vast sums of money if advertising revenues do not reflect street sales figures. This was the case in the early years of *USA Today*, introduced as a "national" newspaper in the early 1980s by the Gannett Corporation and first distributed in select U.S. cities only through box sales and at news-stands. Initial reader response, reflected in circulation fig-ures, was gratifying, but because national advertisers were chary of the new product, advertising revenues lagged be-hind what gross circulation alone would have dictated they should be. In its first years and despite increasing circula-tion, *USA Today* therefore lost hundreds of millions of dol-lars, affecting the balance sheet of its parent corporation.[19] The initial success of the newspaper among readers was offset by its failure as an advertising medium, and Gannett stock prices reflected the drain on corporate resources caused by the newspaper's total production and distribution cost.

A result of the industry at large's primary reliance on advertising revenues is that the economics of news produc-tion favors large corporations that operate multiple outlets and can effectively employ economies of scale. "From the time of the introduction of press advertising, therefore, working-class and radical papers have been at a serious disadvantage. Their readers have tended to be of modest means, a factor that has always affected advertiser inter-est."[20] Another result has been the ability and willingness of advertisers to withhold revenue from publications whose editorial positions or general news perspective is displeasing to them. This power is as relevent to public broadcasting, whose subsidies come from federal sources and corporate "sponsors" (whose financial support is typically acknowl-edged at both the beginning and end of each show), as it is of the print and private broadcast corporations that print or run messages written and produced by the overt sponsor.

Public Broadcasting

In a 1988 proposal on public broadcasting, for example, a working group of long-time academics and news profes-sionals argued that "the current state of financing and the present umbrella structure, as set up by the Public Broad-casting Act of 1967, have opened the door to improper politi-cal influence on its [National Public Radio's] programming."[21] The argument is made but not substantiated in the report that federal financing under the act has led to attempts to control program content by political administrators. Further, the report argued that cuts in federal funding for public broadcasting had led to increased dependency on "corporate underwriting, increasing the chances that corporations could dictate choice of programs and content. Producers now find, for example, they must avoid proposals that corporate executives might deem controversial, and tailor their ideas to fit the general bias of commercial supporters."[22]

The assumption that supporting capital imposes a bias on news production is not new. Examples of such occurrences can be easily recounted. The *Economist*, for example, cited sponsor reaction to a documentary aired on U.S. public television station WNET. The subject was the purchase of large tracts of Third World land by multinationals and so angered a corporate sponsor, Gulf + Western, that the company withdrew its sponsorship because, as its chief executive wrote to the station, the decision to air the report "had not been that of a friend." The *Economist* noted editorially that "Most people believe that WNET would not make the same mistake today."[23] The thesis is clear: both corporate funding and federal grants compromise public broadcast news professionals, and make them unable to act independently and forcefully as watchdogs of business, government, and academe, modern society's prior estates.

What is not clear is how the context of public broadcasters differs from that of news professionals in the private sector whose funding is solely derived from the corporate sector in return for advertising to be displayed. Without even the possibility of congressional subsidies, private sector journalists are totally reliant on corporate support (as well as, in the case of magazines and newspapers, subscription sales). They thus should be even more at risk to capital's view of their product. But the idea of a "free press" that sells a portion of its space or time to advertisers is so well accepted that the potential for abuse is rarely even discussed. In both cases—public and private—the result is the same: time (or space) in a public information vehicle is traded for financial subsidies. Certainly, advertisers have used their patronage to support publications that advanced sympathetic positions and withheld advertising from those whose articles were not complimentary. Columnist Roger Simon pointed out in 1989, for example, that Japanese automakers pulled their advertisements from the August 21 issues of *Time* and *U.S. News & World Report* when these magazines ran special issues commemorating the fiftieth anniversary of the beginning of World War II.[24] *Newsweek*, however, which did not run a retrospective war issue, carried advertisements from Japanese automakers that week.

Thus the existence of news is defined and its continuance assured, publication by publication, only to the degree that its managers can attract paid, corporate subsidies that gain legitimacy by appearing on the newspaper page or in the same time block as the news itself. Public broadcasters, while not offering "advertising," require corporate underwriting (for which acknowledgment is given prominently) and federal monies whose continuance may be determined in part by editorial choices and decisions.

News Professionals

Daily journalists, like their employers, are faced with balancing economic necessity against both the institutional and the instrumental myths that culturally define their professional function. Mainstream reporters and editors directly serve not the public at large but, rather, the economic necessities of those corporations that hire and pay them. Those news corporations, in turn, exist to provide advertising space for the advertisements whose sale may guarantee sustaining financial returns. Thus the journalist's work exists, on one level, as adornment to the advertising space their employers offer for sale. The writer, reporter, or researcher is assigned, as a rule, by an editor or producer to attend an event or interview the participant in some news event. Whether there is print space or broadcast time for that report, however, depends on the "news hole," the total page space or broadcast time not sold to paying advertisers. Reporters' and editors' livelihoods and the journalistic forum itself thus continually must balance functional self-interest (the necessity for sustained corporate profits) with professional values of "objectivity" and the self-esteem and professional acclaim that accrues from the acquisition of a journalistic coup.

There are those who believe this weighing of personal,

professional, and corporate necessities to be an impossible balancing act. Miller, who suggested TV political reporters exist to boost ratings and not serve the public, is not alone. Chomsky has also argued the relation between capital and production in news, combining a historical perspective and a textual analysis of the news "product" in a devastating critique of foreign reportage by U.S. news media.[25] The primary reportorial function, in this economic view, is to serve as shill for the paid advertisers, and whatever that requires in terms of news packaging or emphasis—"to boost ratings"—will be done. If television news reporters have a vested interest in increasing ratings and thus assuring their employer's profitability and continuance, print reporters have a similar interest in the viability of their news organs. Indeed, the folk wisdom is that good stories draw viewers or readers and that reports by excellent journalists—in any medium—attract readers or viewers and thus increase advertising revenues, which are based on the size of a publication's circulation or broadcast station's audience.

While the editorial decisions of news professionals are, in theory, completely separate from those of advertising colleagues, the relation is clear and inevitable. The very space available to print a news report on any given day is defined by the amount of advertising space that has been sold. The more advertising space that has been purchased, the more pages a single edition will require and thus the larger the "news hole" that will be available. The greater the revenues from advertising, the larger the news staff must be to fill the pages that accompany advertising or the larger the group of broadcast journalists whose reports create the context in which corporate messages can be heard. "Whether the girdle manufacturer decides to buy his space on a given day may determine whether a secondary story about labor unrest in Sweden gets in. And sometimes possibility [of publication] is very much the result of principled decisions about [news staff] manpower."[26] Thus the social goals of both journalists and media corporations—the presentation without favor of information important to the general citizenry—are limited to the degree a publication or broadcasting station attracts corporate sponsors who assure the corporate goal of profitability.[27]

CULTURAL IMPERATIVES

Both media officials and newswriters or reporters thus have a primary economic function in relation to their respective parent corporations, and secondarily a social function presumed to be based on society's need for accurate and complete information. These roles are balanced through the choice of stories that, when published or broadcast, determine what information will be presented (and, as importantly, how it will be presented) to the public. Not surprisingly, the yardstick by which stories are measured for inclusion in a news program or page is defined, at least in part, by a story's adherence to general social values that reflect those of the bourgeois owner, advertiser, and news executive.

To the extent that any journalist or news organization attempts to fulfill its instrumental goal of "unbiased" or "objective" reportage, it must do so within the context of a process through which events are daily excluded from the page or broadcast period while others are included. No media organization—despite the *New York Times'* hoary masthead boast—can print, publish, or broadcast "all the news that's fit to print." As *Time* magazine writer William Henry III put it: "Journalism at best only approximates reality, because writers must inevitably select and compress."[28] While fulfilling their assumed social role as providers of information to the public sphere, news professionals constantly, consistently, and of necessity must exclude some events while following and emphasizing others.

Thus editors, newswriters, and broadcast producers function by definition as information gatekeepers, channeling specific types of information into publication or broadcast presentation while excluding others. The concept of the news professional as gatekeeper was introduced in 1950 by David White[29] and since then has been applied by various researchers to a wide range of news studies.[30] What is included and what is excluded is not haphazard, however. These decisions obey a consistent set of social and political values that are generally acknowledged to reflect the view of publishers, politicians, and the status quo.

Other mechanisms have been described that assign positions of relative importance to each story accepted for publication and thus deemed suitable by the gatekeepers for the public sphere. These can be thought of as the channels through which the gatekeeper acts and are usually defined as the "agenda-setting" function of news.[31] Socially, "agenda-setting theory maintains that gatekeepeing serves a valuable societal function. It reduces the array of issues before the public, presents a manageable agenda and helps bring about a society consensus."[32] Practically, the assumption is that audiences respond to cues presented by news editors and broadcasters—frequency of story repetition over time, length of time (or column inches) given to a story, use of visuals with a story—as keys to the relative importance of any topic covered. These and other factors thus define the specific medium's, the general media's, and, by extension, society's agenda of important issues. The accepted assumption is that these decisions are made by those who report the news, assign journalists to cover events, and edit those discrete stories into a newspaper page or broadcast package. As Maxwell McCombs and Donald Shaw said in their frequently cited 1972 study: "In choosing and displaying news, editors, newsroom staff, and broadcaster play an important part in shaping political reality."[33]

Proponents maintain that it is through this active shaping of the public vision that "the press serves a valuable societal function."[34] Further, there is typically in any news market a high degree of unanimity among news professionals on the importance of any single story and, usually, on the way it will be covered.[35] This unanimity is due in part, as we will see, to the degree to which news value is primarily defined by public or corporate officials through personal statements or press releases. Supporters of the agenda-setting theory, which has gained wide currency among academic journalists and communication theorists, argue its efficacy whatever the specific subject. It has been applied to political issues,[36] environmental issues,[37] and the general composition of a television news hour's story lineup.

But none of the hundreds of newsroom decisions, each of which defines the way a specific event will be treated, are value-free. The news is not objective but rather a continuous series of decisions that reflect general social and cultural principles. As Gaye Tuchman has written: "News is a win-

dow on the world . . . but like any frame that delineates the
world, the news frame may be considered problematic. The
view through the window depends on whether the window is
large or small, has many panes or few, whether the glass is
opaque or clear."[38]

Discussions of gate keeping and agenda setting are ways
to define the size of the window and the angle at which it
either reflects or refracts specific events. The theory assumes that the decision on what to let in or through the gate,
and the placement of a story or stories in the society's
agenda, are determined by the professional judgment of
news producers and editors. Within this general frame,
writers of most persuasions agree, is a consistent ideology
whose values reflect those of advertisers, media owners, and
the ruling elite. This perspective has been summarized by
Herb Gans as "the hidden values of moderation as opposed to
extremism, individualism as opposed to collectivism, reform
as opposed to tearing down the system, independence, the
dignity of work, enlightened democracy, responsible capitalism."[39] Not surprisingly, these values, which define what
will be the news, are also those held by the ruling, "equestrian class," which owns the media and sets the nation's
political tone. As Lewis H. Lapham, editor of *Harper's Magazine* and a self-avowed member of the "equestrian class,"
has said:

> The media's long-standing alliance with the monied
> interests should surprise nobody except the young-
> est student at the Columbia School of Journalism.
> Among the 400 Richest Americans memorialized in
> 1986 by *Forbes* magazine, 83 of them derived their
> fortunes from newspaper, television and publishing
> properties. Only the oil industry, which contributed
> 48 names to the list, could make even a modest claim
> to such pecuniary glory.[40]

Thus journalistic gatekeepers and agenda setters operate within the society from a perspective dominated by a
general political stance amenable to the corporate, capitalist
ideology of their owners. Gatekeepers allow through that
material which fits a specific social, political, and economic

vision of society's components and excludes other stories
which may challenge the dominant view. The philosophy on
which news is written and editorial stances are taken is one
amenable to corporate officials who own the news outlet and
the politicians whose actions are a primary focus of its
thematic output. The relation between news as business and
news as public function reflects a more general social perspective in which "the business of America is business."
Excesses may occur, and inappropriate behavior may be
described, but the general tenor will be favorable to corporate and political institutions, which are founded on individualism, reform, and a benevolent leadership.

Business as a Bias

There are those who argue that coverage of corporate
excesses is consistently soft-pedaled not only because large
businesses are major advertisers but also because consistently negative business stories would suggest a critical
view of commerce in general, a posture that is socially
unacceptable in mainstream publications. To understand
this apparent bias, a study of the way in which newspapers
handled major business stories in which corporations were
found to have acted illegally is instructive. One researcher,
James R. Bennett, examined news coverage given to large
corporations involved in major pollution or similarly critical
problems; the chemical pollution of Love Canal in New York
State by Hooker Chemical is perhaps his best-known example. Stories reviewed by Bennett on these public events,
most of which involved court action, were tracked in the
Denver Post, the *Chicago Tribune,* the *Arkansas Gazette,* the
Washington Post, the *New York Times,* and the *Atlanta
Constitution.* But, Bennett concludes, "none of the newspapers surveyed provided its readers with the readily available facts about Hooker's consistent irresponsibility in
dumping extremely toxic wastes and in suppressing information, except for one report in the *Chicago Tribune.*"[41]
In each of Bennett's twelve case studies, coverage of the
specific event complex (pollution, charges, court decisions,
etc.) was consistently less than complete, although general
facts were published.

Nor is reportage of official involvement in corporate excesses like the Love Canal toxic waste dump necessarily more critical. In 1990, for example, the *Buffalo News* carried a story quoting the statements of Mrs. Luella Kenny, a former Love Canal area resident, who told a citizen action group that public officials had attempted to cover up the cause of her seven-year-old son's dioxin-related death. "The state's whole investigation into my son's death was superficial, and it was meant to just placate me," she said.[42] A lab worker whose husband is a chemist, Kenny finally hired an independent toxicologist to review the results of her son's autopsy. Her expert's report was far different from the state's, targeting dioxin presumably leaked from the Love Canal site as a primary agent in her son's death.

When Kenny's charges were published in 1990, they were recorded without analysis, investigation, or editorial comment. Further, her statements to a community meeting occurred a decade after her son's death, a period in which no regional publication or broadcast news team examined—critically or even superficially—the extent to which official investigations of this or other deaths resulting from improperly stored contaminants were effective. A strong case can be made that the responsibility for the problem of toxic contaminants, of which Love Canal has become a symbol, lies not solely or even primarily with the companies who from 1958 to the 1970s followed federal and state guidelines in their waste disposal, but rather with those federal agencies charged with environmental protection and the imposition of chemical waste standards. The dangers of dioxin, and a host of other chemicals, were well documented long before official standards were first proposed and then finally implemented. And yet the failure of those regulatory agencies to put their knowledge to use before long-term environmental damage occurred, and before deaths resulted, has rarely been the subject of newspaper stories in the regional press.

This failure to report on federal or corporate culpability is not isolated. Love Canal can stand for not only a whole class of environmental problems but, for our purposes, as a symbol of a whole style of reportorial bias. On the same day that Kenny's statements were published in the *Buffalo News*, for example, the paper reported statements by Kenneth Worth, a former manager of the Niagara Transformer Corporation, who explained to a Cheektowaga town meeting that then recently discovered high levels of PCBs in the soil were likely a result of his former employer's practice of burying the toxic carcinogen in local landfill sites. "The owners dumped it, and now it's leaching out," Worth said, adding that the landfill site burial of inadequately contained PCBs began in 1958 and ended when the government restricted the practice in the late 1970s.[43] The president of Niagara Transformer in 1990, Fred W. Darby, told the *Buffalo News* reporter that he did not know if Worth's statements were correct. During the period in question, Darby explained, he was working elsewhere. Still, that ignorance did not prevent him from characterizing Worth as a "disgruntled former employee," a label printed by the *News*.

It is easy to see the consistent limits of news coverage both in the early reportage of the Love Canal disaster and the more recent stories on toxic waste in the region. The widely reported assurances of government officials that toxin-related deaths would be investigated, responsibility for those deaths assessed, and the environment restored were recorded but not examined by local journalists, and thus the breaking of those promises was not reported earlier. As Kenny told the action committee, cover-ups of her son's death—and perhaps others—appeared to have been carried out by state officials and only now, in 1990, is her story, delivered at a community meeting, being reported. Nor were early promises by corporate and government officials to review all toxic waste problems and make the region safe for its citizens ever kept. The only reason Niagara Transformer's problems were published in the 1990s, although dumping occurred through the 1970s, was because of local concern over the very high concentration of toxins discovered in a drainage ditch behind the company's plant.

Still, newspeople appear never to have investigated these issues with even a minimum of rigor. They did not monitor government investigations, look for official cover-ups or explore the possibility that other potentially hazardous and yet unreported dump sites might exist. They seem to have done little but report what officials and survivors of the Love Canal said in their varying, often separate forums. Nor did area reporters, presumably sensitized to toxic waste problems by the Love Canal experience, ask Darby in 1990 why his company had not reviewed its earlier storage procedures for carcinogenic PCBs after the danger of landfill storage became evident. After all, the dangers of PCBs had been a matter of public record since at least the early 1970s and their use restricted by the federal government since the late 1970s. Surely it would have been easy for a local reporter to check the accuracy of Worth's statements with official agencies or other Niagara Transformer employees rather than simply quoting Darby's dismissal of Worth as a "disgruntled former employee." The company president's dismissal of the former manager, presumably included in the story in the name of reportorial "objectivity," was not substantiated (maybe Worth left Niagara Transformer for a better job) and certainly bore no relation to the information the former manager presented. Its publication only served the corporation's then presumably urgent need to diminish the weight of Worth's statements, which were based on observation and participation, as manager, in the then-legal dumping. It also allowed the newspaper to avoid coming to grips with the truly critical issues these stories raised—had PCBs and other clearly hazardous chemicals been stored improperly in Niagara Frontier communities? Had local companies and regulatory agencies been consistently lax in addressing these problems and, perhaps, involved in covering up the extent of the deaths and the effects of these underground toxic storage sites?

It will be argued later that these journalistic failures, both those examined by Bennett and these more recent examples from the Buffalo newspaper, were not the result of simple, reportorial incompetence, a media bias toward big business (and advertisers), or journalistic toadying to those government officials and agencies who, in retrospect, can be seen as having failed in their role as guardians of the health and safety of the region's citizens. Instead it will be shown that the apparent official and corporate bias in these and other stories more likely resulted from a systemic failure in the balance between news writer and subject. In each case a report's inadequacies can be shown to stem from the context in which news "facts" were gathered (from press conferences called by company officials, court testimony, press releases) and by historically limiting aspects of the narrative form of the news.

National Biases

It is hard to separate the corporate emphasis from the political perspective. Lapham and others speak of them as synonymous. Individuals with political power and economic influence are, in this view, interchangeable vehicles of the status quo and, it is true, often move from government office to private industry and back again. This conjunction of the corporate and political is defined in part by the degree to which the majority of news corporations define their product not through a critical analysis of national issues but rather by their support of broad and patriotic objectives.

The interrelation of news, business, and politics was never clearer than when the Gannett Corporation launched *USA Today* in 1982 with a front-page credo by then Chairman Allan Neuharth promising that the newly established paper was conceived "to serve as a forum for better understanding and unity to make the USA truly one nation."[44] Just as *Time* magazine was launched with the stated objective of interpreting the news for readers from an American perspective (and thus with a specific political bias), so *USA Today* was launched with a patriotic agenda through which its stories would be filtered. With so nationalistic a goal, it is perhaps not surprising that the newspaper was officially launched at a lavish party on the Washington Mall with then U.S. President Ronald Reagan, Speaker of the House Thomas P. O'Neill and Senate majority leader (and later Gannett board member) Howard Baker as honored guests in attendance.

One of the national Gannett newspaper's significant contributions to North American journalism has been the introduction of the first person plural to describe communal propriety and allegiance within a specific medium's circulation district or broadcast region. Local and regional newspapers and television stations have adopted the *USA Today* style of referring to "our" nation, "we Americans," "our young," "our" (official) policies, and "our" cities or streets. In this insistence on identifying with the reader and "his" or "her" specific geographic allegiance, any pretense to standards of objectivity is discarded. If the newspaper writes about "our" government, it will not attack its values or its organizations any more than children will naturally admit that their parent is an ineffectual wage earner or unsuccessful parent. One may admit to blemishes in one's character, but rarely to its underlying and structural faults.

As *Newsweek* columnist Meg Greenfield said: "Everything, in other words, is received and discussed primarily as an American question, a reflection of some kind on what we were already doing and thinking. It is a kind of intellectual isolationism, and it is shared by Democrats and Republicans, liberals and conservatives."[45]

Racism

The degree to which story selection and treatment is defined by a series of cultural filters that tend to ignore disadvantaged minority citizens, except as crime story perpetrators can be seen, historically, in studies of the U.S. media's treatment of black citizens.[46]

In his study of a U.S. black urban ghetto, for example, Canadian geographer David Ley used the concept of gate keeping to describe the role of the subject city's media in interracial communication. Ley found that local TV and print news providers exhibited two distorting properties. "They both filter information, that is, sort out information considered insignificant or offensive to the readership, and they code information, that is, present it in a form palatable to and consistent with the norms of their readers."[47] More specifically, what was excluded from the news was information that editors considered or assumed would be insignificant or offensive and what was presented was in a form that news editors and producers presumed would be consistent with reader or viewer and advertiser norms.

Thus Ley noted that stories documenting harassment of black families by the police were a regular feature in the alternative, minority press but rarely reported in the main line, bourgeoisie-dominant media.[48] Walter Gieber described more bluntly how the exclusion function works when he quoted a reporter who said his paper had a racist bias: "When I covered a fire or police story in the slum area the desk asked: 'Is this a nigger story?' If I said yes, they told me to forget it. . . . After a while I didn't bother."[49]

It is unclear at this point whether those stories were eliminated because of a simple, editorial decision that blacks as a class did not matter, an editorial policy based on the assumption that blacks were not readers of the region's bourgeois newspapers (and therefore need not be reported), or because blacks were presumed to be poor and therefore without sufficient disposable income to make them a group of even potential importance to major advertisers. Certainly, there was operative at the time of both Ley's and Gieber's studies a general, cultural rule that made blacks a largely invisible race[50] in the greater bourgeois culture.

Similar rules of invisibility and non-news have been applied to other minorities at other times. At the *Springfield* (Mass.) *Union* in the early 1970s, Puerto Ricans and other Central American peoples were similarly ignored. Stories describing members of or activities involving the Latin community were almost exclusively limited to major fires (especially those resulting in the loss of life) or arrests of community members by the police for drug trafficking or burglary. Reportage of the black community was set at a similar level because, as then editor-in-chief Joe Mooney explained, studies had shown that subscriptions and corner box sales were minimal in both the black and Latin communities. If members of those minorities did not buy his newspaper, news advertisers did not care if they existed and, Mooney continued, their coverage became uneconomic and therefore unnecessary. But it was also clear that many reporters, photographers, and editors believed the non-white communities to be dangerous places filled with "non-citizens."[51]

Propagandists

Those who lament the limits placed on public information by editorial gatekeepers and agenda setters agree that certain perspectives and views are excluded from the public sphere and argue that such exclusion is by definition prejudicial to the supposedly impartial functioning of a "free press." The insistence on an ideology acceptable to owners and the elite is not a benign component of the media's construction of a shared social reality. Rather it is propaganda, the presentation of a partial description of reality favorable to a specific ideology, group, or interest. Ley's example, in which harassment of citizens for racial reasons was unreported in the mainstream media, is instructive. It was excluded, at least in part, because the portrayal of America as racist, with unequal treatment of citizens on the basis of their religion, color, or economic status, was, even if accurate, certainly antithetical to the readers', presumably the editors', and certainly the advertisers' perception of the greater society as one in which all individuals have equal opportunity within the socioeconomic system. The news judgment that dictated its exclusion by journalistic gate-keepers thus was justified not only on economic grounds but also to the degree that the purpose of news is to manufacture consent and self-esteem—Neuharth's "unity"—within the culture. To report objectively on America's least pleasant national characteristics—racism, violence, sexism, military adventurism, etcetera—would, while perhaps fulfilling the media's institutional objective, also almost certainly be antithetical to the posture of advertisers and officials who advertise in and grant interviews to the specific newspaper or broadcast station.

Chomsky argues persuasively and on the basis of an extensive analysis of U.S. news coverage of international affairs that the enforcement of an officially sanctioned, national perspective amenable to government officials and the corporate view is the central function of contemporary news:

> In the advanced industrial societies the problem is typically approached by a variety of measures to deprive democratic political structures of substantive content, while leaving them formally intact. A large part of this task is assumed by ideological institutions that channel thought and attitudes within

acceptable bounds, deflecting any potential challenge to established privilege and authority before it
can take form and gather strength. The enterprise
has many facets and agents. I will be primarily
concerned with one aspect: thought control, as conducted through the agency of the national media and
related elements of the elite intellectual culture.[52]

Chomsky's propaganda model of the news defines
boundaries of permissible dissent within the public agenda
and demonstrates the degree to which information published in newspapers and periodicals excludes data that
would exceed those limits. While Chomsky's research has
focused primarily on U.S. publications, it is important to
note that his model is based on a view of the relation between
capital and labor in contemporary, postindustrial, capitalist
societies, of which the United States is but one example. In
such societies, the purpose of the news becomes, he suggests,
the manufacturing of consent[53] among the electorate rather
than a service providing unbiased reportage of events whose
inclusion in the day's news is based on "objective" criteria. It
is a natural expectation, he argues, that journalists will
reflect the broad perspective and interests of their media's
owners, the newspaper or broadcast station's advertisers,
and politicians at large. Massachusetts reporter Al Giordino,
writing in the *Washington Journalism Review*, stated this
view as a rule: "Journalism follows whatever the national
agenda is. The president determines that, and the media
reports what's being said."[54] At other levels of society it is
the mayor, the police chief, the university president, or the
corporate chief executive officer who sets the agenda that
reporters and editors will follow.

A similar view is expressed by Alan Rachlin, who argues
that contemporary U.S. news agencies are committed to an
editorial posture supporting a vision of American hegemony.
In a detailed analysis of U.S. media coverage of the downing
of Korean Flight 007 by a Soviet airplane in 1983, he demonstrates the degree to which specific facts, reported elsewhere
and presumably equally available to U.S. newspeople, were
not found in U.S. newspaper and periodical reports on the
incident. Thus coverage by *Time* magazine and the *New York*

Times, for example, quoted copiously and followed editorially the often self-serving expressions of outrage, horror, and condemnation by United States officials who would later attempt to explain away the shooting down by U.S. military forces of a civilian airline in 1988 in the Middle East. In the first incident, *New York Times* editorial writers condemned the Soviet action, arguing "there is no conceivable excuse for any nation shooting down a harmless airline." But when Iran Air's civilian Flight 655 was destroyed in the second incident, the *Times* blamed not the Americans but the general Middle East situation. Clearly, when the Americans did the killing, there was a conceivable excuse.[55] Rachlin also demonstrates that the tone, slant, and data used by U.S. newspapers to cover these structurally similar stories differed markedly from the presentation in, for example, the Canadian *Globe and Mail*.[56]

Jeff Cohen of *Accuracy in Media* calls this the "home team bias. That's the only way I can describe it. It's root, root, root for the home team."[57] The gatekeepers promote this "home team bias," which is rooted in a view of American hegemony, by describing and defining information and editorial perspective in accord with the vision of the American political and economic elite. As *Harper's* editor Lapham says succinctly, "The American press is, and always has been, a booster press, its editorial pages characteristically advancing the same arguments as the paid advertising copy."[58]

Legitimacy

All these arguments have as a central principle the assertion that a critical function of contemporary American news is to establish the legitimacy of official, governmental action, either through the selection of information presented or through the means by which specific views are advanced or withheld in the public agenda. "Legitimacy denotes the positive valuation and acceptance enjoyed by a system of power and its bearers, who 'voluntarily' accept their masters as valid and deserving and their own subordination as an obligatory fate."[59] The principle of legitimacy as a function of the news is a theme inherent in Chomsky's propaganda model, Rachlin's hegemonic model, and the less politically overt sociologists' models. The argument is simple in its broad outlines. For the system to function, there must be compliance with society's laws, rules, and general agenda. Since democratic principles prohibit more than a limited use of force to assure that compliance, Western societies like the United States and Canada rely instead on other means— like the news—to bring citizens to accept the actions and priorities of their leaders.

No other explanation of agendas, gatekeepers, and propagandists has been found that so clearly states the central thrust of these analytic views. Further, legitimacy includes as a corollary the positive valuation of the corporate as well as the general political system. To the extent that politicians and political systems are dependent on the compliance of their constituents, it becomes ever more critical that news professionals support and thus legitimate the general worldview of the nation's leaders. If this positive valuation involves deception, exclusions, or arbitrary decisions by those officials, such deviations will not normally be questioned. This is what Gilbert Cranbert called the rule of the "compliant press." Writing about the U.S. invasion of Panama in 1989, he noted in "A Flimsy Story and a Compliant Press" that if officials "sound the 'protect American lives' refrain [even when those lives are not truly at risk] . . . Americans will fall for it every time. If aided and abetted, that is, by a compliant press."[60]

Thus the pervading view of the media is of necessity that of a booster press that supports the broad tenets of its government while presenting an ideology compatible with the conservative view of its owners and investors. Even when American blacks were denied equal access to public transportation and lunch counters, for example, U.S. newspapers and broadcast news teams did not accuse their readers or countrymen of being racist. When U.S. companies provided patently unsafe working conditions for employees, the media of the day spoke, as a rule, in favor of the jobs those unsafe conditions provide to the greater economy and dismissed or downplayed resulting deaths or injuries.[61] Lapham states clearly the general dictum that governs media coverage of social problems and issues:

Together with the teachers in the schools, the national media preserve the myths that the society
deems precious, reassuring their patrons . . . that all
is well, that the American truths remain securely in
place, that the banks are safe, our generals competent, our presidents interested in the common welfare, our artists capable of masterpieces, our weapons invincible and our democratic institutions the
wonder of an admiring world.[62]

There is, therefore, an area of broad consensus between
those who view news as a valuable and relatively unfettered
democratic forum, and those who view the media as a tool to
manufacture consent for the benefit of the elite by the
systematic exclusion of specific views. Both groups agree,
although using different languages, that there is a consistent ideology operative among gatekeepers and agenda setters that editors and broadcast news producers apply, perhaps unconsciously, to the stories that cross their desks.
This ideology is, not surprisingly, that of the corporate and
political rulers whose press conferences reporters attend
and whose attributed statements journalists daily quote as
fact in attributed paragraphs ("Exxon officials said Thursday," "Police Chief Daniel Shea said at a news conference
today," "President Bush told reporters who gathered at his
helicopter before he flew to Camp David for the weekend
that," etc.). Moreover, the pervasiveness of this bias in
contemporary media reports severely limits the institutional and instrumental goals of journalists, which here
have been called myths. The question arises, then, as to the
nature of the mechanics by which this ideology is applied and
the means by which the agenda is set.

THE MECHANICS OF LEGITIMACY

This book begins, then, with the reality that there is a
general and consistent bias in contemporary news, irrespective of the medium of dissemination—radio, television, or
print—or frequency (daily or weekly) of publication or

broadcast. Further, it assumes this perspective can be defined in part as an ideology supportive of the general goals of the nation's political and corporate leaders. That is, the perspective of officials, CEOs, and "experts" will not be easily challenged by journalists, even if specific details of individual events may be questioned. Others have demonstrated the power of gatekeepers and agenda setters as well as the consistency of their editorial policies. But even if one accepts that the media primarily reflect the needs of corporations selling audiences to other businesses, the specific mechanisms by which the news is constrained are unclear. Who is the gatekeeper, and how is a consistent agenda set? Even if one grants that corporate necessities and financial pressure create a single set of values, how is this imposed upon the news itself? Chomsky has argued that the whole is based on ideology and self-interest:

> Those who occupy managerial positions in the media, or gain status within them as commentators, belong to the same privileged elites, and might be expected to share the perceptions, aspirations, and attitudes of their associates, reflecting their own class interests as well. Journalists entering the system are unlikely to make their way unless they conform to these ideological pressures, generally by internalizing the values; it is not easy to say one thing and believe another, and those who fail to conform will tend to be weeded out by familiar mechanisms.[63]

Others have suggested that such an explanation of conscious bias on the part of news professionals is too simple and, even if accepted, incomplete. Sigelman, like V.O. Key, has suggested that bias in the news is less a matter of conspiracy and direct misinformation by reporters and editors, although certainly both may occur, and more likely the result of cooperation and shared professional satisfactions.[64] This book argues that to the extent structural and systemic misdirection occurs, the journalist may be as much victim as perpetrator, as deceived by his experts and sources as is the audience that accepts as "fact" the flawed news product eventually printed or aired.

NEWS AS ASSIGNMENT

Central to almost all the previous analysis is the apparently natural assumption that news professionals are both active and principal agents in the setting of the news agenda. It is common sense to assume, as have most past researchers, that news, assignment, city, and copy editors were the practical gatekeepers and daily agenda setters of the media. Their identification as the determiners of news is so obvious that it has never been adequately examined or seriously questioned. These are the lower level but upwardly mobile managers whom Chomsky mentions, the "gatekeepers" and "agenda setters" identified by sociologists. Based on a cursory analysis of the mechanisms by which individual stories are generated and produced, the assumption is reasonable. Here are the print editors and broadcast producers who assign reporters to cover specific events, supervise the editing of the resulting copy, and determine its eventual placement (including length and relation to other stories on any day) in the final news product. The largely unexamined assumption of most critics and students has been that those editors, producers, and reporters involved in this communal set of tasks actively and consciously set the agenda for the media in which they work. "The mass media force attention to certain issues. They build up public images of political figures. They are constantly presenting objects suggesting what individuals in the mass should think about, should know about, have feelings about."[65]

Were members of the mass media able to exercise such power, self-consciously and freely, they would be powerful and potent people within the greater culture. Were journalists able consistently to "force attention to certain issues," even within the limits imposed by corporate restraints and ideology, their force as watchdog and agent within the culture would be great indeed. But in fact journalists do not set the agenda they publish and broadcast. Instead they affirm and reflect the decisions of others.

Story Origins

The traditional assumption has been that reporters, or
at least their editors, determine what events will be covered
and, therefore, are conscious contributors to any bias in the
news. In reality, news professionals are almost totally dependent on press releases and the public statements of
sanctioned "experts" and officials. The distinction has been
made elsewhere between the boundary event—an occurrence in which individuals die, are injured, or are otherwise
affected—and the journalistic event that follows it in which
a public official or expert discusses the prior boundary
occurrence.[66] Editors assign reporters to follow publicly
sanctioned, journalistic events and not to investigate their
antecedent boundary occurrences. Thus reporters will cover
a speech by President George Bush and report his statement
that drugs are an urgent threat to American society, but
those same reporters will not investigate the reality of the
reported "drug culture" or the literature of addiction and
habituation that addresses the roots of substance abuse. If a
provincial or regional coroner holds an inquest into the
death of a child, reporters will cover the inquest (and report
its findings) but will rarely consider independently the circumstances of that death and its official investigation.[67]

An example of the distance between these two levels of
occurrence—and the expectations that arise from them—
was provided in late 1989 and early 1990 by the Charles
Stuart murder case in Boston. The nation's attention was
captured when on October 23, 1989, Stuart used his car
telephone to call 911 for help after both he and his pregnant
wife, Carol, were shot while driving in Roxbury, Boston's
predominantly lower-class, black ghetto. Severely wounded,
Stuart used the cellular telephone's signals to direct the
police to his car's location (which he did not know by street
address), and later said their assailants had been black
males intent on robbery. It was a wonderful story, and
footage of Boston police at the scene was played around the
continent and the world, with the audible portion of the 911
taped recording of Stuart's call as soundtrack. Stuart's wife
died as a result of the injuries incurred and her fetus,
delivered by Caesarean section, died soon after. A police

manhunt for the black assailants was then carried out across Roxbury. But early in 1990, Stuart committed suicide and left a note saying, "I'm sorry." Police then admitted that they had believed for weeks the man had in fact shot his wife and then himself, but lacked sufficient evidence to charge him. At the time of Stuart's suicide, his brother provided police with virtually incontrovertible evidence that Stuart had killed his wife for insurance monies.

In January 1990, following Stuart's suicide, Roxbury community members criticized both the police investigation (which focused on the community's predominantly black citizenry) and news coverage of the incident. They organized a boycott of the *Boston Globe,* which, critics said, had been all too willing to assign blame to blacks for the death. *Globe* columnist Ellen Goodman publicly admitted that her newspaper had been wrong in its facts but defended its coverage by saying that, although newspaper reporters had chased down "every lead," the information they received had been deficient and that what they had written was correct at the time of publication even though events proved the story wrong. *Newsweek*, which had also covered the original event, joined in criticism of press coverage of the Stuart shooting and the failure of Boston reporters to fulfill a "primary job description"—"skepticism"—and consider the possibility that the surviving victim, Charles Stuart, was in fact the perpetrator of the crime.[68]

But what *Boston Globe* journalists, and those working for other media, covered was what police investigators, emergency officials and the families of the victims said after the shooting. The journalistic event was the official investigation, not the boundary event of the shooting of two people and one fetus in a car at night. Police investigated the circumstances of the shooting; newspeople reported what officials (clergy, city officials, police, etc.) said at the resulting press conferences. Reporters "chasing leads," in Goodman's phrase, did not examine insurance records (Stuart had taken out a policy on his family several weeks before the shooting), because finding and examining such data is not their job. They do not have legal access to an individual's personal records or, usually, the skill to interpret such records when in receipt of them. Instead, *Boston Globe* reporters (and other newspeople covering the story) did what most journalists do: reported as rapidly as possible the newest information provided by officials, in this case the police and hospital personnel involved in the case.

For representatives of the black community—or *Newsweek*'s writers—to criticize the *Globe*'s reporters for not "investigating" the possibility of a bizarre insurance slaying while reporting everything the police, clergy, family members, and hospital spokespeople said on the record is to assume that the instrumental level of news description is at the level of boundary event (the shooting) and not the level of journalistic event (the police investigation). In her public apology, Goodman perpetuated the myth that police reporters routinely investigate such incidents, when in fact they do not. Newspeople report on what officials say, and their investigatory skills are limited in the main to gaining as much information as possible from those formal sources (the police, the mayor, community relations councils, etc.). They do not chase down murderers.

Blood relatives of the dead woman, on the other hand, criticized not the media but the police. They insisted the police should have informed the victim's family at the earliest moment of the possible complicity of their son-in-law, Stuart. In the time between the shooting and Stuart's death, they treated him as a victim and, perhaps, martyr and not as the slayer of a family member. Police had suspected the man's responsibility, but until sufficient legally admissible evidence was obtained told neither the family nor the press, which followed, as it must, the twists and turns of the information released, the "facts" as they were defined by the police at the level of journalistic information.

Goodman was wrong. It wasn't a case of skilled reportorial investigators being fooled by a clever murderer who later killed himself. They did their job very well indeed. Only that job was not (and is not) to find the truth about a killing but, rather, to report on what those whose job that is may do and say in an official context. But Goodman's public admission of her employer's shortcomings in this case served an important function. It affirmed the myth of an investigative, independent, active press aspiring to fulfill journalism's institutional and instrumental goals. Had she said with a shrug that newspeople report what cops and other officials say (the journalistic event) and, in this case, the official line was wrong about the (boundary) events of October 23, 1989, the newspaper's responsibility for misleading the public would have been mitigated. But admitting the distinction between what newspeople actually do at the level of the journalistic event and what they are believed to do as investigators of boundary events would have exploded the myth of a free, independent press.

Almost all students of the media confuse these two levels of occurrence. Certainly the literature on agenda setting ignores, in the main, the fact that officials set the agenda through press conferences, court hearings, and news releases. Reporters quote and synthesize attributed statements. Journalists—skeptical or not—reflect that agenda through their coverage of statements made at the level of journalistic event. In the Stuart case, police defined the parameters of the story from the first 911 call by Stuart in 1989 to an official announcement of the man's suicide in January 1990. Those who, like *Newsweek*'s writers or the *Globe*'s Goodman, wish to deny this inherent limit on contemporary news must endure the assumption of journalistic failure when, as in the Stuart case, the media's reliance on officially attributed statements is made clear.

Both critics and advocates of the media assume the editorial sanctity of the news, while at the same time they acknowledge parenthetically the degree to which news in fact affirms the agendas of others. McCombs and Shaw, for example, concluded on the basis of their study of salience in a political campaign that:

> The Media appear to have exerted a considerable impact on voters' judgments of what they considered the major issues of the campaign. The correlation between the major item emphasis on the main campaign issues carried by the media and the voters' independent judgments of what were the important issues was +.967. Between minor item emphasis on the main campaign issues and voters' judgements, the correlation was +.979. In short, the data suggest a very strong relationship between the emphasis

placed on different campaign issues by the media *(reflecting to a considerable degree the emphasis by candidates)* and the judgments of voters as to the salience and importance of various campaign topics [italics added].[69]

Reporters covering the campaign did not choose the issues that candidates discussed and that the news therefore reported. They did not decide when and where debates—if any—would be held or critically question the candidates on their policies, positions, or the issues. When the "war on crime" was an issue, reporters relayed the candidates' positions but did not, for example, ask about the degree to which previous policies administered by the candidates (professional politicians whose administration records were available for examination) may have contributed to a climate conducive to crime. Stories not reflecting the candidates' emphasis were largely stories reviewing "how the campaign is doing," a selection of articles on candidate statements regarding their individual campaign's progress, reports on public survey poll results (often commissioned by the candidates themselves), and editorials about the campaign in general. Thus the news chosen by editorial decision makers was based on the prior choices (reflected in official speeches presented at press conferences and planned rallies) of the candidates. The agenda was set by the political principals and confirmed by reporters who, covering campaign events, repeated "objectively"—without critical consideration—what each politician said.

This pattern is largely ignored by news and communication theorists, who almost universally assume that news professionals set the agenda and investigate events independent of official sanction or influence. The literature, including the agenda-setting literature, "has focused primarily on effects at the cognitive level and on variables within the audience, such as salience and attention to the media, which influence the strength of the agenda-setting effect. Less attention has been given to variables within the media."[70] The editorial origin of the stories whose salience has been the subject of such discussion—the antecedent choices—has not been adequately examined.

If an official or expert states, at a press conference, that a death was suicide and not murder,[71] that the use of a specific chemical or drug is evil, that an invasion by U.S. troops of another country is justified, or that similar actions by a foreign nation are criminal—reporters must, by the rules of their trade, write for broadcast those statements as if they were fact. Questioning by reporters is carried out within the boundaries set by the official who has called the press conference, issued the press release or is making public an in-house study. Reporters rarely question independently the legitimacy of the speakers' statements, and truth is reduced to the reasonably accurate reportage of what an official says in press conference or at a simiarly public forum. The result is a compliant press whose job is to report and relay what officials tell them to write. Thus during the U.S. invasion of Panama in 1989, "Nearly a hundred and twenty-five journalists, after spending less than twelve hours in Panama without leaving Howard Air Base, where they were informed that there was shooting in the streets of Panama City ("It is war out there," the briefing officer told them), had accepted the Southern Command's offer of a charter flight back to Miami."[72]

When such examples are brought up at journalism conferences, the position of media defenders is that such coverage is "bad journalism" and not an appropriate example of the trade's real state. As an article of faith, most news professionals insist they and their colleagues are independent investigators free of allegiances and "objective" in their professional presentation. The argument here is that those who reported on the U.S. invasion of Panama from a Howard Air Force Base briefing room were simply following the normal practice of relaying official statements to the public through their respective media organs. Reporters at every level—from the city police beat to the White House press corps—demonstrate a similar dependence on officially presented information as the basis for their stories. The example quoted from the United States' Panamanian incursion only made overt what is typically hidden beneath the chimera of instrumental and institutional myths.

The power of officials to set the news agenda and control the media is increasingly evident the higher one goes on the political or economic ladder. In regional markets, local officials, state or federal senators and representatives, university presidents, and corporate presidents (e.g., the CEO of Eastman Kodak in Rochester, New York, or the chairman of Coca Cola in Atlanta, Georgia) have the power to determine the next day's news and to direct the attention of that region's newspeople toward or away from an issue whose parameters those officials themselves define. As television reporter Jeff Greenfield admitted on *Nightline*, "When the president—any president—says that something is news, it is news."[73] The degree to which this reflexive pattern of news judgment diminishes any pretense of objectivity or intelligent inquiry was underlined by former newsman and current Harvard University professor Marvin Kalb on the same broadcast: "When watching the networks' reaction to the President's speech on drugs, my wife and I wondered whether we were still in a free society, or whether we were back covering the Soviet Union in the pre-*glasnost* days, because it seemed to both of us that the White House called a shot and all three networks galloped after the shot as if there were no other story in the world."[74]

The extraordinary percentage of stories originating from public officials or corporate offices—announced by press releases or attributed to statements made in press conferences (called by the public or private official) indicates the extent to which control of the news agenda has been relegated by news officials to their subjects. For years, researchers have noted the degree to which stories in the mainstream media reflected government sources and were attributed to and originated by official spokespeople. Gans lamented, as have others, that the vast majority of stories published in both the *New York Times* and the *Washington Post* were based primarily or exclusively on information attributed to public officials.[75] Studies of news content also have documented a more general reliance by the media on press releases from all sources. Scott Cutlip, for example, found in the early 1960s that public relations professionals were responsible for 35 percent of newspaper content.[76] Since the 1960s, researchers have continued to find frequent usage of press releases in news generation.

Within this focus is a second bias toward reportage of the statements of and positions enunciated by the wealthy. "Most news is about affluent people, almost by definition, since the main actors in the news are public officials whose incomes are in the top one to five percent of the [national] income distribution."[77] The power of the official lies not, however, solely in personal worth or acumen, but in the ability, ceded by the press, to call a press conference or make a statement to news professionals that will be both credited and attributed in print or on air to the official. It is in this way, through the printed or broadcast attribution which becomes public record, that the word of officialdom becomes published fact, whatever its objective truth. Mark Schudson bluntly summarized the situation: "Much of the news the press reports is given to it by public officials who can pass it out routinely or with fanfare, urgently or casually, all at once or in pieces, depending on what kind of effect they want to achieve."[78] Journalistic events are defined, in large, not only by official statements but through the support of experts whose opinions are solicited by newspeople to give a story at least the impression of objectivity. Henry Kissinger, once the most quoted man in America, defined such experts as "those who have a vested interest in commonly held opinions: elaborating and defining its consensus at a high level has, after all, made him an expert."[79]

News, in short, is utterly dependent on the opinions of such officials or their designated experts, who typically choose the forum and time the release of their views, often stated as "facts," to the media. This phenomenon is not new. The early American publisher Ben Franklin, for example, said that the business of printing "has chiefly to do with Men's Opinions,"[80] those "men" being males of position, substance, and responsibilty. Since then, the idea of official statement masquarading as "fact" has evolved into a central facet of the narrative form of the "news." Chomsky explains it as an economic necessity dictated by the media's need for news that is exploited by officials who know when and how to leak information to their own advantage and to gain the best coverage. Journalistic reliance on official statement and expert opinion to the exclusion of independent and objective inquiry represents, in his view:

A symbiotic relationship with powerful sources of information by economic necessity and reciprocity of interest. The media need a steady, reliable flow of the raw material of news. They have daily news demands and imperative news schedules that they must meet. They cannot afford to have reporters and cameras at all places where important stories may break. Economics dictates that they concentrate their resources where significant news often occurs, where important rumors and leaks abound, and where regular conferences are held. The White House, the Pentagon, and the State Department are central nodes of such news activity.[81]

What concerns many students of journalism or communications is not simply that official perspectives are reported but that they are reported uncritically. There is little need for official experts to voice opinions or take positions that resemble an objective reality or truth because journalists are taught not to question seriously but rather to relay, in their stories, only what was said on a single day at a specific news conference by a single official on a discrete subject. Journalists are trained to be not investigators or skeptical critics but, rather, disseminators or relays for an official's or expert's point of view. The more important the sanctioned speaker or the delegate, the greater the attention paid to his or her words. The importance of the designated expert is, as Kissinger noted (and demonstrated), a function of consensus with the dominant ideology and the speaker's position within the ruling bureaucracy.

Reporters and editors are disposed to accept official accounts as truth without the critical examination of each press release or news conference statement that could, were it attempted, lead to an unbiased account. Mark Fishman sees the functional relation between newspeople and sources as one whose purpose and effect are the enforcement of society's normative political and social order—Rachline's "hegemony" and the political scientist's "legitimacy."

News workers are predisposed to treat bureaucratic accounts as factual because news personnel participate in upholding a normative order of authorized knowers in society. Reporters operate with the attitude that officials ought to know what it is their job to know. . . . In particular, a news worker will recognize an official's claim to knowledge not merely as a claim, but as a credible, complete piece of knowledge. This amounts to a moral division of labor: officials have and give the facts; reporters merely get them.[82]

Thus the reporter must follow the agenda of others. Of critical importance is the fact that few governmental or corporate stories are generated by reportorial interest or editorial curiosity alone. Rather, they originate with and are offered by the eventual subjects of those stories themselves. A president, governor, mayor, city councilor, corporate officer or public relations specialist will call a press conference or issue a news release whose purpose is to place specific information into the public domain. The newsperson does not act but reacts, passing on the information provided by others rather than either generating it or evaluating independently.

Because that journalist (and by extension the supervising editor or producer) is dependent on an official's knowledge as well as the legitimacy of his or her office, the newsperson cannot critically examine the information officials determine should be relayed. The relationship is too close, too personal, and too critical for both writer and subject to allow the newsperson to be an adversarial and unbiased critic of his or her source. This dependence is central to modern journalism, a critical, causative agent which has created the narrative form that defines, in large part, the content of public information, irrespective of the specific medium, by news writers and reporters. Edward Jay Epstein summed up the issue succinctly in the following way: "The problem of journalism in America proceeds from a simple but inescapable bind: journalists are rarely, if ever, in a position to establish the truth about an issue for themselves, and they are therefore almost entirely dependent on self-interested "sources" for the version of reality that they report."[83]

Others have noted that reporters identify with their sources; newspeople tend to trust and credit those who constantly provide information "for the very human reason that he prefers to be treated pleasantly when he walks into an office, rather than to be treated as though he were poison."[84] Reporters confront their sources again and again, every day and face-to-face. These individuals become not merely professional assets critical to the performance of an editorial task, but also colleagues with whom one spends the day. "It is natural for a reporter who spends more time in city hall than in the newsroom to begin identifying his own interest as being more in common with the city manager than with the city editor."[85] In this identification of reporter and source, it has been common practice for journalists to function as public relations counselors, restructuring and rewriting "quotes" to assure that the subject sounds informed, logical, and correct. As Associated Press president Louis Boccardi told *Newsweek*: "Traditionally, the rule was to clean it up [grammatically], not make them [subjects of stories] look foolish, because they couldn't protect themselves."[86] Despite Boccardi's use of the past tense, there is no indication that this practice has stopped. Its benefits are undeniable, both emphasizing the source's information (which becomes, in the process, intelligible and usable) while making the reporter indispensable to the informant, whose normal speech may be grammatically unintelligible (as President Ronald Reagan's often was), filled with expletives (as was President Lyndon Johnson's), or presented in some other style or manner assumed to be socially unacceptable.

The reporter's objectivity is thus hemmed on one side by the economic necessities of news publishing or broadcasting, which impose limits of time and space on the daily story, and on the other by personal relations with "sources" and "contacts," whose statements are the basis of the content of the news. That the quoted individuals tend to be official or corporate spokespeople whose ideology is likely to be conducive to that of station owners and publishers is no surprise.

This system of privileged sources whose relations with a newsperson may shield their acts from public reportage is not limited to the personal relationship between reporter and subject. Newspaper editors and publishers often have similar relations with officials whom their lower-level reporters and editors are required to shield and treat carefully in their stories. Tom Goldstein, a former *New York Times* reporter, described how the relations between his editorial superiors and a Federal Appeals Court judge were kept under wraps and away from the newspaper's pages, affecting in the process the content of the news:

> At the *Times*, I was forbidden to write about probably the best story I knew—the close relationship between Irving Kaufman, a Federal Appeals Court judge, and the *Times* . . . the *Times* flattered him in its news columns and frequently had him write for the paper. The tightness of the bond was well known to many leading lawyers, and the overwhelming praise and absence of criticism of the judge in the newspaper's pages gave evidence to these lawyers that the coverage by the *Times* was far from objective.[87]

Further, even if the reporter wished to critically examine the information an official presented, journalists typically have little expertise and even less direct involvement in the subjects on which they are called to report. Dean Robart, a former *Wall Street Journal* reporter who publishes the *Journalist & Financial Reporting Newsletter*, summarized the situation neatly when he suggested to corporation clients that "reporters can be bought" and advised executives to shop for a few through whom news could be funneled in a manner appropriate to the specific corporation's public posture.[88] The medium of purchase, he explained, is not money but rather information, the very thing reporters need desperately and executives possess in excess. When an expert or official provides a reporter with data favorable to that subject, the journalist obtains the basis of the story he or she needs and the interviewee defines, by controlling that information, the coverage that will ensue. Robart suggests, by way of an example of the efficacy of this system, that early signs of illegal dealings by inside traders Ivan Boesky and Martin Siegal, who routinely shared information with Wall Street beat reporters, were ignored while those relating to the more aloof Michael Milken were seized upon and quickly published.[89]

One result of this reliance on sources for information is a system of "beats" in which journalists are assigned to narrowly prescribed areas of reportage in which they presumably develop an expertise. "Business writers" cover corporations, "cop reporters" spend their days with the police, "medical reporters" are the conduit for information from medical and hospital associations, and "court reporters" are responsible for legal actions and issues. On any beat, a reporter or editor is only as good as the source, whom the newsperson is pledged to protect at all costs. Thus the description of a situation in which the legal and commercial and medical areas combine—for example a suit against a hospital by the relatives of a patient who died during surgery—will pit reporters (each briefed by a different source whose personal interests will be unique) against each other. Because there is no way to test any datum individually, the accumulated information becomes fragmented, before the first story is written, by the conflicting allegiances of the reporters.

Narrative Form

This review of the literature argues the persistent failure of contemporary journalism to fulfill its instrumental and institutional goals. If news is legitimacy, offering not "objective" editorial decision but the agenda of its editorial subjects, then its supposedly dispassionate service "to the people," in Reston's phrase and, in Kurault's, to the country at large, is compromised. One might argue that the media's constant reliance on the statements and agenda of sanctioned experts (corporate, academic, and governmental) is at base economic. It could also be said that the steady presentation of readily available and easily attained information is a hidden subsidy of the news. The media protect their sources because they provide usable material whose cost, in time and manpower (for story generation, research, fact checking), is minimal. Certainly it is less expensive (and legally safer) to rely on the public statement of a powerful and acknowledged person than to independently investigate a specific event.

Another explanation is that the practice of basing news on the largely unexamined statements of experts and officials is the result of journalism's narrative form. The "5 Ws" of journalism demand of each story "who," "what," "when," "where," and "why" elements, which define the narrowest locational parameters possible in a story.[90] The more important the "who" and the more precise the "where" and "when," the better the form works. If President George Bush states at a White House press conference that the U.S. invasion of Panama was a tactical and moral success, that judgment will be reported (immediately) as the fact of "what" was said. That he may, in the past, have condemned as morally repulsive the use of military force in China, Eastern Europe, and Afghanistan will be excluded because the story is about Bush's statement uttered in the White House on January 5. He is the president. That's what he said. Today. An independent, journalistic judgment of success or failure, morality or immorality, right or wrong does not fit the narrative form of the news as it is conceived of today. "The conditions of journalistic practice and the literary forms journalists inherited together strictly limit the degree to which daily journalism can answer how or why. How something happens or how someone accomplishes something demands the journalist's close, detailed attention to the flow of facts which culminate in a happening."[91]

But contemporary journalists who are locked into the pattern of a narrowly defined story based on expert testimony drawn from public statements are therefore typically largely barred from perceiving or describing that critical "flow of facts which culminate in a happening." What the president, coroner, CEO, senator, physician, or expert said today or yesterday is what the news is about. It presents a chimera of objectivity, the odor of information sanctified by attribution, but the result is the isolated datum, the statement separated from any context and thus deprived of its value as information.

The Oral Tradition

Objectivity, journalism's instrumental myth, depends upon a context, the placing of data into a perspective by which the resulting information can be judged by reader or reviewer. Objectivity, to the extent that it is possible, depends on the dispassionate organization of independent data into a coherent narrative that involves each isolated event in a greater pattern of occurrence. This goal is virtually impossible with current journalistic definitions because contemporary journalists operate under the series of economic, bureaucratic, social, and professional restrictions that have been reviewed in this chapter.

One reason news professionals are unable to fulfill their instrumental and, therefore, their institutional goals lies in the oral tradition of news. The journalist's narrative form, reliance on personal relations between newsperson and source, and the reportage as fact of the statements of the expert or official are all, at heart, results of an oral tradition of information diffusion that makes facts of declarative but not necessarily substantiated statements and translates arguments into apparently powerful but often spurious opinions. The form's narrow spatial and temporal boundaries (e.g., "President Bush said today in an impromptu press conference at the White House") isolate what needs to be conveyed into small, easily repeatable segments.

The history of the press is marked technically by two separate streams of innovation. One has allowed for the ever more economic production and dissemination of information through increasingly efficient presses and distribution systems (trains to trucks to airplanes to satellites). In the 1980s the ability to send electronic impulses via satellite to secondary printing facilities allowed, for example, the creation of regional editions of individual newspapers (*USA Today*, the *Wall Street Journal*) and weekly publications (for example, *Time* magazine) at previously impossible economies. Another theme of innovation has been the increasing ability to transmit with ever greater speed and efficiency the reporter's or writer's text from distant locations to the editorial facility. In this category one finds the national (and international) mails being superseded by the telegraph, which was in turn almost totally replaced as an information system by the telephone. To the extent that the remote computer terminal linked to a news office has been accepted today, it represents another, faster method of transferring the reporter's words to the editorial desk.

But the information that is to be translated remains primarily the reporter's version of what an individual said at a given place and time. Until now, technology has provided no real advance in the methods of data accumulation which could affect the information to be transmitted. Journalists lacked in the nineteenth century and largely lack today a form or method through which evidence can be systematically adduced and statements considered critically:

> In the absence of any foolproof criterion for choosing sources who are likely to provide valid information, journalists are uncertain about whom to believe. They cope with uncertainty by continuing to rely on authoritative sources. The presumption of hierarchy, that those at the top of any organization are the people in charge and that those in subordinate positions do what their superiors tell them too, underlies the journalist's criterion for selected sources even though journalists themselves recognize that this presumption is often of doubtful validity.[92]

In 1920, Walter Lippmann said that journalists had to trust officials because "the books and papers are in their offices."[93] And for most journalists, that statement remains true today. Lippmann's "books and papers" represent the accumulated data made possible by print, and that material—the context in which information can be objectively considered—has traditionally been beyond the reporter's reach. In 1850, 1920, and 1989, reporters covering an inquest, commission, congressional hearing, or police news conference have been unable to weigh critically or judge astutely the information officials present to them. They did not and do not have any basis of information, any context in which to place and evaluate officials' statements because:

The journalists' typical tools, particularly the telephone interview, are inadequate to a task that demands far more varied resources. Journalists cannot subpoena witnesses, no one is required to talk to
them. As a result, "how," the detail, must await
agencies outside of journalism such as the grand
jury, the common trial, the blue-ribbon commission,
social surveys, congressional investigating com-
mittees, or other, more leisured and wide-ranging
forms of journalistic inquiry: the extended series,
magazine article or book."[94]

One possible objection to this position is that much of the
modern journalist's information comes in the form of written
(or faxed) press releases crafted by public relations professionals in other offices. But a press release from President Bush's office, the mayor's office, or the coroner's office
has as its sole function the presentation in written form of
that official's statement of position. It is, like the news story,
a written record of an oral event in which someone says "I
want a press release about 'x' and here $(x_1, x_2, \ldots, x_n)$ is what
I want that release to say." That it is transmitted in written
form and not spoken does not affect the message's content or
its use in the crafting of a news story. Certainly, newspapers
have files and copies of previous releases or reports, but, to
the extent that they are used, they offer other, similar
records of prior, official statements that do not in themselves
necessarily provide any broader context for the newest official or expert quote. If a man lies consistently it should not
become truth, but the current system of information accumulation accepted without question by journalists provides
no criteria by which the truth or falsity of an official statement—spoken or written—can be objectively judged.
    Another objection might be that contemporary news-
people are better educated and have access to print libraries
in which they can independently research issues the news
makers may raise. The problem is that such resources are
rarely used in the production of news stories. The use of
specialized libraries requires specific skills that the typical
reporter does not have, as well as time for that research
which is often not granted. To use a law library, or medical

library, research a question in engineering, or sift through the literature of modern biotechnology is, even for a skilled librarian, a sometimes complex and time-consuming enterprise. Reporters rarely have the required skills, and even more rarely is that research seen as necessary for the production of the news. To the extent that the news is a system of oral transmission, libraries are superfluous.

In 1967, when Irving Kristol publically lamented the lack of critical, intellectual expertise in *New York Times* reportage, Clifford Daniel, then a managing editor at the newspaper, rose in defence of his employer. Not only were there scores of university-educated people on staff at the *Times,* Daniel said, but the newspaper had a large library filled with critical facts and pertinent information that allowed *Times* people to be accurate, factual, and on the ball. Kristol responded that all the books in the world were of little use if they were not read, and he pointed out that most reportage—at the *Times* or any other daily news organ—did not read as if it had been written by newswriters who had perused fifteen journal articles or even five basic texts in their particular field.[95]

News as we conceive it is, supposedly, if not about information—the presentation of data in a comprehensible and coherent context—then least about "facts": what occurred at a specific moment with a single series of actors. But, as Alan White said: "Facts, unlike events, situations, states of affairs, or objects, have no date or location. Facts, unlike objects, cannot be created or destroyed, pointed to or avoided. We cannot be overtaken by, involved in, or predict facts as we can events."[96] The "fact" is that a body ceased existence in an operating room on a specific day; that five thousand men flew from one area (with the political designation of the United States) to another, distant geographic region (Vietnam, Grenada, Panama, etc.) where they fought with other men. The "success" or "failure," "rightness" or "wrongness" of those events, whoever may voice them, are not facts but opinions. They are interpretations within a wider cultural system, and to evaluate them newspeople must, if they wish to be "objective," be able to perceive and acknowledge the context of the whole. To understand these events in any reasonable or minimally objective fashion requires an approach that is not exclusively oral but literate as well, not narrowly defined in time or space (because "facts" do not accept such boundaries) but bounded by a broader, locational definition.

For even the most minimally objective reportage to occur, newswriters, researchers, and editors need a method by which the oral statements of officials can be verified from a perspective beyond that of the press conference or press release. The assertion, for example, that "drugs are evil" and that only more monies will combat their spread is not truth but a premise, albeit one accepted daily by reporters who write and editors who run stories based on its validity. To cover the issue of addiction and free itself from a solely legitimizing function, news requires a system and technology that will allow it to examine and verify the assumptions that subjects state as "fact" and are typically reported without comment as "truth."

Without such a perspective, the "news" is a progression of essentially trivial statements, the march of unrelated and unevaluated individual data pronounced by one or another subject at the level of the publicly sanctioned, journalistic event. But no context for the events of public importance can be gained simply through reliance on an oral assertion by one or more individuals, even if those individuals are judged to be "experts." The context must come from outside, from elsewhere than the specific, journalistic event. It is this objectifying context, which is critical to the instrumental goal of public information writers, that electronic databases can provide.

For the first time, these resources open the accumulated information of libraries and create a system in which the data presented by other journalists can be fashioned, quickly and efficiently, into an objective context for the news. The essential argument of this book is that online communication technologies will transform the news from a system of oral transmission to one organized around print technologies. The result will empower the writer and change the context of contemporary news.

NOTES

1. James Reston, "The Job of the Reporter," in *The Newspaper: Its Making and Its Meaning* (New York: Scribners, 1945), 93-94. Quoted in Lee Sigelman, "Reporting the News: An Organizational Analysis," *American Journal of Sociology* 79:1 (July 1973), 133.

2. The definition of an "institutional myth" as an attempt to "state in language of uplift and idealism, what is distinctive about the aims and methods of the enterprise" was introduced by Philip Selznick, *Leadership and Organization* (Chicago: Rand McNally, 1957), 151. It was then applied to journalism by Sigelman in his study of news organization and socialization. Sigelman, "Reporting the News."

3. Sigelman, "Reporting the News."

4. Jeff Greenfield, "'Pack Journalism': Horde Copy," *Nightline*, September 27, 1989. Show no. 2178. The show's participants discussed the degree to which journalists in general allow the U.S. president to dictate their subjects and approach. I am indebted to Muriel McDaniel of *Nightline* for a video and transcript of the presentation.

5. Charles W. Baily, review of Tom Goldstein, ed., *Killing the Messenger: 100 Years of Media Criticism* (New York: Columbia University Press, 1989), in "A Century of Media Critics," *Washington Journalism Review* 11:7 (September 1989), 46.

6. Mark Crispin Miller, "TV's Anti-Liberal Bias," *New York Times*, November 17, 1988.

7. Charles Kuralt in a foreword to Peter S. Prichard, *The Making of McPaper: The Inside Story of USA Today* (New York: St. Martin's Press, 1987), xvii.

8. Carlin Romano, "The Grisly Truth about Bare Facts," in Robert Karl Manoff and Michael Schudson, eds., *Reading the News* (New York, Pantheon: 1986), 51. Content studies of major news publications have shown a consistent reliance on officially released reports. This has been true historically both of "newspapers of record" like the *New York Times*, whose foreign and national reportage is largely based on the administration's perspective, and for papers of "commercial

record" like the *Wall Street Journal*. For an exhaustive treatment of foreign coverage by major U.S. newspapers, see Noam Chomsky, *Necessary Illusions* (Toronto, Canada: CBC Enterprises, 1989). For a discussion of the use of corporate announcements in the *Wall Street Journal*, see Joanne Ambrosio, "It's in the *Journal*: But This Is Reporting?" *Columbia Journalism Review* (March 1989), 34.

9. Historians of print, printing, and literature generally prefer the phrase *printing revolution* to the more common *print technology* in the belief it better describes the complex of technology, social change, and economic development that transformed an oral and then scribal society into one whose information base was built upon mass-produced and commercially printed publications. That general preference, discussed by Alvin Kernan in *Printing Technology, Letters and Samuel Johnson* (Princeton: Princeton University Press, 1987), xv, is followed here.

10. Kernan is at some pains to demonstrate the degree to which all these changes were related to the printing revolution and to each other. As a summary of the effect of the printing revolution on public information in Great Britain, his work provides a superb introduction. But Kernan makes clear that his text focuses, in the study of Samuel Johnson, on the work of others who have described the broader history of the printing revolution. Among those cited by him whose work is critical to this area are: Elizabeth Eisenstein, *The Printing Press as an Agent of Change*, 2 vols. (Cambridge: Cambridge University Press, 1979); Robert Darnton, *The Business of Enlightenment: A Publishing History of the 'Encyclopedie' 1775-1800* (Cambridge, Mass.: Harvard University Press, 1979).

11. Kernan, *Printing Technology*. His work focuses on the work of Samuel Johnson, placing the body of Johnson's writing within the general context of the printing revolution. Others have examined the same period as a result of the philosophies of the Enlightenment as they moved through the English-speaking world. See, for example, J. Herbert Altschull, *From Milton to McLuhan: The Ideas Behind American Journalism* (White Plains, N.Y.: Longman, 1990)

for an attempt to put contemporary news theory within a historical and philosophic tradition.

12. Various aspects of Johnson's professional life and personal world have been studied and analyzed for two centuries. For an introduction to Johnson's life and work, see John Wain, *Samuel Johnson: A Biography* (New York: Viking Press, 1974); W. Jackson Bate, *Samuel Johnson* (New York: Harcourt Brace Jovanovich, 1975); and any edition of Boswell's *Life of Johnson.* Some scholarly editions include valuable indexes, for example, George Birkeck Hill, *Boswell's Life of Johnson*, 6 vols. (New York: Harper and Brothers, 1891).

13. Kernan, *Printing Technology*, 103.

14. Leon V. Sigal, "Sources Make the News," in Manoff and Schudson, *Reading the News*, 15.

15. Stratford P. Sherman, "Smart Ways to Handle the Press," *Fortune*, June 19, 1989, 69.

16. In North America, newspapers and periodicals are sold, while broadcast news has typically been disseminated without daily or subscription charge. But the issue of "free" news to all who can receive a broadcast is not that simple. In the 1980s, with the growth of cable television, specialty news channels became a commodity sold by subscription. In the early days of broadcast, RCA sold receivers, created news shows (on which it advertised) through its news subsidiaries and created markets for both through free access to those who had paid for a receiving set. Currently, certain online newsletters and "forums" are free to those who have purchased expensive computer equipment. One can argue that it makes no difference, at least to the consumer, if the capital cost is paid for a receiver or if it is paid in daily or weekly "subscription" or "newsstand" installments. I am indebted to Denis Wood of North Carolina State University for this argument. Denis Wood, private communication, December 13, 1989.

17. Edward S. Herman and Noam Chomsky, *Manufacturing Consent: The Political Economy of the Mass Media* (New York: Pantheon, 1988), 14-18.

18. Cited by Noam Chomsky, *Necessary Illusions*, 358, from Jerome A. Barron, "Access to the Press—A New First

Amendment Right," *Harvard Law Review* 80 (1967). The
original quote is found in Vladimir O. Key, *Public Opinion
and Democracy* (New York: Knopf, 1961).

19. Because *USA Today* was a new newspaper with an
undefined market, created as a journalistic entity that had
to demonstrate its economic viability, it provides a fascinat-
ing study of the complex masters any news publication must
simultaneously serve. See Prichard, *The Making of McPaper*,
for the authorized history of the daily's history.

20. This is critical to Herman and Chomsky's discussion
of the death of a labor-oriented and radical press. Herman
and Chomsky, *Manufacturing Consent*, 15.

21. John Wicklein, ed., *Public Broadcasting: A National
Asset to be Preserved, Promoted and Protected* (Columbus, Ohio:
Ohio State University School of Journalism, Working Group
for Public Broadcasting, December 1988), 1. A partial list of
working group members includes Wicklein, Ben H. Bag-
dikian from the University of California at Berkeley, Henry
Geller of the Center for Public Policy Research, Andrew
Schwartzman of the Media Access Project, and the National
Council of Churches' executive director, William Fore.

22. Wicklein, *Public Broadcasting*.

23. *Economist*, December 5, 1987. Quoted in Chomsky,
Necessary Illusions, 8.

24. Roger Simon, "Simon Says Ad-Pulling Is a Form of
Censorship," *Ka Leo O Hawai'i*, September 20, 1989, 4. Simon's
column is carried by a number of student newspapers, including the University of Hawaii's *Ka Leo* in which I happened to read this one.

25. See, for example, Herman and Chomsky, *Manufacturing Consent*, chapter 1.

26. Carlin Romano, "The Grisly Truth about Bare Facts,"
49.

27. Were the issue one simply of paying for publication,
the amount of advertising required would be far less. Whatever the media's public role, the corporate purpose of not
simply continuance but, as importantly, profitability is what
fuels the aggressive drive for ever more advertising time or
space to be sold.

28. William A. Henry III, "The Right to Fake Quotes," *Time*, August 21, 1989, 49.

29. David M. White, "'The Gate-Keeper': A Case Study in the Selection of News," *Journalism Quarterly* 27 (1950), 383-90.

30. See, for example: L. Donohue, "Newspaper Gate-Keepers and Forces in the News Channel," *Public Opinion Quarterly* 31 (1967), 61-68; Kurt Levin, "Frontiers in Group Dynamics II," *Human Relations* 1:47 (1947), 143-53.

31. This has become a large literature in its own right. For a sampling, see: Carrie Heeter, Natalie Brown, Stan Soffin, Cynthia Stanley, and Michael Salwenet, "Agenda-Setting by Electronic Text News," *Journalism Research* (Summer 1989); Maxwell E. McCombs and Donald L. Shaw, "The Agenda Setting Function of the Mass Media," *Public Opinion Quarterly* 36 (1972), 176-87; Maxwell E. McCombs, "The Agenda-Setting Approach," in Dan D. Nimmo and Keith R. Sanders, *Handbook of Political Communication* (Beverly Hills: Sage, 1981); Donald L. Shaw and Maxwell E. McCombs, eds., *The Emergence of American Political Issues: The Agenda-Setting Function of the Press* (St. Paul, Minn.: West, 1977).

32. Heeter et al., "Agenda-Setting," 101.

33. McCombs and Shaw, "Agenda-Setting Function," 176.

34. Heeter, et al., "Agenda-Setting."

35. In a study of presidential election coverage, media across the spectrum demonstrated very high correlations suggesting "consensus on news values, especially on major news items." McCombs and Shaw, "Agenda-Setting Function," 184. For an interesting view of the degree of conformity and the predictability of news coverage in another subject area, see T. Joseph Scanlon and Suzanne Alldred, "Media Coverage of Disasters: The Same Old Story," *Emergency Planning Digest* (October, 1982), 13-19.

36. See, for example, Shaw and McCombs, eds., *Emergence of American Political Issues.*

37. Michael B. Salwenet, *Agenda Setting with Environmental Issues: A Study of Time Process, Media Dependency, Audience Salience and Newspaper Reading,* Ph.D. diss.,

Michigan State University, 1985). Quoted in Heeter et al., "Agenda-Setting," 1989.

38. Gaye Tuchman, *Making News: A Study in the Construction of Reality* (New York: Free Press, 1978).

39. Herb Gans, *Deciding What's News* (New York: Pantheon Books, 1979). Quoted in Edwin Diamond, *The Last Days of Television* (Cambridge, Mass.: MIT Press, 1982), 148.

40. Lewis P. Lapham, *Money and Class in America* (New York: Ballantine Books, 1988), 50. Lapham takes it as self-evident that corporate concern with the economic viability of public information organizations has clear and consistent ramifications on the content of the end product.

41. James R. Bennett, "Newspaper Reporting of U.S. Business Crime in 1980," *Newspaper Research Journal* 3:1 (October 1981) quoted in Rusty Todd, "Research: Media Watchers Gag Reporters," *IRE Journal* 5:3 (Summer 1982), 6.

42. Anthony Carinale, "Mother Warns Not to Trust Officials on Dioxin," *Buffalo News*, April 26, 1990, A14.

43. Susan Schulman, "Ex-manager Says Plant Dumped PCBs at Site," *Buffalo News*, April 26, 1990, A1.

44. Neuharth's credo was included in a personal statement published on the front page of *USA Today*'s first edition (September 15, 1982) and is quoted in Prichard, *The Making of McPaper,* 8.

45. Meg Greenfield, "I Didn't Tell You So," *Newsweek,* November 27, 1989, 104.

46. Again it needs to be stressed that while this work focuses on U.S. examples, the issues raised are not unique to that country. To the extent that cultural values and technologies are evident, similar patterns can be found elsewhere. For a discussion of racism in a Canadian publication, for example, see Doreen M. Indra, "South Asian Stereotypes in the Vancouver Press," *Ethnic and Racial Studies* 2:2 (April 1979).

47. David Ley, *The Black Inner City as Frontier Outpost: Images and Behavior of a Philadelphia Neighborhood* (Washington, D.C.: American Association of Geographers, 1974), 32.

48. Ley, *The Black Inner City.*

49. Walter Gieber, "Two Communicators of the News: A Study of the Roles of Sources and Reporters," *Social Forces* 39 (October 1960), 80. Quoted in Sigelman, *Reporting the News*, 138.

50. See, for example, R.D. Cole, "Negro Image in the Mass Media: A Case Study in Social Change," *Journalism Quarterly* 45 (1968), 55-60. Cole noted that at that time a black could be seen on television only once every 2.5 hours.

51. I was a reporter at the *Springfield Union* from 1972 to 1974. During that time I was also the only bilingual, Spanish-speaking reporter on staff at either the *Union* or its sister publication, the *Daily News*. These "facts of life" were explained to me by Mooney and other editors amused at my desire to increase coverage of the Spanish-speaking community in which I lived at that time.

52. Noam Chomsky, *Necessary Illusions*, vii-viii.

53. Herman and Chomsky, *Manufacturing Consent*.

54. Al Giordino, "The War on Drugs: Who Drafted the Press?" *Washington Journalism Review* 12:1 (January 1990), 23.

55. A *"New York Times* editorial writer said, of his newspaper's coverage, that the contexts of the two situations are entirely different." Martin Mittelstaedt, "Is It Really All the News That's Fit to Print?" *Globe and Mail*, October 8, 1988, D3. One difference between the two situations was, according to David Pearson writing in *The Nation*, that U.S. intelligence officials were necessarily aware of the divergence of Flight 007 from its flight path and could have averted the tragedy. The Soviet Union, on the other hand, had no way of preventing the U.S. downing of the Iran Air flight. For a brilliant analysis of what is and is not known about Flight 007, see David Pearson, "007: What the U.S. Knew and When We Knew It," *The Nation,* August 18, 1984, 105-23. Reportage of this issue will be returned to in Chapter 3, "Transformations: Scale and Focus."

56. In 1990, the U.S. Defense Department honored Captain Will Rogers III and Lieutenant-Commander Scott Lustig of the SS *Vincennes* for their conduct during a July 3, 1988, skirmish in the Persian Gulf. Those citations were for actions resulting in the downing of the Iran Air Flight 655.

Even *Time*, which reported the awards, thought it excessive for the nation to honor its officers for the unintentional obliteration of a civilian plane. As the magazine writer editorialized, "The Defense Department has a strange way with awards." See "American Notes: Commending The Vincennes," *Time*, May 7, 1990, 37.

57. Mittelstaedt, "Is It Really," D1.

58. Lapham, *Money and Class,* 50.

59. John Keane, *Public Life and Late Capitalism* (New York: Cambridge University Press, 1984), 224.

60. Gilbert Cranberg, "A Flimsy Story and a Compliant Press," *Washington Journalism Review* (March 1990), 48. His article discusses how flimsy the rationale was for the Panamanian invasion by U.S. forces.

61. This is especially true when the injuries result from technology used by the news industry itself. Failure adequately to report on the health dangers resulting from prolonged use of VDTs is perhaps the best and most recent example. See Paul Brodeur, "Annals of Radiation, The Hazards of Electronic Fields," *New Yorker*, June 26, 1989, 39-68. This article was the last of a three-part series that has been published in book form. Paul Brodeur, *Currents of Death: Power Lines, Computer Terminals and the Attempt to Cover Up Their Threat to Your Health* (New York: Simon and Schuster, 1989).

62. Lewis H. Lapham, *Money and Class,* 50.

63. Noam Chomsky, *Necessary Illusions,* 8.

64. Sigelman, "Reporting the News."

65. Kurt Lang and Gladys Engle Lang, "The Mass Media and Voting," in Bernard Berelson and Morris Janowitz, eds., *Readings in Public Opinion and Communication*, 2nd ed. (New York: Free Press, 1966), 466. Quoted in McCombs and Shaw, "Agenda-Setting Function."

66. Tom Koch, *The News as Myth: Fact and Context in Journalism* (Westport, Conn.: Greenwood Press, 1990).

67. For a detailed analysis of how this affects coverage of boundary events, see Koch, *The News as Myth,* 122-43.

68. Jonathan Alter and Mark Star, "Race and Hype in a Divided City," *Newsweek*, January 22, 1990, 21-22. The crucial passage reads, in part: "The press abandoned its pri-

mary job requirement—skepticism. The pack mentality was so strong that even a stream of tips and rumors about Stuart's involvement in his wife's death did not lead reporters to do any real digging. . . . Because old-fashioned independent crime reporting is a lost art in most newsrooms, reporters assigned to the story mostly lapped up uncorroborated police leaks."

69. McCombs and Shaw, "Agenda-Setting Function," 180-81.

70. Steve K. Toggerson, "Media Coverage and Information-Seeking Behavior, *Journalism Quarterly* 58 (Spring 1981), 89.

71. For example, consider the coverage by the Hawaiian media of the attempted murder in 1981 of Honolulu judge Harry Y. Shintaku. Print reportage of this case is reviewed and analyzed in Koch, *The News as Myth*, 5-9, 91-109.

72. Joan Didion, "Letter from Los Angeles," *New Yorker*, February 26, 1990, 96. Didion was writing about the *Los Angeles Times* and quoting from a January 1, 1990 story by its reporter in Panama, Kenneth Freed.

73. Greenfield, "Pack Journalism." Mr. Greenfield is a network reporter interested in the performance of the media and an occasional commentator on that subject.

74. Greenfield, "Pack Journalism." Mr. Kalb was a guest on the *Nightline* segment.

75. In the story he quotes, the figure is 80 percent of 2,850 separate stories examined. Herb Gans, *Deciding What's News*, (New York: Pantheon, 1979), 25. Quoted in Edwin Diamond, *The Last Days of Television* (Cambridge, Mass.: MIT Press, 1982), 148. More recent studies have continued to show a consistent emphasis in the news on stories quoting and reflecting official positions. Others have found slightly different figures in subsequent studies, but the number is always above 70 percent.

76. Scott M. Cutlip, "Third of Newspapers' Content PR-Inspired," *Editor and Publisher*, May 26, 1962, 68, quoted in William P. Martin and Michael W. Singletary, "Newspaper Treatment of State Government Releases," *Journalism Quarterly* 58 (Spring 1981), 93, which provides a summary of several other articles on the relations between press

releases and journalism. A wide literature exists on maximizing information use in public relations, and, despite occasional denials by journalists, the symbiotic nature of both professions is attested by joint master's programs in schools of journalism and mass communications across the country.

77. Gans, *Deciding What's News,* 25.

78. Mark Schudson, "Deadlines, Datelines and History," in Robert Karl Manoff and Michael Schudson, eds., *Reading the News* (New York: Pantheon, 1986), 81.

79. Quoted in Chomsky, *Necessary Illusions*, 47.

80. Quoted in J. Herbert Altschull, *From Milton to McLuhan* (White Plains, N.Y.: Longman, 1990), 108.

81. Herman and Chomsky, *Manufacturing Consent*, 18-19.

82. Mark Fishman, *Manufacturing the News* (Austin, Tex. University of of Texas Press, 1980), 143. Quoted in Herman and Chomsky, *Manufacturing Consent,* 19.

83. Edward J. Epstein, *Between Fact and Fiction: The Problem of Journalism* (New York: Vintage Books, 1974), 3. Also quoted in Altschull, *From Milton to McLuhan.*

84. James McCartney, "The Vested Interests of the Reporter," in Louis Lyons, ed., *Reporting the News* (Cambridge, Mass.: Belknap Press, 1965), 65.

85. Robert P. Judd, "The Newspaper Reporter in a Suburban City," *Journalism Quarterly* 38 (Winter 1961), 38.

86. Jonathan Alter, "The Art of the Profile," *Newsweek*, January 22, 1990, 54.

87. Tom Goldstein, *The News at Any Cost* (New York: Simon and Schuster, 1985), 55. Also quoted in Romano, "Grisly Truth," Manoff and Schudson, eds., *Reading the News,* 55.

88. Stratford P. Sherman, "Smart Ways to Handle the Press," *Fortune,* June 26, 1989, 72.

89. Sherman, "Smart Ways."

90. See, for example, John Ullmann, "Introduction," in John Ullmann and Steve Honeyman, eds. *The Reporter's Handbook* (New York: St. Martin's Press, 1983), 3. For an extensive analysis of news writing as a narrative form see

Tom Koch, *The News as Myth,* chapter 2. For another view, see Manoff and Schudson, eds., *Reading the News*.

91. James W. Carey, "The Dark Continent of American Journalism," Manoff and Schudson, eds., *Reading the News,* 166.

92. Sigal, "Sources Make the News," 20.

93. Walter Lippmann, *Public Opinion* (New York: Free Press, 1965), 157.

94. Carey, *"Dark Continent,"* 166.

95. Clifford Daniel and Irving Kristol, "The Times: An Exchange," *Public Interest* 7 (1967), 119-123. The original article by Kristol appeared in *Public Interest* 6 (1966), but its main points are recapitulated by both Daniel and Kristol in this exchange.

2

Online News:
Trivial, Contextual,
and Structural

A number of separate but related factors impose upon the daily journalist's ability to fulfill either instrumental or institutional goals. Newspeople are constrained by economic imperatives, social perspectives, institutional restrictions, and a narrative form that organizes orally received data and makes it suitable for public dissemination. Electronic database technologies are not a panacea that will seamlessly or magically transform the news into a reasonably objective social service. But it is a new technology, and to the extent that news is structural and systemic, to alter a part is to affect the whole. This chapter attempts to show what online information systems can and, to some extent, have done. Because the use of these systems in contemporary newsrooms is so new and so tenuous, the analysis of their benefits must, to some extent, be speculative. The general argument is that these technologies will free journalists from a total reliance on the individual and thus, by definition, from limited views voiced by specific experts and officials. This freedom will allow reporters and editors themselves to define the context of a news story, thus regaining control of their own agenda and, perhaps, better approximate the profession's instrumental goals.

This advance is crucial, if limited. It is limited to the extent that it directly affects only one of the many social, cultural, and economic factors that shape the news. It is important because journalists cannot function as even minimally objective chroniclers unless they have sufficient information to question their subjects intelligently. To interview critically a physician, city engineer, corporate lawyer, or U.S. president or senator, reporters require independent access to information equal to the subject's on the event being discussed. But at present, unless a competitor or outside agency of legitimacy equal to the subject's offers a dissenting view, journalists are forced to rely on their subjects for data on the topic that the expert or official wishes to speak about.

Objectivity thus becomes a tautology in which contemporary reporters—constrained by ignorance—ask officials about events for which those officials are, in fact, responsible. To gain access to this information they have to be, if not welcomed, at least acknowledged and accepted by the police official, mayoral staff, presidential adviser, corporation chairman, or senator's aide, and this toleration is paid for in the coin of legitimizing copy. The story is defined narrowly and to the subject's benefit as what the CEO, hospital administrator, "Presidential Drug Czar William Bennett," or "chief of police" said at a specific moment. The cost of the whole is a story that puts forward as fact the subject's point of view, even though it may be inaccurate, biased, and self-serving.

The only way to break this impasse and thus to create a potential for critical and objective reportage is to free the newsperson from absolute dependence on information provided by sanctioned experts and officials. That will not remove the economic and social constraints supporting the editorial status quo or necessarily change the natural conservatism of many news managers. But for those who seek to understand and accurately describe current events, the ability rapidly to place an official datum into a broader context of information would and does change the relations between journalistic writer and editorial subject. It is this task that online technologies are able to perform, and the empowerment, when utilized, can be revolutionary.

ONLINE TECHNOLOGIES

Online technologies—usually called "databases" or, less frequently, "online libraries"—efficiently place an enormous amount of information at the command of the reporter or writer. Further, they do so with incredible specificity. Data available from online sources are so vast that it would take an expert months or years to search through them manually for the pertinent fact or the seminal article. But because these databases can be searched using specific key words and carefully crafted search phrases, the mass of accumulated literature in almost any field can be narrowed to the appropriate and crucial information within minutes by a competent data searcher. "The ability to search millions of pages of information in seconds to find a single mention of, say, a person's name, illustrates the awesome specificity of computerized information retrieval."[1]

Online libraries currently exist that are made up of the past editions of a variety of newspapers and magazines. These databases for the first time place at the individual journalist's disposal the work of colleagues from across North America and, increasingly, the world. A reporter in Honolulu, Hawaii, can rapidly and efficiently search through the news files of over 60 U.S. newspapers, more than 150 magazines, Japan's Kyodo News Agency, England's *Manchester Guardian,* and (in translation) the Soviet agency Tass for information on any single issue or event. A reporter writing on nosocomial illness in Portland, Oregon, can seek pertinent data, quickly and efficiently, not only through a selection of international medical journals and U.S. court records, but through the published work of newspaper and magazine colleagues around the world.

So empowered, the reporter or public affairs writer can critically question the hospital spokesman, coroner, pathologist, or judge with information equal to or, at times, greater than the official's. "You say this was a unique death, a 'freak occurrence,' but thirty others were reported in 1987," the reporter states. "Why didn't you know about this, and isn't it your job to make sure that equipment is safe in your facility?" When the official says no, it is not his responsibility, the reporter can say, with authority, "But the courts have found time and again that hospitals and their physicians are liable in this type of situation. The principle of law [quoted in an Ohio newspaper dispatch] is *res ipsa loquitor*." If a hospital official dismisses a patient's death at an official inquest as "unfortunate, a one-in-a-million accident," reporters need not accept this statistical judgment on faith.[2] In an hour or less online, that newsperson can check the available medical literature, court records, or the libraries of scores of newspapers to determine if, indeed, that death was a "freak"event or one of scores occurring under similar conditions in any given year.[3]

Such aggressiveness will not win the journalist powerful friends. Corporate officials may not seek out those journalists as confidants worthy of leaked information, but the loss of some contacts is more than offset by the ability to question critically when events occur. The specificity of online information searching allows a reporter to draw from the widest range of public information and to focus the results of those searches on a narrowly defined problem.

ORAL, PRINT, ELECTRONIC

Perhaps the best way to describe the potential of this electronic information system to journalism is to suggest that online information databases will bring the benefits of the eighteenth-century print revolution to late twenty-first-century journalism. The system will allow daily and weekly periodical writers not only to base their reports on "what was said today by 'X'" but as well to put that statement in the broad context of a deep stream of previous work and research. One can state with some assurance that this development will occur because it happened before when, in the eighteenth century, printing technologies gave rise to a mass-market publication system. To understand the diffusion and potential of electronic information today, it is helpful to review briefly the transformations that occurred during the first printing revolution. As a number of writers have been at pains to demonstrate, the very idea of "objective fact" owes its existence in great part to the eighteenth-century revolution in printing technology and the resulting growth in commercial, mass publication.

Alvin Kernan, for example, shows that a result of the acceptance of these technologies was "the [textual] authenticity that is probably the absolute mark of a print culture, a generally accepted view that what is printed is true, or at least truer than any other type of record."[4] By fixing a fact, idea, word, or dialogue onto a page that can be read, reread, and considered by many people over time, print allowed individuals for the first time to see and consider an occurrence or idea as stable and discrete. This ability is, in Kernan's words, the "power of print to fix and objectify."[5] Marshall McLuhan defines it as the "interiorization of technology," the process by which knowledge was transformed through the diffusion of printed materials from open, oral data to closed, abstract, fixed, and isolated information.[6]

Further, by allowing for the relatively inexpensive, mass production of multiple volumes and editions of books, news-letters, and pamphlets, print as a system of knowledge created, for the first time, an intellectual context in which the views or findings of many different people on a single topic could be dispassionately—"objectively"—compared. "Print, with its logic of systemization orders information, thus making it useful by placing it firmly in a structure of knowledge."[7] The development of this structure and its potential for objective reflection was the essence of the print revolution, which resulted in, among other benefits, a "scientific" system of knowledge placing individual statements or data within a context.

That "X" says "y" at a certain time and place is not information. It is an essentially trivial datum because there is no way to evaluate X's assertion, no context for its objective consideration. Before print, the royalty and clergy had the power to pronounce, and except in a narrow circle of the landed and wealthy, those statements were accepted as fact because the general population had no context other than the crown or church's claim of legitimacy in which to evaluate their pronouncements. Print, which allowed for the rapid diffusion of an enormous amount of information at minimal cost, created not only the periodical report but such a wealth of written material that vast libraries had to be created to be created. Over time, these libraries became a public resource whose information was, at least in theory, available to everyone and thus promised, through the creation of an educated and informed electorate, an inherent check against the unbridled excesses of the ruling class. An electorate so armed with information and an independent perspective was feared, at one point, by the small class of intelligentsia (essentially large landowners, clergy, and royalty), but the transformation to literacy—and its resulting democratization of knowledge—was unstoppable.

Before the eighteenth century, to be literate was to know a small body of classical literature, to have read perhaps (in Chaucer's day) twenty books and certainly no more than two hundred. But in the eighteenth century libraries with thousands of works came into being, and in the late nineteenth century the popular library movement gained momentum. With the increasing production and accumulation of printed materials, new ways of reading developed in which the works of one person, or information contained in one edition of a text, were critically compared with the writings of other individuals or editions of a single text. Kernan defines this fundamental change as the development of the "Gutenberg reader," an individual who reads and compares the information found in various texts, weighing the various statements against the accumulation of available information.

This transformation of society's information base was profoundly democratic. Before print, the power of information was solely in the hands of society's clear rulers—the clergy and the crown—but in the eighteenth century the commercial press gave rise, first in Britain and, soon after, in the colonies, to a print-based, information system increasingly controlled not by the crown alone but by independent publishers and individual writers who maintained the commercial information machine. Printing technology became an indispensable part of both the official posture—government printing offices, for example—and a dissenting position marked by pamphlets, polemics, editorials, and a populist press.

NEWS AND PRINT

Because this book is not a historical analysis of the relation of news to technology, it is unnecessary to discuss at length the reasons that periodicals retained a fundamentally oral system of information in the print era.[8] But it is perhaps pertinent to note in passing how rare and precious libraries and print resources were before this century. "Journalists" had little access to the work of other writers, and the technology that extended their geographic reach—first the telegraph, then the telephone, and now the satellite—emphasized not critical evaluation but simple transmission of what was said at a distant place. Even if a reporter in New York wanted to consider, to question what President Theodore Roosevelt said on the campaign trail, that reporter lacked ready access to the work of other daily news professionals writing in Chicago, Boston, Buffalo, or San Francisco. Technological advances facilitated the journalist's means of transmission while creating economies of scale for the media investor, but left the process of information gathering relatively unchanged.

The growth of daily newspapers as a business extended the need for copy at the same time that technology (the boat, train, automobile, and, finally, the airplane) extended the range of society as a whole. In this rush to cover increasing areas of the globe where national interests lay, the time and resources for placing the accumulated statements into a broader context were minimal. The custom of news became set, and reporters were defined by the increasingly specialized ability to translate rapidly what someone said into so many column inches of print for the next day. There could be nothing more and, as Walter Lippmann said in 1920, one of necessity accepted, in the main, the statements of officials because "the books and papers are in their [the officials'] offices."[9]

Even when public libraries became a nearly ubiquitous fixture of the North American city in this century, daily hacks were seldom given the time required for their use. Even if they had the time, the expertise required to search legal, financial, or medical literature was rarely a part of the journalists' kit bag, and the work of colleagues at geographically distant publications was rarely available for their perusal. Nor, of course, was the lack of such research tools perceived as a liability by the vast majority of editors and reporters. Few news professionals had the requisite skills to be a "Gutenberg reader," even had they been granted the time to use the library as a professional resource and seek through legal, medical or general texts to fashion a context for their stories. Reporters wrote and editors printed what people said. Lacking the crucial "books and papers," which remained on the desks of officials and officially designated experts—or the time to utilize and reflect on those which were available—reportage became by default a public address system in which the narrative form of the news lacked any critical structure. The best one could hope for was contradiction by dissenting, but still official actors participating in a specific event. The way to break a story was to quote what some other, "real" investigator said. To a great extent, the situation remains the same today.

> In the absence of any foolproof criterion for choosing sources who are likely to provide valid information, journalists are uncertain about whom to believe. They cope with uncertainty by continuing to rely on authoritative sources. The presumption of hierarchy, that those at the top of any organization are the people in charge and that those in subordinate positions do what their superiors tell them to— underlies the journalist's criterion for selected sources even though journalists themselves recognize that this presumption is often of doubtful validity.[10]

DATABASE TECHNOLOGIES: AN EXAMPLE

Electronic information databases provide the potential for the typical journalist to develop, story by story and issue by issue, criteria for evaluating the statements of their sources. These databases take the "books and papers" from the offices of officials and place them in the hands of journalists and other public information writers who can use them to question critically a subject's statements. An example of exactly how this process works at its best may provide a better understanding of the degree to which online information technologies can transform the reportorial function and, by extension, that of any writer or advocate interested in a specific issue. To evaluate this and other examples used in this book, the reader will find it helpful to distinguish between three different levels of story, each level defined by the type of information it carries. These definitions are tentative guidelines, but will serve not only to demonstrate how the use of electronic databases can affect news content but to distinguish later among various databases themselves:

1. *Trivial or Ephemeral Story.* This is the commonplace, contemporary news report that describes "what" was said by "who" (an official or expert), "where" (here), and "when" (today). It is in the main composed of isolated and discrete data, whose accuracy is unevaluated by the newsperson, reflecting or repeating narrowly prescribed statements of one or more participants in some event. The individual data have no greater context and are of limited interest. As Tim Miller said, "Not only does the print newspaper [story] have the life span of the May fly, it also has about the same migratory range."[11] The ephemeral story, as a category, presents an isolated datum that, the day after publication, is quickly forgotten.

2. *Contextual Story.* This narrative takes the individual datum and places it within one or more contexts in which its importance can be evaluated. The context is typically one of a recurring class of events for which information has been accumulated and causes assigned. In the conventional news paradigm, this story would focus on the broad "what" happened or "how" an event is to be understood. It thus places a single event—a death, fire, medical condition, government regulation, or political occurrence—within a broader context, much as legal precedents serve to define issues of responsibility within the civil court system.

3. *Structural Story.* To the extent that events are related, they can be seen within the greater context of social issues and forces. "Why" a pattern emerges is often the

result of political, economic, or cultural forces that, while not immediately evident in the trivial or contextual category, may be manifest in another situation. Thus a structural story makes overt the links connecting an event or series of events and broader social issues or policies.

To see how each level is related and how contextual and structural elements are made accessible to the generalist reporter familiar with computer databases, consider the following story on tort reform and its relation to the issue of medical costs in the United States.

TORT REFORM

Since the 1970s, state legislators, the U.S. Congress, the American Medical Association, and the Association of Trial Lawyers of America have become increasingly concerned about the rising cost to society of medical treatment in the United States. Thousands of newspaper stories and magazine articles have been written about the problem, many of them dealing with the debate over legislation commonly referred to as tort reform. Sparked by the California legislature's Medical Injury Compensation Reform Act (MICRA), passed in 1975, the idea has been to reduce medical costs, or at least the rapidity of their increase, by placing a limit on jury awards for pain and suffering to victims of medical malpractice. Proponents of tort reform have insisted this limit would reduce the overall costs of medical care by decreasing the stunning increases in malpractice insurance premiums which physicians have been forced to pay. Holding down the amount of court-ordered awards would save insurers money, decrease the cost of premiums to physicians, and in theory those savings would be passed on to society at large.

In this debate, heard each time tort reform is introduced (in states ranging from New York to Hawaii), the two sides have been adamant and clear. Lawyers opposing tort reform consistently argue that increasing malpractice premiums are the result of fair compensation to the victims of bad medical practice; and the answer to increasing health insurance costs, therefore, not legal but medical. The American

Medical Association and insurers argue that avaricious lawyers and greedy, if grieving clients are indeed the problem
and, further, that the sacred patient-doctor relationship is
being destroyed by an increasingly adversarial legal system,
which has made litigants of the partnership between caring
healer and needy patient.

News reporters cover these issues at legislative hearings and press conferences called by one or another side.
They do not take sides or independently examine the central
questions raised by the debate. They quote one or another
official representative of a medical association, a legal organization, or an insurance company executive who testified at
a hearing or called a press conference to state the specific
organization's position. These are the "facts" presented to
readers or viewers in daily stories chronicling opposing
views.

The *Wall Street Journal*

A good example of standard reportage on this issue is a
Wall Street Journal article that reported on a "debate" between the president of the Association of Trial Lawyers of
America, Robert Habash, and a "surgeon and a top official of
the American Medical Association," Dr. James Todd.[12] The
long, two-column story was accompanied by a sidebar on the
Canadian system titled, "In Canada, Different Legal and
Popular Views Prevail." The whole presentation appears to
be a model of contemporary journalism, objectively balancing two opposing views, each articulated by a leading "expert"
in his field, in a "debate" over the perceived problem of
malpractice liability premiums. The whole is preceded by
Journal reporter Michael Waldholz's introduction, which
summarizes both legal and medical positions through the
statements of the participants themselves:

> Malpractice liability has lately become one of the
> most divisive issues among doctors and lawyers.
> "Physicians are leaving the profession in unheard-
> of droves because of a system they don't under-
> stand, they can't cope with, and which is getting

worse," says James Todd, a surgeon and a top official of the American Medical Association. At fault for the burgeoning lawsuits and staggeringly high premiums many doctors pay, he argues, are a legal system that encourages meritless litigation and trial lawyers who profit exorbitantly from malpractice cases.

"Malpractice lawsuits result from malpractice," counters Robert Habash, a partner with the Milwaukee law firm Habash, Habash and Davis and president-elect of the Association of Trial Lawyers of America. Mr. Habash says that present laws help protect patients' rights and ensure their access to the courts. He believes the situation calls for changes in the insurance industry and more careful monitoring by doctors of competence in the profession.

What follows is a debate organized by *The Wall Street Journal* between Dr. Todd and Mr. Habash.

The Introduction
This story is, for all its appearance of "objective" debate, a synthetic and mediated product, consistently slanted in its presentation despite the premise of objectivity presumably guaranteed by the body of the text, which is composed entirely of excerpts from the participants' speeches. Even though Waldholz is supposedly silent and "objective," his introduction makes clear what his—or his newspaper's—posture and interests are. In fact, before the body of the "debate" has begun, the biases of both participants and the newspaper are evident. This *Journal* "top" sanctifies as fact a series of assumptions through its summation, thus defining all that will follow.

We do not question, for example, the bylined story's assertion, attributed to Todd, that "physicians are leaving the profession in unheard-of droves" because if it were not true, why would the *Journal* print it, and if it were not a problem, would there be any need for a debate at all? Nor do we doubt that these career changes are directly related to the problem of malpractice liability, despite a total lack of substantiation for that position in the text. The lead paragraph—short and direct—insists we accept this linkage.

Todd's assertion that this terrifying image of a future bereft of physicians is due to "a system they [physicians] don't understand, they can't cope with, and which is getting worse" is not substantiated by the story and effectively places the onus for these problems on the debate's "other side," the lawyers and their representative, Habash.

But it is not "the system," understood or not, that is at issue. Rather, this story is about "staggeringly high premiums" and "lawyers who profit exorbitantly"—phrases of the journalist and not of the debators. Waldholz uses adjectives to editorialize in the time honored, *Time* magazine style of condemnation by adjective and modifier. We credit him in part because this is the *Wall Street Journal* on issues of money and business, the commercial daily's métier. We accept on faith that premiums are too high (But too high compared with what? As a function of total gross revenues for doctors? Real income?) and that lawyers profit exorbitantly. Precisely what system is misunderstood by physicians—and the actual state of their confusion—is unstated here, and perhaps it is just as well.

Thus the *Journal* agrees from the start with Todd's position that the issue is malpractice liability premiums, a posture Habash, for his part, rejects. Despite its pretense of objectivity and the reporter's apparent role as moderator, the newspaper has taken a stand squarely on the physicians' side of the argument. In the body of the "debate," Habash insists the problem is elsewhere than in fleeing physicians, in lawyers profiting exhorbitantly, or in a system that befuddles the hardworking physician. He tries to reframe the context of the debate to include prevention of malpractice through tighter regulation of physicians as a class. But Todd disagrees and the body of the *Journal*'s introduction to Habash emphasizes not the lawyer's main argument, that "malpractice lawsuits result from malpractice," but his position on necessary changes in the insurance, medical, and legal industries.

Underscoring the *Journal*'s bias is the simple fact that Todd, a "top official" of the American Medical Association, is given higher billing than the president of the Association of Trial Lawyers of America. One would expect that an association president would be asked to speak first and, where the two speakers are equal in status, the person whose last name begins with the letter closest to "A" would be given precedence. But the first quotes in the introduction are given to Todd and Habash is left for rebuttal. Presumably this order is a result of the fact that the doctor's position, like the *Journal*'s, emphasizes the economics of malpractice liability and not the messy and more complex issue of physician responsibility.

The "Debate"

Thus the "debate" begins with a bias toward Todd's posture. He is the first speaker and the one most clearly focused on the "divisive" issue of the cost of malpractice liability. The whole text then alternates, paragraph by paragraph, with statements by one or the other man. We presume, but are not told, that the story is composed of edited excerpts from a longer interview session. Rarely do individuals—especially those so clearly involved in their topic as these men—speak in one- or two-paragraph bursts. Nor, one suspects, would two such men never interrupt each other or allow topics to be changed and discussion over a "divisive issue" to flow as easily as this "debate" suggests. The whole piece is thus an artificial dialogue excerpted, condensed, and formulated to fit both the *Journal's* editorial perspective and its available news hole on a single day. What, then, do the two men say?

Todd argues that juries composed of lay individuals cannot judge malpractice cases, that a doctor's only "peers" are other physicians. Juries of lay people, he implies, are manipulated by crafty lawyers and higher rates are the result. He denies that bad medicine by incompetent doctors is the problem but agrees that "medicine can do a better job disciplining [incompetent] doctors." The real problem, Todd insists, lies with inequities in the legal system that make everyone resort to litigation. It is that tendancy to litigate that has caused an increase in malpractice suits and the size of resulting awards. The result of these inequities is that physicians are leaving their practice and profession, hurt and befuddled by a system that they do not understand and cannot afford. "If the medical profession is guilty of a thing," he insists, "it is overselling its wares. Everyone no expects a perfect result." The people profiting from all this— the real villains in Todd's view—are malpractice lawyers. The principal victim is society-at-large, which suffers through higher costs and decreased care as physicians leave practice (or refuse to practice in a specific state) because of high malpractice insurance costs and the deleterious effect on their lives of contentious malpractice suits.

The answer, Todd says, is tort reform, which would limit the amount juries can award for "pain and suffering" to $250,000, with payment spread over a period of time instead of ordered in a lump sum.

Habash, on the other hand, says that tort reform would not solve the problem which he defines, more generally, as botched operations by incompetent physicians. He even quotes a statement attributed to Todd in 1984 that, "there's just too much incompetence and negligence in the medical profession." Habash insists that the root of the problem is not the U.S. system of litigation but, instead, the fact that bad physicians are allowed to practice medicine. "It's the incompetent doctors who are causing the problem," he says. "In Pennsylvania, 1 percent of the doctors accounted for 25 percent of medical malpractice payments." Thus Habash suggests that if only those "few bad apples" were excised from the community of physicians, the problem would be resolved. Unfortunately, Habash suggests, statistics show that physicians are not doing the job. Medical malpractice suits with high awards thus protect the public, in the lawyer's view, by focusing public attention through the courts on incompetent doctors, and serve the public by championing the victims of bad medicine.

To limit awards in any area would, Habash concludes, accomplish little except "taking rights away from victims." Not surprisingly, Todd takes strong exception to Habash's characterization of claimants in malpractice suits as victims. Habash suggests (and Todd denies) that malpractice litigation is just a convenient target for physicians who don't want to address more central and crucial problems.

he Context

" is an essentially trivial story. It excerpts, stories, from a longer discussion between ojects and then records elements of what ̣said on a single day. It provides, really, no information from which a concerned citizen could choose or judge between the positions offered. The whole is a procession of individual, unexamined, and unsubstantiated data which the reader, like the reporter, cannot evaluate without recourse to independent research. Todd sounds like an honest, sincere guy. So does Habash. Todd is really worried about doctors leaving their practices because they can't afford the malpractice bill. Habash says, in effect, nuts and good riddance. Bad doctors are the issue. Of course, one would expect a lawyer to defend the legal side and a physician to defend the medical profession. There are nuggets of potential information tucked away, of course, that a truly interested reader or reporter could pursue. Did Todd really say, before he became a spokesman, that medicine is riddled with "incompetence" and, if so, did he think then what he denies here—that medical incompetence is a part of this problem? How many cases of malpractice are attributed to a small group of bad physicians? Todd says it's not the issue. Habash says it is.

There is no way to judge between Habash's and Todd's respective positions on the basis of information provided by the *Journal*, and the story joins a huge bank of ephemeral data on a topic that cries to be pulled into a context that would give the reader real information. Who is correct—physicians, represented by Todd, or lawyers, who presumably stand behind Habash? If we put the question another way, can a reporter determine if either bad medicine or litigious patients (teamed with avaricious lawyers) constitute the real, root problem? What are the central issues in the tort reform argument, and to what extent can blame in fact be laid either at the door of doctors (for improper procedures that cause the injuries that result in suits) or of venal lawyers (who encourage legal action at the drop of a hat)? Would a cap on payments for "pain and suffering" really make a difference, and while we're asking, how much is awarded by juries to litigants as a rule? Maybe "pain and suffering" awards are an insignificant part of the typical jury award and thus of the issue of malpractice award costs. The participants in the*Wall Street Journal* debate each had vested interests. What would an objective treatment of this whole subject mean to a reporter?

One way to examine the issues raised by this debate would be to look at the findings of court cases in which juries had made awards to the victims of malpractice. Since this issue is state-wide—tort reform is legislated at that level—and nation-wide because the cost of health care is a federal concern, pertinent cases from most U.S. legal jurisdictions would bear on it. These cases would show how and where blame in fact was laid and, further, allow a journalist to break down jury-awarded monies: so much for pain and suffering, so much to keep a person in hospital, so much for loss of consortium (in the case of a spouse or child) or future earning power for a family's principal wage earner. That research, which would provide one context for the respective statements of both Habash and Todd, could be done in a law library, of course, but legal research is a rather specialized field that few reporters have studied. Since newspapers typically report on large jury awards—and large awards in cases of medical misadventure are the issue—it might be possible to search principal newspapers in each state for stories of large awards. Using traditional, nonelectronic methods, that search would require writing scores of letters to city editors or librarians around the country and waiting for them to reply.

To search forty or more newspapers online for stories dealing with court malpractice awards is, however, well within the range of the possible. One service that facilitates such research is Vu/Text, a company that specializes in transferring newspaper files into a computerized database for ease of storage and access. Some of the costs of that exercise are recovered for those clients who agree to allow Vu/Text to offer their files online to other subscribers. At present, over sixty-five newspapers have signed up for that service, and all can be searched globally (at once) for any single search word or phrase.

The question is what to ask; and the issue of crafting appropriate search language is addressed in Chapter 4. For the moment, consider that just looking for articles on "tort reform" would return newspaper accounts of legislative debates like the *Wall Street Journal* story—more of the same. If news is, as we contend, primarily the printed record of oral statements, it is unlikely one will find in these accounts an unbiased context for review of the issues enjoined by this specific "debate." Habash suggests the problem is incompetent and undisciplined physicians, but looking for court cases involving physician discipline is not the answer. Stories on surgery and injury or death would be helpful but these phrases are also too general. We talk about deadly "surgical strikes," for instance, so such a search would bring up stories about military exercises. In many newspapers (like the ones where I have worked) there are files of stories, and many involve anesthesia and problems related to its use. Since anesthesia is used in most surgery, perhaps it is a crucial element, and searching for stories involving anesthesia and injury or death to patients should be narrow enough.[13] Searching the whole database with this phrase is worth a try.[14]

Between January 1, 1987, and October 22, 1988, forty U.S. newspapers whose files are stored on Vu/Text carried over thirty stories describing court cases involving death or injury resulting from anesthesia. Several of those stories described court cases in which a single physician was found guilty of up to sixteen deaths or injuries[15] that resulted in court action, so, in fact, the number of relevant cases was far higher than the number of returned stories noted here would suggest. In most cases, the newspaper stories reported on court evidence which showed that death or permanent injury resulted when physicians either failed to monitor their patients adequately during a procedure, used incorrect drugs during a procedure, or otherwise failed to follow established medical procedures.

There were a few spectacularly large awards. One story involved a $28 million award,[16] but the average size of settlements was $4.5 million. Further, the monies awarded were largely for medical expenses[17] to maintain patients who had been permanently disabled by a physician's mistake or to provide continued life support for those who had been left by medical misadventures in a "vegetative state."[18] Patients so injured often received awards in excess of $1 million but, according to these newspaper accounts of statements made in court, those monies were awarded by a judge or jury to pay for the cost of maintaining a disabled person—Todd insists they are not "victims"—in a diminished (quadriplegia, paraplegia, extensive brain dysfunction, etc.) or vegetative state.[19] The amount awarded for pain and suffering sometimes equaled but rarely surpassed and was typically far less than that given by juries to victims for medical maintenance, an area of cost that tort reform would not affect. The whole search took about fifteen minutes, although reading the recovered stories took three hours and analysis of award amounts several hours more. It was, perhaps, a full day's work.

One for the lawyers. Jury awards were based primarily on medical necessity. Compensation to families of those who died or were permanently injured during surgery also included monies for "loss of consortium," which would allow, for example, a widower to hire a housekeeper or nanny to assist him in the care of his children after his wife died in an anesthetic-related mishap. Awards were made for "pain and suffering," and, sometimes, they were large. But the whole of this evidence of reportage of court awards emphasized the cost of malpractice in which the physician(s) were judged to be at fault.

Todd says right off the top in the *Wall Street Journal* story that lay people can't judge medical issues, that only physicians can function as peers for other doctors. So maybe judges and juries were swayed in all these cases by tricky and avaricious lawyers, as the American Medical Association's high official suggests. But in the search for news stories answering the phrase "anesthesia and death or injury," several non-court stories were captured that suggest the opposite. The *Sacramento Bee,* for example, quoted a Harvard Medical School researcher who said that at least two thousand people die annually, and more are injured, because of improperly administered anesthetic. Further, these deaths and injuries were all described as preventable.[20] Dr. John Eichorn told the *Bee* that a review of all anesthetic-related fatalities at Beth Israel Hospital in Boston over the previous decade had concluded that 70 percent of the deaths would not have occurred had physicians followed established standards of anesthetic administration.

Reducing the number of deaths by 70 percent would certainly cut the cost of malpractice insurance by reducing incidents which result in legal action. Further, the story offered strong support for the trial lawyers' association's position that bad medicine, not high awards, was the major villain in medical malpractice awards. But, frankly, I would not want to take a single story from the *Sacramento Bee* (or any other individual newspaper story) to the bank when talking about something so important. Beth Israel Hospital runs a medical database in which articles from all major medical journals are collected and indexed. Checking that service, called PaperChase, for articles by John Eichorn uncovered the critical article[21] which presumably sparked the *Sacramento Bee* interview with him, as well as other, more recent articles that cited Eichorn's research. This body of information (which in turn is based on separate studies done at several geographically distant hospitals) also insisted that if physicians only used appropriate monitoring equipment and followed established procedures, many lives would be saved and permanent injuries prevented. Further, one or more articles analyzed the cost of monitoring equipment that, if used, would radically reduce anesthetic-related problems and found the cost trivial when compared with the savings that would result from decreased litigation.[22] Medical journal articles estimated that health care professionals were responsible for anesthetic-related "catastrophic errors" occurring in surgery from 50 to 90 percent of the time.[23]

The cost of the Vu/Text and PaperChase searches together was under one hundred dollars and required less than an hour to execute. Reading and analyzing the material returned by those searches took about six hours. Were reporters really industrious, they also could have searched a database like *WestLaw* for the text of cases mentioned in news reports or for the principles of law stated in some stories. Thus, a *Columbus Dispatch* story reported that an Ohio jury was instructed by its judge in an anesthetic-related case that the principle of law pertinent to judgments in this area was *res ipsa loquitor*—which means that if something occurred, someone is to blame.[24] On *WestLaw's* legal database, searching for other cases in which this principle was stated made clear that the issue of compensation when someone is at fault is deeply embedded in the legal system and applicable not only to medical malpractice, but to all injury cases as well. That raises the interesting question of why malpractice awards should be isolated, as Todd thinks they should be, as the only category of personal injury where compensation under the principle would be denied. Further, specific cases searched through *WestLaw* provided in-depth treatment of both the precise types of medical injury sustained by individuals and clear statements of the effective causes of those injuries and justification of the awards (whether the money was for maintenance of a person in a vegetative state, for pain and suffering, or for loss of consortium).

All this information, while not necessarily pertinent to any single, specific story, becomes valuable and powerful when a journalist attempts to put a recent, journalistically defined event into a broader context. If, for example, an individual has been injured in surgery and the physician's lawyer says, because the cause of that injury was atypical and unusual that the physician should not be held responsible, the traditional reportorial response has been to quote that statement, seek a "balancing" quote from the claimant's attorney ("Your opponent says the physician's not at fault. What do you say?"), and then go home. Traditionally, reporters could, as a rule, do little more because they knew no more. Now they can understand a bit of the law behind such events and, certainly, draw (as do lawyers) from other cases, legal precedents, and a vast medical literature that make responsibility and liability relatively precise and objective terms.

On the basis of this research, which could be localized by reporters to focus on cases occurring in their circulation or immediate broadcast areas, the conclusions are inescapable. Cases of death and injury in surgery could be reduced significantly—estimates ranged from between 50 and 70 percent—if physicians followed established procedures and used appropriate monitoring equipment when a patient was anesthetized. That reduction would result in savings not only of dollars but of lives far in excess of anything that proponents of tort reform have anticipated for their plan. Reducing incidence of death or permanent injury would eliminate not only large awards for pain and suffering—the sole result of tort reform—but also reduce or eliminate other, costlier awards for maintenance of the injured, compensation for lost ability to work, loss of consortium, burial expenses, etcetera.

Further, failure to follow established procedures may be based on not only physician error but physician incompetence. A significant percentage of supposedly licensed physicians are, in fact, bogus doctors practicing without proper training. Other physicians suffer from alcohol and drug abuse—estimates run as high as one in five—while residents who carry the brunt of hospital work are often forced to work so long without a break that they may literally fall asleep during a surgical procedure.[25] This information is in both popular and technical journals and reports.

Other Approaches

This approach has required the reporter to choose what points require examination, to fashion a hypothesis from the subject's statement, and then to test it against the written record. The database approach forces public information writers to make independent choices as they build a story. Other searches could also have been carried out. A simple question raised by Todd, and amenable to examination, is whether there is a real possibility that the United States faces a shortage of physicians because so many are leaving the profession—for whatever reason. If there is a real possibility of a shortage, then the question may be why those doctors are quitting. Are malpractice premiums the only reason? By searching newspapers for the words "physician and shortage," Todd's concern can be quickly laid to rest. In 1990, for example, Louis Sullivan, secretary of the United States Department of Health and Human Services, told Congress that the current supply of physicians would be at least adequate through the turn of the century.[26] Certainly, physicians were leaving the profession in the 1980s, presumably for a variety of reasons, but not in numbers sufficient to adversely affect the health care of the average citizen. Sullivan also noted, as have others in previous reports, a real and growing shortage of nurses that may impact on long-term health care.

Habash stated that the failure of physician organizations to adequately police their own sometimes results in deadly medicine by bad doctors. Todd, for his part, not only said that physicians can supervise their own professional community but went further and argued that, in his opinion (and the opinion, therefore, of the American Medical Association), no one but a physician can adequately judge another doctor's performance. Is Habash right—are doctors unable to police their own? Or is Todd right when he says physicians and only physicians can regulate their professional brethren? This is a topic which can be framed as a hypothesis and checked against the written record.

One tends to be skeptical of Todd's insistence that physicians and only physicians should review the work of their colleagues. There is an element of self-protection and self-interest in that argument that has been noted by individuals other than Habash. A *New York Times* article, for example, suggested that physicians reviewing the performance of their colleagues is at best a conflict of interest when it asked "whether the medical association, whose central purpose is to represent the interest of doctors, should take the lead in disciplining them."[27] That story did not answer the question, but information found in a basic computer search shows that, at least in the past, physicians have been quite unable adequately to police their own. The *Detroit News* summed up the point nicely when it stated that physicians "reporting an incompetent or impaired doctor to a county, state or national medical organization is like [a motorist] reporting a bad driver to the American Automobile Association. The organizations might deplore the behavior but neither is equipped, legally or politically, to deal with the problem."[28]

Daily newspaper databases carry a wealth of anecdotal, regional stories about the failure of medical organizations in various jurisdictions to discipline or restrict the practices of incompetent or unqualified members. Taken together, they become a damning indictment of Todd's position. The medical literature also concludes that physicians have been extremely reluctant to examine critically the performance or

even the credentials of their members. A 1985 report in the
New England Journal of Medicine, for example, showed that
in 1982 some states reported no disciplinary action against
even one member per thousand and the number of states
that disciplined more than three members per thousand was
only fourteen. The report's author, a physician, said dryly
that "it is difficult to believe that in any given year any state
or territory would not have at least one physician per thousand who posed a threat to the health and safety of its
citizens and yet, in 1982, 4 states reported less than that
number of disciplinary actions."[29] In 1985 the situation had
not significantly improved. In that year, only 2,108 of the
United States' estimated 405,000 physicians (.00468 percent) were disciplined, although perhaps 20 percent of U.S.
doctors were, according to other studies, abusing drugs or
alcohol[30] and at least 6 percent of those who practiced
medicine as physicians were, in fact, not licensed and may
have had no formal medical training.[31] Thus a significant
percentage of the currently practicing physicians to whom
Todd wanted society to turn over exclusive judgment of their
colleagues are unlicensed, "bogus" doctors,[32] the very lay-
persons he insisted could not adequately judge the competence of licensed professionals.

The Computer-Researched Story

The information generated online to test statements by
Todd and Habash would make a respectable story, sidebar,
or part of a series on the issues of contemporary medicine.
Whatever approach is taken, the story has become not simply that doctors and lawyers disagree but, rather defini-
tively, that "malpractice is expensive practice." Statements
by Habash and Todd, proponents for groups with economic
and professional interests in the issues, have been placed in
a broader context which allows the writer—hack, flack, or
advocate—to examine critically the individual statements.
Information resulting from the online search, localized by
journalists with examples from their specific circulation or
broadcast area,[33] would include the following facts:

• Medical authorities admit that incidence of death and injury resulting from surgery are usually the avoidable result of bad medicine.

• Many physicians do not follow widely accepted procedures or use effective and recommended monitoring techniques. This failure causes as much as 70 percent of the anesthetic-related deaths occurring nationally in surgery.

• One result of these failures has been increased insurance costs as malpractice suits multiplied, causing, among other problems, the "medical insurance crisis."

• Medical associations have been lax in disciplining their members, weeding out "bogus" or inferior practitioners, and, generally, in assuring fulfillment of the profession's institutional and instrumental goals: to heal the sick through administration of specific protocols and procedures.

• Physicians agree that if proper medical procedures were followed in surgery and if anesthetists used appropriate monitoring equipment, incidents of injury and death—and therefore the number of court awards involving malpractice—would decrease dramatically.

Further, these statements are "facts" not in the sense that newspapers typically use the word but, rather, in one approximating the objective sense it carries in logic and science. Typically, a "fact" in news means someone in a position of authority stated that "x" was true. It is a fact only to the degree that the "fact" reflects a true statement at the level of the journalistic event—that is, what was actually said by the official, president, coroner, chief of police, CEO, professor, or designated spokesperson. The validity of that statement in relation to the antecedent subject is outside the journalist's typical arena of inquiry. It is a datum bounded by both the level of information of its source and the time frame of that statement. Newspaper "facts" are like the Watergate defendants' defense: everything is modified by the phrases "at that one point in time" or "in that time frame." If the police announce that a man's death was suicide, the fact is not necessarily that of an individual's successful action to end his own life. In the absence of other information from dissenting but still official sources, one may assume the truthfulness of the police chief's statement, but without corroborating evidence, nothing more.[34]

The "facts" in this computer-assisted story are a little different. They put the issues raised by Todd and Habash within the context of a score of medical studies, public reports, and court decisions written and rendered over time. There are to the stories, decisions, and reports returned by this search a depth and breadth which require of the print reporter, broadcast journalist, or magazine writer a critical focus and input as the statements of a Habash or a Todd are weighed against outside information. The reporter or editorial writer can say with some certainty that, to the best of our knowledge, something is true not because an official says it is so but that it is true on the basis of a wide range of public information. Thus a computer-assisted story on the subject of tort reform, which subjected the statements of Habash and Todd to an electronic review, might include the following:

Malpractice is "Malpractice"

A newspaper staff investigation suggests strongly that those lawyers who argue that "bad medicine" is at the root of the medical cost crisis are correct.

Forcing physicians to follow established procedure would save hundreds of lives and the millions of dollars required to maintain individuals placed in a "vegetative state" by improperly administered anesthesia during surgery.

Medical experts admit that the failure of physicians to follow basic procedures or use readily available equipment that medical studies and medical schools recommend is responsible for more than 50 percent of the deaths or permanent injuries that result from surgery in the nation's hospitals.

"There's just too much incompetence and negligence in the medical profession," Dr. James Todd, a high official in the American Medical Association, stated in 1984. Here are examples of what incompetence and negligence mean to individuals:

The story would then include a localized discussion of issues like:
- cases involving failure to monitor
- cases involving use of inappropriate drugs
- cases involving equipment failure leading to death
- the failure of medical associations to supervise their members or to assure that members have proper credentials and training.

WHAT HAS CHANGED

It is important to see the limits as well as the strengths of this approach. The general agenda remains in the hands of lawyers, physicians, and legislators who have raised the issue of medical costs to society and framed it in terms of compensation to victims or their families. Problems are still defined not in terms of an individual's quality of life or the root causes of illness and preventable injury (many of which are social and environmental) but in terms of an economic bottom line. The main issue—cost of compensation after medical misadventure—was defined by the speakers and followed by the reporter. The story has become not how to eliminate illness resulting in deaths and injuries but, rather, how to cut medical insurance costs by evaluating a class of medical events. Nobody has questioned that economics is the essential issue in the malpractice debate or that lawyers and physicians are the appropriate people to make these decisions. The position of nurses, for example, has not been solicited on the issue of medical costs or procedure. Nor has the idea been raised of scrapping fee-for-service medicine for a more socialized medical system like Canada's or New Zealand's, a change which would, some believe, increase the quality of health care while decreasing total cost to the nation.[35] The *Wall Street Journal*'s sidebar on the Canadian medical system was limited solely to statements on that country's system of malpractice litigation. Nobody has entertained suggestions that supervision of physicians—

and their licensing—be taken from medical organizations and given to an independent body composed, perhaps, of nurses, emergency technicians, lay people, and physicians. The physician's present status in society and the means by which medical services are rendered remain unquestioned.

Further, the agenda in which medical and legal officials focus on malpractice as the critical factor in rising health care costs has been retained without examination. There is a wealth of stories in both the professional and popular literature describing the degree to which other elements contribute to national medical costs. For example, both professional journal and news writers have shown that in some cases Directed Release Groups (DRGs), introduced in the 1980s in the United States as a cost-cutting measure, have resulted in an increase in deaths or post-operative complications by forcing the too rapid release of patients from hospitals. Further, the issue of not only iatrogenic (physician-created) disorders but also of nosocomial illness (those caused by the hospital environment) is not addressed, though it is the root of a whole class of illness, adding to the nation's total medical bill.[36] These range from the spreading of infections on hospital wards by hospital staff members who fail to wash their hands between patient visits to the disastrous effects of incorrect medication of patients by hospital and pharmacy staffs.[37] Leading systemic causes of injury and illness—automobile accidents and sustained abuse of tobacco and alcohol—contribute significantly to lost work hours among the populace, injuries leading to hospital admission and thus the general national health bill. To address the issues of health care costs would require an examination of these and other problems, which are, in fact, discussed in medical and social literature. But because the story's "hook" is a legislative debate focusing solely on the cost of malpractice insurance rates for physicians, this computer-researched story is limited in the main to that context as well.

But within the parameters of the specific legislative agenda—tort reform—this online approach has led to significant changes in text and procedure. Reportage has become active rather than reactive. Positions are not simply relayed, oral statement to printed paragraph, but examined from the perspective of an enormous body of information drawn from the medical, legal, and popular literature to bear precisely on the essential point: people are injured or killed in hospital and seek, in person or through their survivors, compensation for those injuries or deaths.

Rather than simply quoting a doctor, lawyer, or representative, reporters can now closely and critically question the participants. Their knowledge of the issues, supported by targeted electronic research, is sufficient to ask appropriate questions and to know when the responses are incorrect. It would have been interesting to ask Todd about Eichorn's study, for example. It would have been fun (as well as interesting) to point out to the AMA official that tort reform's cap on pain and suffering would barely dent the total amount awarded, during the year reviewed here, in malpractice suits. Certainly, medical journal articles, information from the Federation of State Medical Boards, and newspaper summaries all suggest strongly that physicians perform laxly as peers policing their own profession. Personally, I may find Todd's suggestion that lay people should not sit in jury on medical cases offensive. Politically, I could argue that it flies in the face of several hundred years of legal and democratic tradition that defines "peer" as not simply a fellow professional or classmate, but rather as a member of the same society. Professionally, I now can take him apart on this point, using evidence available in the public domain to show that physicians have not, in the past, been able to police their own adequately and that the failure of doctors to follow what they themselves agree are appropriate procedures in anesthetic administration has significantly affected the incidence of injury and thus of malpractice in general.

Hack journalists trained to quote subjects uncritically, to write ephemeral stories based on the unquestioned statements of authorities or officials, have been empowered by information approximating that possessed by their subjects. The form is not destroyed—they still quote interview subjects who largely define the agenda, but both the questions a reporter might ask and the context in which the responses are framed can now, for the first time, occur from within the broader context of that information already in the public domain. The difference, quite simply, is between a lapdog and a watchdog press.

Newsroom Effect: The Beat

Perhaps as importantly, this method, based on electronic information has broken down barriers that in the past have kept reporters locked in a "beat system." The general assignment reporter has covered and brought together material that would normally have fallen into the separate domains of the court reporter (what is the liability? what do the courts find?), legislative reporter (where tort reform is to be debated), medical reporter (Eichorn's and other researchers' work is noted), financial reporter (rising health care costs as a function of insurance, effect on business payments for medical insurance), and a general, human interest writer (one who can pull from the cases described in the literature or personalize a story through local, individual tales).

In short, not only are individual data from a variety of sources no longer necessarily isolated, but reporters once blocked by the newsroom's internal fiefdoms ("Ask reporter Ralph—he's business." "Ask reporter Koch—he's our medical man.") have been freed to pursue a story across those internal barriers. Because data comes from outside as well as inside the realm of the cultivated source, the reporter's traditionally absolute reliance on personal relations with officials is also lessened. This change will affect, perhaps radically, the relations of newspeople to their individual sources or experts because no longer can the head of the local hospital, who has cultivated reporter "X," be assured that "his" or "her" reporter will be the one present when tough questions are raised. As reporters move beyond the traditional system of "exclusive" beat information and absolute reliance on the official sources each has cultivated in his or her "beat," the traditional news subject's ability to control and slant stories by feeding information to a specific reporter will be diminished to the degree that newspeople can gain independent background information. Creating an information system that decreases reliance on any single source or the necessity for cultivating ties to a professonal category weakens the beat system, diminishes reportorial fiefdoms, and gives newspeople a method for the objective evaluation of public statements.

Writers have found a context broader than the narrow political viewpoint of adversaries or the definitions of the newsroom itself. They are empowered to examine, discuss, or focus a story through intelligent questioning based on a large background of objective information. Writers, in short, have the opportunity, if not independently to set the general agenda, then at least to modify it, and in the process to become the gatekeepers of their own stories—wherever they may lead. The electronically generated, informational background allows the newsperson, advocate, public relations writer, or interested citizen to access a context greater than that ordained by a partisan but necessary source or subject.

Story Levels: The *Wall Street Journal*

Another way of understanding what has changed is to see the degree to which this database approach has altered the story's signifier and what that image signifies. *Signifier* is defined by semiologists as the original subject, the boundary event that becomes, through the mediation of the news story, a sign. In the case of a photograph, for example, the signifier is a pattern of dots on paper that makes an image we take, at the most elementary level, as a photograph representing "x" at a moment in time. That photo, however, is not a value-free representation any more than Todd's statements were value-free, but one to be interpreted and perceived through social and political filters. Semiology provides a perspective allowing for the decoding of cultural events and was developed from attempts by linguists to describe the structure of language. In a very general sense, it is the type of intuitive abstraction that good political cartoonists employ when creating and applying symbols across the text of news reports to individual illustrations. As a system of understanding, semiology was pioneered by Roland Barthes[38] and offers a useful perspective on precisely what cultural artifacts, in this case news stories, do or do not say.

In the *Wall Street Journal* story, the signifier is a class: lawsuits that are filed by lawyers against doctors. The headline, "Malpractice Liability: Can the Law Serve Both Doctors and Patients?" makes this clear. The ability of the law to serve patients is, however, not the focus or the subject of the story because, as the lead paragraph states, malpractice liability is itself defined and treated as a divisive issue between doctors and lawyers. In the body of the text, Habash introduces the issue of patient suffering but Todd refuses it. Objecting to the word *victims*, Todd addresses only the social and practical cost of malpractice suits. Both men steer clear, perhaps by previous agreement, of any case examples. So while the story's signifier is the burgeoning case load of medical malpractice cases, what is signified is increasing cost to physicians and society.

The story's sign, at the most elementary level, is a dollar sign: cost in insurance premiums (to doctors) and in physician care (to society). At a more abstract, political level, however, that dollar sign is interpreted in very different ways by the two men. Todd and the *Wall Street Journal* interpret the subject of malpractice liability as a signifier composed of "burgeoning lawsuits" and "staggering premiums" (malpractice liability), which, in their turn, signify "merciless litigation" and exorbitant profits for members of the legal profession. Doctors can't do their job. They're leaving their practices in droves. Malpractice liability (and, by extension, avaricious lawyers playing on the trauma of the patients mentioned in the headline) is robbing doctors of their work and the population of medical care. In Todd's analysis, the whole signifies, at a more general level, embattled, humanitarian physicians beset by onerous costs and avaricious lawyers—the whole business that interferes with their job of caring and treating.

Habash's recitation defines the second and third levels more generally. While accepting the basic sign, he, like Todd, virtually ignores the patients. In his version, "bad doctors," not "burgeoning lawsuits," are the signifier of this tale. He quotes federal statistics which suggest 5 percent of the nation's physicians are incompetent. He quotes "an outstanding physician [Todd]" on "incompetence and negligence in the medical profession." The problem is not medicine in general or physicians as a class but a few bad apples in the medical barrel. What is signified by incompetent physicians is injured patients. At a political level, this signifies the necessity for lawyers to represent the injured and lawyers thus become not the problem but the answer, signifying redress and not, as Todd argued, the problem.

What is signified in Habash's view is the lawyer as guardian, attorneys as defenders and protectors. Todd's statements signified the physician as healer, the good doctor under attack by a "system" which is beggaring his profession. Thus both men reinforce the myths of their respective professions throughout the whole argument. Todd has the healer befuddled by laws, lawyers, and malpractice suits, followers of a healing art who cannot understand (although clearly Todd does—very well) the issues behind increasing malpractice premiums. For his part, Habash cleverly enforces and underlines the advocate's image as guardian both of the injured (the client) and (because the law helps weed out bad doctors) of medicine itself.

The whole is pretty much a standoff. What the story does do supremely well is allow the issue of medical care to be defined in terms of cost and to create a text that affirms simultaneously the social posture of both lawyers and physicians, two primary categories of *Journal* subscribers. The context of the story has, as its elementary signifiers, a physician, a lawyer, and a *Journal* reporter together. It signifies reasonable and responsible discourse. After all, the lawyer, the doctor, and the reporter are sitting together, "debating," finding common ground and defining honest differences. In this process the *Journal* (through its reporter's participation) is coequal, a facilitator and partner among professionals in the search for solutions to society's problems, which are, the whole says, at base business-related. Signified is an entire process of problem identification and solution in which the publication takes on the role of both society's informant and its surrogate. The story signifies, in its present form, the newspaper as consensus builder in the realm of power because, after all, it brought together a high official of the American Medical Association and the president of the Association of Trial Lawyers of America. Habash says that Todd is "an outstanding physican,"

although on what he bases his assertion is unclear. Todd
clearly listens to and respects Habash's opinion, even though
he sees lawyers as a class as the problem. Both exist within
the context of the *Journal*'s editorial pages.

The "Daily Journal of the American Dream" comes off
the clear winner because the whole exercise signifies its
power, "objectivity," and attraction to wealthy clients who
are or serve physicians and lawyers. Lost in these abstrac-
tions from the start, however, was the issue of injured
patients who may file suit against physicians and then use
lawyers as their representatives. When introduced into the
debate at all, patients were ciphers mentioned as a class by
Habash and then only in the briefest, most general terms.
Also ignored were questions regarding the context (iatrogenic
and nosocomial) that causes specific health problems, as
well as attention to other factors directly affecting the social
cost of health care (e.g., fee-for-service medicine, under-
utilization of nurses). These subjects are central to the cost
of medical treatment (and the efficacy of American medicine
in general) and, at another level, the overall cost of health
care in the United States. The whole has been dehumanized,
reduced to an abstraction of professional stances which are
not challenged and costs which are not critically considered.

A reader in 1986 could scan this story or study it and
come away uninformed. Doctors will agree, presumably,
with their surrogate while lawyers will support their leader.
Uninvolved readers can say with satisfaction that "there is
right and wrong on both sides" but cannot come away with
anything other than the occasional, disembodied factoid. For
example, the government says that at least twenty thousand
of America's four hundred thousand doctors are incompetent
(whatever that means); 1 percent of the doctors in Pennsylvania account for 25 percent of the malpractice claims (Are
they all in high-risk specialties? Is Pennsylvania unique?);
and physicians are leaving the profession in droves ("Not in
my neighborhood," a reader might say dismissively. "I support five of them myself.").

The whole does not inform from the start because it
presents no data in context, no information other than self-
serving statements by representatives of two groups: physicians and lawyers. It deals not with illness, the sick, or those

injured by medicine but rather with an aspect of the cost of bad medicine to society. It is smoke and mirrors, like Todd's argument that only physicians are qualified to judge the performance of their own class. The *Journal* has presented information that affirms its role as chronicler of society's commercial issues, but at the cost of the type of information news publications are pledged to provide (full and unbiased) if they are to fulfill their institutional and instrumental goals. The real loser in this approach has been the United States as a dynamic social system whose legal and scientific communities act to assure the life, liberty, and potential for its citizens' contentment. Attempts by the medical, legal, judicial, and legislative communities to define and then redress the root problems of society through research, case law, medical protocol, etcetera—the wealth of data uncovered in the computer search—are ignored in this traditional news approach. This lack of context implies by that exclusion that cost is the only issue and that what is important is the self-interest of wealthy, professional groups.

Story Levels: Contextual

The story resulting from the computer search changes the system of signifier, signified, and sign throughout the whole. It places the question of malpractice litigation and the resulting costs within the context of an aspect of contemporary surgery in which a large percentage of suits originates. The basic signifier is "individuals injured by improperly administered anesthesia during surgery." What is signified is not money or dollars but corpses or critically disabled people whose deficits are the direct result of physician malpractice. At another level of meaning, those victims (that is what they have become, despite Todd's objections) stand for the failure of physicians as a class to monitor their own and enforce upon individual members even the most basic standards of competence. Physicians are not, in this version, part of the solution but instead constitute a central aspect of the problem. Lawyers become, at this level, tangential to the problem. If the issue is not costs but the cause of the injuries that give rise to the suits, then the question of avaricious lawyers is not even relevant.

Illustration 2.1
Goals and Myths: Malpractice

	Institutional A	Instrumental B	Functional C
Reporters -1-	To serve through providing information	that is unbiased and complete.	Earn adequate hourly wage.
Physicians -2-	To cure the sick and injured	through recognized protocols and procedures.	Make a profit through fees charged per patient.
Lawyers -3-	To defend the injured or wronged	through successful litigation.	Make a profit by fee or percentage of awards per case.

At one more level, physicians are seen not as Todd insists they must be, as caregivers besieged by financial concerns and a legal system they cannot understand but, rather, as a class of technicians who lack appropriate monitoring and control. In a contextual story, lawyers are neither agents of avarice or of justice. They become a conduit for the redress of the injured and, as such, are valued neither positively nor negatively because the issue of the nature and causes of those injuries has become the central issue. From such contextual or structural reportage comes a radically changed image of the newspaper. Here the signs affirm not the other professions but rather that of the journalist, whose contextual investigation "suggests strongly" that a specific problem exists that can be precisely defined on the basis of objective documentation, and one which therefore can be clearly explained. By examining medical texts, legal cases, and the printed reports of colleagues from other geographical regions, the newsperson has gathered a series of cases in which individuals were injured. By drawing on the published work of medical and legal experts, the public information writer can suggest authoritatively how those injuries might, in the future, be diminished or eliminated. Cost has become not the issue but a result and, in the process, the newspaper has fulfilled, at least to some degree, its instrumental goal of objectivity. It has examined an issue, identified its components, and then reported from within a context that fit the "facts" together to create a coherent description of the issue at hand. It has, simultaneously, approached its institutional goal by providing information of social importance in such a way that both layperson and official may be informed by the story the newspaper puts forward. Things might even change.

Precisely what has happened is summarized in Illustration 2.1, which sets out the institutional, instrumental, and functional goals of the debate's participants: reporters, physicians, and lawyers. Todd, for his part, emphasized to the *Journal* the physicians' *institutional* goal and warned that because the physicians *functional* goal was under attack (malpractice suits cost money and time; malpractice premiums are expensive), many doctors were abandoning their professions and thus their socially desirable, instrumental goal. In short, they were refusing to attend to the *instrumental* goal because malpractice insurance costs were making it uneconomical for those physicians to continue to cure the sick. Habash suggests the real problem is at the physicians' *instrumental* level, that the recognized protocols are not being employed and, therefore, the physicians' *institutional* goal (to cure the sick) is not being fulfilled. In fact, he says, the reverse often occurs and people are made sicker. That argument is amenable to computer information searching and is the one both examined and tentatively confirmed by our story.

Todd and the *Journal*'s introduction emphasize the lawyer's functional goal and downplay or deny the institutional goal and institutional myths of the legal profession. They ignore the root cause of a "burgeoning" number of lawsuits or the reasoning behind the high awards that have resulted in increased premiums. Thus they define lawyers earning contingency fees as the problem. Habash, for his part, skillfully counters by emphasizing his profession's instrumental goal—defense of the injured through socially approved litigation—and allows the reader to perceive the institutional value of these acts. He is also careful—a good technique in legal arguments—to take the high road. By complimenting Todd—"an outstanding physician"—he does not attack the institutional image of physicians as healers and helpers (something many people believe in[39]) but rather the instrumental failure of a subset (bad doctors) who injure the legal profession's clients.

The advantage of the story based on computer-generated information is its ability, through proper searching of popular, professional, and technical literature, to make overt the difference between what people say in defense of their own institutional myths, and what they may, in fact, want at the functional level. Further, it allows the layperson to compare institutional goals with the evidence of observable performance at the instrumental level. Actions at this level are typically well documented and therefore particularly amenable to contextual, computer-generated analysis. The *Journal*, with no real information of its own, credited and placed prominently in its introduction Todd's statement that physicians are abandoning their practices because of "a [malpractice insurance] system they don't understand, [and] they can't cope with." But Todd, a physician as well as spokesman, clearly understands it very well. The issue as he states it is one of functional economics (they don't want to pay more) and the degree to which instrumental goals (people are injured, not cured) are being unfulfilled. It is also one, as Todd suggests, of power and control. Will courts with lay juries continue to judge physicians demonstrably incapable of overseeing themselves? Or will physicians be freed from general, social accountability, as Todd argues they should be, presumably to judge themselves in solitude? From this perspective, the issue is one of balancing the autonomy of a profession with the social accountability of its individual members—whose record in self-regulation as a class is, on the evidence, anything but reassuring.

This computer-assisted, contextual approach has laid bare the grammar of the "debate" and thus allowed the reader to evaluate its constituent parts. Through the perspective of outside research it has made overt the interests of the respective speakers and the means by which one or another used the *Journal* as a forum to advance a specific profession's agenda or interests. Sigelman's sociology and

Barthes' semiology provide different languages which allow us to analyze the whole. But both gain, in this case, through the ability to test the conclusions and examine the debate's dialectic through reference to outside data. Indeed, this extended exegesis would not have been possible without the use of these technologies. Through this process the newspaper and its reporter have gone from being a silent conduit for the polemics of others to an active participant in a social debate. The newspaper, through its reporter, now listens to the positions enunciated by interview subjects and not only relays those positions but places them in a more objective context. It accepts oral statements as a starting point and tests them in the context of what has been written by "experts" on the general subject and against what has happened of a similar nature in other circulation or broadcast jurisdictions. Thus the newswriter and the publication acknowledge and approach, perhaps for the first time, the journalist's instrumental goal of unbiased, objective coverage and, through this, the institutional myth has a chance of becoming a reality. The effect of this approach on publishers' and writers' functional goals is at present untested.

Structural Context

The contextual level is one in which statements by interview subjects can be examined against the records of previous cases and their analysis in a general or professional literature. If Habash says a small number of unqualified physicians cause a large number of complaints, that statement can be checked. If Todd says that physicians can adequately police their colleagues and judge the competence of their fellows, that statement, too, need not be accepted on faith. A structural story might take the whole further and attempt to determine the degree to which elements causing a specific problem are, in fact, merely symptoms of a deeper social perspective or context.

If the issue is the cost of health care to society at large, examining the cost of malpractice as a single problem will not serve. As the contextual approach made clear, health costs are a subset of larger issues in medicine and in society. Using a series of electronic databases, it would not be difficult to define the problem by first examinig the major types of illness (nosocomial, environmental, viral and bacterial, accidental, etc.), defining general categories of health care costs (pharmaceutical, physician-related, nursing, etc.), reviewing the costs of specific medical procedures, and referencing the whole against the demographics of illness (at what ages are people most likely to become ill and to what extent are their medical bills paid for by society at large).

Further, there are nations with federal health insurance programs where indices of health are higher while health care costs are lower. The efficiency of those programs, and thus their potential suitability for the United States (or any other country), can be determined through the examination of any number of health service indices. Armed with this information, the public can judge for itself the wisdom of adopting a federal health insurance program. The structural issues thus become efficient use, appropriate compensation, and adequate supervision of health care professionals as a class, of political allocations and decisions. Classes of disease are defined as the result of environmental, industrial, and social policy choices. In this whole, Todd's agenda and Habash's perspective are but single elements of the greater, immediate whole, and the issues of cost which they present will be seen very differently from a structural perspective.

Thus, in the structural story, the writer or broadcaster takes full control of the agenda. The designated speaker's signifier is diminished as the reporter defines and redefines the context of an issue as one of root causes and systemic problems. In this process, which tests immediate concerns against antecedent knowledge, the system of signifiers and signs traditionally accepted as public fact becomes obviously biased data. A structural story by definition changes the initial focus from that of an individual issue to the more general, cultural perspective by absorbing the original speaker's signifier into a broader class of events or research. One example is the current American war on drugs, declared in the early 1980s by President Ronald Reagan and carried on with enthusiasm by his successor, President George Bush.[40] A brief overview of its coverage and the issues that it raises is an instructive lesson in the limits of orally transmitted news.

THE WAR ON DRUGS

Throughout the 1980s, the chemical addiction of U.S. citizens to a long list of controlled substances—heroin, marijuana, and cocaine being the best publicized—was trumpeted as a critical danger to the national body. The interdiction of drug supplies through the use of military, police, and judicial resources, a growth industry during President Reagan's tenure, escalated during the term of his successor, President Bush, who used the "drug war" as an excuse for, among other things, the invasion of Panama and the removal of its leader, General Manuel Noriega. Between 1980 and 1988, the United States spent several hundred billion dollars to first interdict narcotics during the transportation of supplies to their market and then to prosecute those responsible for the wholesale preparation and distribution of controlled substances.[41] In 1989, President Bush asked the U.S. congress for $9.5 billion more and his 1990 budget included direct allocations of $10 billion in drug war monies. These funds were allocated during a period of systematic federal cutbacks in funding for social programs, education, and general services.

The war against illegal drugs has been covered at each step by daily journalists who typically report the arrest and trial of dealers in their circulation area, lament the continued presence of drugs in their home region, and editorially laud government and community efforts to remove a chemical tumor from the body of the American politic. As Jeff Greenfield of ABC News noted, national television coverage of the war on drugs has been voluminous, if unedifying.[42] In a two-week period in 1989, for example, the three major networks carried 163 drug-related stories and several "special reports" on their national news shows. CBS named its coverage, "One Nation under Siege," and ABC titled its stories, "A Plague upon the Land."[43] Regionally, trivial stories across the nation have recorded, in newspapers and on broadcast news shows, the amounts and estimated street value of illegal substances seized by local or federal police departments in thousands of separate raids. They have also disseminated, without consideration or thought, thousands of official statements made by law enforcement officers and politicians insistent on the necessity for increasing police and military action in the war on drugs.

As Massachusetts reporter Al Giordano said of his fellow journalists involved in covering the war on drugs:

> With a few exceptions, they have neglected their self-proclaimed task of providing objective or critical coverage of the issue. Although there is a wealth of academic research that finds most casual users of non-nicotine drugs do not become addicted, press coverage continues to stigmatize (or is it deglamorize?) addicts and scapegoat users of illegal drugs for social problems that existed long before crack arrived. Journalists have failed to differentiate between types of illegal drugs and have accepted legal definitions of drug abuse as medical and factual—which they are not.[44]

There are two basic patterns to the ephemeral story on drugs. One chronicles, on the authority of local police, federal investigators, or army officials "who" was arrested (today), the value estimated by officials of the drugs seized, and "what" a police chief, president, army officer, or administration "drug czar" said about those drugs (yesterday). The second quotes those same officials when they reiterate the danger—to the individual and to society—of any drug use, the importance of decreasing chemical dependency among the citizenry, and the official position that a "drug-free America" can only be reached through interdiction and the apparatus of the judicial system.

This reflexive reportage clearly serves a legitimizing function, affirming the official postures not only that drugs create an evil, chemical dependency among users but that police action and a tough judicial posture are the only possible cures. In January 1990, NBC broadcast a mini-series—*Drug Wars: The Camarena Story*—which presented both a fictionalized account of the death of a Drug Enforcement Adminstration (DEA) agent, Enrique Camarena, and the attempts of his fellow officers to bring his killers to trial. Following the nightly series segment, NBC national news anchor Tom Brokaw hosted and participated in "panel discussions" on the drug problem, which were broadcast from a DEA laboratory. Clearly, NBC News, through its participation in these "discussions," was lending its considerable prestige and voice not only to the U.S. government's war on drugs but also to its foreign adventures in drug interdiction. In one segment Brokaw insisted, for example, that Mexico, like Panama, was a drug villain ("In every part of the country there is a local Noriega, a commandante, a general, a governor getting rich.").[45] In this series NBC's principal newsman, and by extension NBC News itself, functioned as an uncritical advocate for both the DEA, whose agents were portrayed (in both the fictional show and the "news" segment) as universally virtuous, patriotic, and hardworking, and for the administration, which has made the war on drugs into a patriotic crusade. In the NBC series, as in most daily or weekly news reportage of the drug, there was little objectivity and virtually no analysis of the assumptions of the war on drugs, no consideration of the structural or contextual issues that it raises.

Like local news stories trumpeting brave police arresting dangerous drug dealers, NBC News' participation in this docudrama's creation of a federal martyr, agent Enrique Camarena, affirmed government action by accurately reflecting official positions without any consideration of the two principal assumptions of the war on drugs: that chemical dependency is a problem in and of itself and that police and judicial action can stop the traffic in illegal substances.

An even simpler question would be whether the program of interdiction has been successful. In 1990, when President Bush asked Congress to allocate an additional $10.5 billion for the war on drugs, one way to deal intelligently with the story would have been to ask if, in a decade of escalating action, there had been any hint of success. The answer is, in fact, no. Those searching for stories on the efficiency of the war on drugs would find, for example, an American Bar Association report, issued in 1988, which stated bluntly:

> Police, prosecutors and judges told the committee that they have been unsuccessful in making a significant impact on the importation, sale and use of illegal drugs, despite devoting much of their re-

sources to the arrest, prosecution and trial of drug offenders. . . . These extraordinary efforts have instead distorted and overwhelmed the criminal justice system, crowding dockets and jails, and diluting law enforcement and judicial efforts to deal with other major criminal cases.[46]

From 1980 to 1988 the cost to customers of most controlled substances (marijuana, cocaine, heroin) dropped as supplies increased, despite the increasingly expensive and constant efforts of local, regional, and federal law enforcement agencies. Interdiction is, apparently, an appalling failure. Further, it is clear from a search of newspaper stories including the words *drugs* and *arrest* or *death* that the war on drugs is not a tightly focused fight. There are, for example, battles to stay the supply of cocaine (from Colombia), marijuana (from Mexico or Hawaii), heroin (from Asia) or, most recently, "crystal methamphetamine" (from Korea). At varying times in the decade, the war on drugs has been defined with reference to each of these substances, as well as alcohol, model airplane glue, crack (synthetic cocaine), tobacco (a "legal drug"), etcetera. At different times each drug has been targeted as a real and present danger, its increasing use supposedly signifying, according to news reports of the day, an ever greater imperative to allocate public resources to the war.

Individuals will, apparently, switch with alacrity from one drug to another depending on cost and availability. That explanation is the only one for the progression of "targeted" drugs, and one found frequently in newspaper stories. A more appropriate question is: Why do individuals use drugs at all? As Greenfield of ABC News said in a *Nightline* report on the "timid" state of contemporary journalism:

A more skeptical press might have asked questions. If drugs have triggered a sudden huge surge in crime, why are national murder and robbery rates down in the last two years? Why were there fewer burglaries in New York and Los Angeles last year than there were back in 1980? They might have asked whether the violence of drug-dealing gangs stems from drug use itself or from the battle to protect the huge profits of dealing in illegal drugs. They might have asked whether drugs are a cause of crime, or a symptom of deeper social pathologies.[47]

Some spokespeople on the fringes of official dissent have raised these issues. Rev. Jesse Jackson, for example, told a congressional panel that "Bush's plan [to stop drugs] does not adequately address 'material and spiritual poverty, which are the preconditions for the drug crisis.'"[48] That statement suggests that drug use is, in fact, a symptom resulting from "material and spiritual poverty." But his is a relatively solitary voice, an apparently unsubstantiated opinion isolated in an ephemeral story from the other side. In the same month, however, the *Wall Street Journal* had a long front-page article on how an Omaha businessman, Ben Gray, hired the head of a local, drug-oriented youth gang because, Gray told the *Journal*, in his opinion the drug problem was "institutional racism and double standards."[49] If drug sellers could be brought into the social and economic mainstream of society, he reasoned, they would give up the quite dangerous business of selling and distributing controlled substances. So this story at least had some meat, a single case study of one man and one drug dealer whom the businessman tried to convert.

The article quoted Gray's gang-leader-turned-employee, Robert Penn, and Federal Bureau of Investigation (FBI) supervisor John Pankonin, who both said drugs are a problem rooted in poverty and that, to decrease drug use, issues of poverty need to be addressed. In the words of the FBI agent: "What alternative have I got for them? What job have I got for a high school dropout that will allow him to get up at noon and make $300 dollars in the afternoon? I don't like to admit it, but they're pretty good capitalists."[50]

This suggests that, on the basis of both the FBI field officer's and Penn's experiences, activist Jackson may be right: poverty and alienation are indeed factors in the continued sale, if not the use, of controlled susbstances. This possibility is especially interesting because throughout the 1980s, newspapers and magazines also chronicled the government's elimination of a whole series of programs aimed at decreasing poverty through increasing literacy, prenatal care, and so on. A result of Reagan's "supply-side" economics and Bush's wars on both drugs and taxes was the destruction of a "social safety net" whose unraveling coincides with increasing drug use, increasing supplies of controlled substances, and increasing federal and regional expenditures in the war on drugs. In fact, there seems to have been an inverse correlation: the more that funding for social programs was cut, the more money was spent on drug interdiction. Further, throughout the 1980s (as several writers make clear) the street prices of most controlled substances—crack, cocaine, heroin—fell. A graph charting these trends would show an increase in money spent for drug interdiction by the government and a decrease in the cost of individual drug dosages as a function of supply outpacing demand. Not since the sale of liquor was prohibited has so much money been spent for so little effect.

If it is all a shuck, if the drug busts, drug wars, and drug legislation are futile exercises unless socioeconomic problems are addressed, why cover the subject at all? A search of magazine articles on drugs and interdiction turned up a tentative answer by *Harper's* editor Lewis P. Lapham, who described the current war on drugs as a safe, political ploy that makes good copy. "Because the human craving for intoxicants cannot be suppressed—not by priests or jailers or acts of Congress—the politicians can bravely confront an allegorical enemy rather than an enemy that takes the corporeal form of the tobacco industry, say, or the Chines, or the oil and banking lobbies."[51] He also blames the media for their slavish coverage of drug busts and drug hysteria but acknowledges that:

The drug war, like all wars, sells papers, and the media, like the politicians, ask for nothing better than a safe and profitable menace. The campaign against drugs involves most of the theatrical devices employed by *Miami Vice*—scenes of crimes in progress (almost always dressed up, for salacious effect, with the cameo appearances of one or two prostitutes, melodramatic villains in the Andes, a vocabulary of high-tech military jargon as reassuring as the acronyms in a Tom Clancy novel, the specter of a crazed lumpen proletariat rising in revolt in the nation's cities).[52]

Great writing and beautifully crafted opinion, but not really substantial. Similar views are also expressed by Charles T. Salmon, who reviews the work of sociologists interested in media coverage of the drug phenomena.[53] But consider, for a moment, the assumptions in Mr. Lapham's piece. Who says the human craving for "intoxicants cannot be suppressed?" Is there, in fact, such a craving at all? What are the biology, psychology, and pharmacology of addiction? Are they the same for all drugs or different for each one?

If the policy of interdiction is a failure, perhaps demand is where the real story lies. Therefore the appropriate contextual question might be: Why do people take drugs at all? The war on drugs is based on an assumption that a broad class of controlled substances (heroin, marijuana, cocaine, etc.) is chemically addictive, creating an absolute physical need on the part of addicts, who will do anything to satisfy their habits. A search of the pharmacology and psychology literatures (using search phrases written as "addiction and (heroine or cocaine)," or "addiction and habituation") suggests that this assumption is, at best, a very partial truth.

Addiction researchers seem unanimous on two general points. One is that chemical dependency is not the single, critical factor in repeated use of either heroin or cocaine.[54] The second point is that prohibition and interdiction cannot and and will not be effective in the curtailment of drug use. Were unrelenting chemical dependency the necessary result of the ingestion (or injection) of proscribed substances, it would be impossible for individuals using cocaine, heroin, marijuana, etcetera, to cease their use voluntarily. But clinical studies have shown consistently that chemically dependent mammals regularly give up drugs on their own when the conditions of their life improve. For example, animal studies have shown that laboratory rats kept in comfortable surroundings do not become addicted while those isolated in small cages rapidly become dependent on morphine.[56] Studies of human addiction have had similar results. A follow-up study of U.S. military veterans, addicted during the Vietnam War, showed that the vast majority voluntarily stopped using controlled substances after their return to the United States.[55] Individuals belonging to self-help groups, which attempt to modify their members' social context, cease inhalation of cocaine, for example, without adverse affects, just as Alcoholics Anonymous assists alcoholics, once freed of their immediate dependency, from again using alcohol as a stress release.[57] In addition, the vast majority of young drug users voluntarily cease use of currently illegal drugs as they mature.[58] Hospital patients are increasingly allowed to self-administer morphine following surgery and not only do they not become addicted to the analgesic but, in fact, they used less narcotic than physicians typically ordered for their comfort.[59] The stated conclusion of these and other studies published in the technical literature has been that individuals became addicts as a response to stress and tensions in their personal lives. U.S. military personnel in the 1960s and early 1970s, for example, used drugs as an escape when their quality of life in Vietnam was intolerable, but when their tours were completed, most voluntarily became drug-free as their lives returned to relative normalcy.

This suggests that interdiction cannot work because those whose quality of life is such as to require relief will use almost any substance that offers escape from an unpleasant and stresful reality. A partial list of drugs whose use newspapers have campaigned against includes alcohol, heroin, airplane glue, morphine, marijuana, cocaine, crack cocaine, amphetamines as a class, and crystal methamphetamine as a specific substance. Street users regularly switch from one drug to another, often on the basis of availability, just as newspaper coverage switches from articles on one drug or drug class to articles on another (marijuana to heroin to cocaine to synthetic drugs) on the basis of what police are confiscating in the current season of drug busts.[60]

The Story

The clear conclusion, based on these and other studies, is that to decrease drug use, it would be necessary to create a series of social programs, for clients of various income levels, that support and help improve lives so diminished that narcotic use became desirable. To the degree that controlled substances are sold or used as a means to escape poverty, social programs whose aim is the long-term elimination of society's economic disparities would need to be implemented. But social programs themselves have been a major casualty of the drug wars. As money was funneled into the war on drugs, the war on poverty became ever more tenuous. And, of course, the war on drugs is based, as was 1920s-style prohibition, on legal penalties and interdiction. Just as prohibition failed to stop the use of alcohol, so must current and structurally similar policies be ineffective in stemming the use of heroin or cocaine, because interdiction does not address the primary causes of any substance's abuse. Jackson was, in retrospect, quite correct. Drug abuse has social, economic, and psychological roots not addressed and, perhaps, exacerbated by Bush's policies.

It is not that the futility of administration policies or the false premises which are at the heart of the administration's war on drugs has gone unnoticed. Even conservative magazines ranging from the *National Review* to the *Economist* have carried articles arguing for some form of drug legalization as a cost-effective alternative to, in Giordano's words, the "prohibition-related crime" that current drug war policies have spawned. In an open letter to the administration on September 7, 1989, economist Milton Friedman argued in the *Wall Street Journal*[61] that repressive administration policies in the war on drugs—more police, more jails, harsher penalties for drug users, military adventurism— "only make a bad situation worse." But these pieces are opinion, like Lapham's argument, submitted through the press and quickly forgotten in the daily march of new statements at news conferences covered by reporters. There is no memory to the oral argument, no careful comparison to be based on it. As in the debate between Todd and Habash, it is barely considered grist for the editorial mill.

I first researched this general subject in 1980, using traditional library resources and local, university-based addiction researchers Barry Beyerstein and Bruce Alexander as my primary sources. A general story based on their laboratory animal studies but including information from research done on prison inmate and U.S. military veteran

Illustration 2.2
Drug Cops and Crime Reporters

	Institutional *A*	Instrumental *B*	Functional *C*
Crime Reporter -1-	To serve through publishing or broadcasting	records of police antidrug activities	and earn salary through exciting, prestigious, socially important work.
Drug Squad Cop -2-	To protect and serve the people	by arresting drug users and suppliers	is a valuable social service worthy of a decent wage and society's respect.

populations was prepared for publication in that year. But it took two years for my employers to run a different and greatly modified version because, as *Province* assistant city editor William Holden, said testily "I just don't believe it, no matter how many eggheads you quote." Holden's aversion to academics, intellectuals, researchers, and other "eggheads," as well as the comments of other *Province* editors, was instructive.

When the story finally ran,[62] the *Province*'s city editor, Donald MacLaughlin, insisted it also include an interview with a local official of the Royal Canadian Mounted Police (RCMP) involved in drug enforcement, who said simply, "I don't buy it." The RCMP officer, like Holden, sneered at academic research and argued that his experience on the streets was sufficient to assure the newspaper's readers that chemical addiction was the real problem and police action the necessary solution. Running this interview served two purposes. It guarded against the *Province*'s apparent endorsement of some flaky academic finding—Holden's "egghead argument"—and, more important to MacLaughlin, assured the *Province* would not lose valuable police contacts that, he said, the newspaper needed. To run the story without giving the police a rebuttal would have been not only "biased" but politically unsound. The newspaper needed

police sources, and allowing the RCMP to critique the conclusions of years of careful research assured the whole could
be finessed as an "egghead" story in which the politically
valuable police were given a chance to insist upon their
raison d'être, drug confiscation and interdiction. Another
assistant editor, Bud Jorgensen, was more than willing to
accept the position of researchers, but he insisted the story
could not run without information on the economics of the
drug business: how much was spent on enforcement and how
much drug users spent on the streets. If the academics were
correct, Jorgensen reasoned, then the taxpayers money was
being misspent. The salient question for him was, by how
much?

Within this one admittedly anecdotal example, the
variety of perspectives affecting news judgment can be seen.
MacLaughlin was concerned about the newspaper's losing
valuable police connections, without which it could not continue
to report on drug busts and other RCMP activities. Since
these were crucial to its style of ephemeral reportage, those
factions had to be placated. Holden did not give credence to
research on principle, trusting instead to the weight of
materials published in his and other newspapers in which
drugs had been socially defined as a menace. What more, he
reasoned, did one really need to know? Jorgenson, a more
experienced and perhaps a better-read editor, understood
that whatever the conclusions of the researchers, readers
and advertisers wanted an economic focus: how much was
spent on these chemical prohibitions and what did this
research mean to some "bottom line"? Thus the final copy
had to balance a number of nontextual constraints in its
attempt to present objective "fact" based on a series of
studies and researcher positions within the broad context of
the daily news process.

In retrospect, all these editorial concerns were justified.
Police were angered because the story attacked not only
their view of the world in general but, specifically, their
instrumental goals. The myth of the drug enforcement program is that, institutionally, police protect the public by
(instrumentally) stopping the flow of harmful substances to
an unwitting public. Functionally, RCMP and city police
drug officers earned their salaries through a system that

deemed it necessary to pay them wages to fight drug suppliers and to capture both suppliers and users.

In this specific example, graphically laid out in Illustration 2.2, newspeople attempt to fulfill their institutional objective (service to the public) by instrumentally publicizing the "successes" of antidrug officials involved in interdiction. A story challenging the assumptions of the drug interdiction program attacked not only the police officers' livelihood, and thus the individual officers' functional support, but also the instrumental myth that governed both the officers' and journalists' professional lives. As Holden was at pains to point out, the story made a mockery of the hundreds of articles and stories the *Province* had run. If the newspaper in fact served the public (institutionally) and made its money (functionally) by publicizing drug arrests, then what would it mean if the newspaper said with any consistency that researchers had known for years these arrests not only were not going to stop drug traffic but would, in fact, have no effect whatsoever (despite the enormous financial cost of interdiction) on drug use? And if drugs are themselves a symptom and not the cause, why was the newspaper devoting substantial news space to stories quoting police, politicians, and civic leaders who might, for one self-interested reason or another, decide to "speak out" on the evil of drugs? The amazing thing, in retrospect, is that my story ran at all.

It is from this perspective that reportage through the 1980s of not only the drug war but, by extension, government policies and actions in general can be understood. To the degree that reporters, editors, and television anchors are limited to information based on the official view, they repeat those official statements without consideration. Their research is limited to "checking facts" in the newspaper morgue or broadcast station's library. And, in both, the principal information base is prior "facts" from previous stories quoting the same sources. There is, simply, no context from which the journalistic event (the press conference, media opportunity, official statement, or press release) can be judged. News research becomes, in the main, a tautology in which the statement of an official today is compared with the "facts" he or she uttered yesterday. There is, with these traditional resources, no possible connection between the boundary event (the addicted or habituated individual) and the journalistic event (the trumpeted war on drugs). It is as if contemporary news were a physics experiment in which light (information) is reflected from mirror to mirror until its final intensity (the story) is measured. One mirror is the journalistic event, a second is the reporter's perception, and the third, perhaps, is the editor's. Information on the original boundary event, the objective context of a prior occurrence or process, is not within the traditional system. So the whole reflects but does not probe, presents but cannot inform, because there is no way to examine the information presented or compare the illumination's source with its final transformation.

This changes when computer-assisted data is included. One result in this case, like that of Todd and Habash, is that the system of meanings alters dramatically. In the *Province*'s typical drug bust story, believed by Holden and protected by MacLaughlin, for example, the elementary signifier is arrestees in chains, led to jail or the booking desk. What is signified by the standard news photo or arrest story is active police closing down drug dealers. At a second level, that news photo image creates a signifier emphasizing not the workaday, mundane officer following orders but the institutional myth of the police, whose motto is To Serve and Protect, as social servant fighting for the individual citizen in the communal war against drugs. Finally, the police are officers of the courts, civil servants whose allegiance is to the jurisdiction that employs them. The success of the RCMP officer (patrol cop, FBI agent, or army private) affirms, at the level of myth, the government's protection of its citizenry and its waging of a war (however senseless, however counterproductive) on behalf of each of us. Ultimately, each drug bust legitimizes by what is signified: government active on the behalf of its members.

The electronic story changes these levels of meaning by changing the interpretation of that original signifier. If drug abuse is a social problem brought on by poverty, lack of opportunity, and failed lives, then the constantly repeated news image of drug dealers arrested or in jail signifies not protection but failure on the part of society's protectors. If interdiction cannot work, then the antidrug machine is spending money not on the problem (poverty, lack of opportunity, racism) but on a symptom. Then the police do not signify protection but become, themselves, signs of a broader social failure to address the issue, dupes whose financial compensation (the functional goal) is a reward for largely valueless work. From this perspective, the police drug raid story cannot signify the honorable motto To Serve and Protect, but becomes, rather, the mercenary's "bust'em and get paid." The whole makes of police what radicals have charged, an army of occupation in the ghetto where the majority of police actions occur, including drug interdictions. Finally, Mr. Bush's government, which proclaims its responsibility for the war on drugs, is signified in turn not as caring but as indifferent, not concerned but opportunistic. They fight the visible symptoms and not the problem itself, a futile exercise whose only result is waste and continued suffering.

These transformations occur on the basis not, however, of radical rhetoric but of studies in recognized journals, even articles from the *Wall Street Journal* and other newspapers that have been pulled into a structural or contextual whole. These changes occur as the story gains depth through structure and context, the conjunction not only of a class of specific events (fifteen drug busts; new drug "epidemics") but of the relation between narrowly defined occurrences and their "what" and "why" written over time.

In this brief analysis, the general issue of police and news objectives and goals has been focused on a single type of reportage and a single type of police activity. In the previous example, the general operational myths of lawyers and physicians were used. But it is important to remember that these are examples whose real utility is to demonstrate the effect of new technologies on news in general and not simply a medical or police story, interesting though they may be. To the degree that the information generated by online resources allows for the examination of the institutional and instrumental myths, it also forces the writer to seek a greater specificity in the definition of a problem or argument. The whole indeed may be hampered by the cultural filters and individual perceptions that news professionals bring to their post, or by the economic necessities that limit individual media outlets. But those assumptions and, to a lesser extent, the economic restraints themselves, are the end result of a historical tradition growing out of the era of the first printing revolution. News is a system of information transfer whose historical function has been to assist in the dissemination of the officially spoken word to geographically dispersed peoples. It grew from the printing revolution and its form remains rooted in the postures of that era. It is argued here that new technologies will result in new economies and cultural forms whose end effect will be to change the cultural assumptions and traditions on which news, a part of the public information system, is based.

CONCLUSION

It is clear that online technologies can significantly affect the content of the news and the ability of contemporary journalists to approach the instrumental goal of "objectivity" that all, in theory, espouse. The typical news story, based on what one or another source said at a specific time and place, is by definition limited to an individual's comments and thus to that subject's specific perspective and information resources. Attempts to "balance" such statements are usually limited at present to fielding other comments, delivered orally, by actors of official import in a specific context (e.g., drug enforcement) or at a specific event (e.g., a district court trial). Current journalistic practice reinforces and is limited to the traditional, supporting media role of relay or conduit for the orally presented statements of officials and experts. Even when the information to be translated from distinct event to public report is printed, it often is treated as if it were a verbal presentation. Thus information from press releases, typically prepared in the standard news narrative's "he said" or "she said" form, is included uncritically in any individual story by newswires. Objectivity, the instrumental goal, is thus impossible to achieve in any but the most limited of senses.

Electronic databases, which make available to the reporter a wide variety of journals, newsletters, and newspaper texts, present the opportunity for a radically different, far more instrumentally satisfactory reportage. Through the

Illustration 2.3
Means and Goals

	Institutional A	Instrumental B	Method C
Reporter -1-	To serve by providing information	which is complete and unbiased coverage	of what officials say.
Police -2-	To Serve and Protect	By arresting crooks and getting them convicted	through investigation of traces of prior events.

"structural" or "contextual" story that this technology makes possible, online resources place the description of any isolated event within the context of a class of similar occurrences so that the journalist is informed by the work and research of other writers—colleagues and academics—involved in and knowledgeable about the event or event class in question. The assertions of news subjects are seen as not necessarily "true," as verified "facts" in and of themselves, but as hypotheses to be examined within a literature's context. This represents a potentially profound shift in the way data can be treated by public information writers and a significant change in the way data is incorporated into the public sphere. At the very least, this potential informs reporters or editors in a significant way, empowering them, through this electronically-gathered, background information, with a perspective that allows them to question critically an official posture, no matter how politically powerful its official source may be.

The result is a diminishment of the source or subject's power to define any story's content in such a way as to advance arbitrarily that person's personal standing or the posture of the subject's professional group. If one accepts as general divisions of interest the categories of institutional, instrumental, and functional goals, this procedure may emphasize the speakers' personal, financial interest in a project or proposed legislation while making overt the degree to which their instrumental procedures or policies are perhaps the real issue at hand. For newswriters, the end result is not only an ability to approximate journalism's own instrumental (and thus institutional) goals but an increasing freedom from the profession's history of absolute reliance on the professional or political subject as crucial and sole information source.

Consider Illustration 2.3 and the confusion that arose following the shooting of Carol Stuart by her husband, Charles, in 1989. As Chapter 1's brief review noted, criticism of coverage in this case presumed that the methods by which the press fulfilled its instrumental and institutional goals were the same as those of the police. But reporters do not have the legal authority or professional expertise to investigate homicides. Just as police were hampered by a lack of evidence against the victim's husband until Stuart's brother came forward, reporters were limited to police reports and—even without any other evidence—had a fantastic story. Similarly, the news professional does not have the institutional goal of To Serve and Protect, as do the police. Rather, the reporter and editor offer to the public, in the traditional news paradigm, information provided by official, police sources.

Thus criticism of *Boston Globe* reportage depended on a confusion of police methods and instrumental goals (Illustration 2.3, B2 and C2) with those of the newspeople who covered the case (B1 and C1). Reporters are not investigators. They report (B1) what police officials find (C1). In cases like the Stuart case, this is an uncomfortable truth for news professionals to accept. Most would, like the *Globe's* Goodman, prefer to argue a failure in reportage and presentation than admit a structural limit to their profession's abilities. But, as the analysis of the *Wall Street Journal*'s story made clear, the confusion of methods and goals is a consistent aspect of contemporary journalism. In this book's context, what makes the Stuart case unusual is that reporters covering it would have gained nothing from online search techniques. It was a totally unique event and thus not conducive to any contextual or structural research. There was, in short, no class of prior events that a reporter could have used to make sense of the whole. While one may know, statistically, that spouses are usually the primary suspects in a murder investigation, the likelihood that a man would shoot himself in the stomach after killing his pregnant wife but before calling for help on a mobile telephone—all as part of a bizarre murder plan—makes the whole situation atypical.

It is far more common to assign reporters to cover events or issues for which there is a body of information amenable to online research, and, in those cases, the journalist's role and function can change. Thus, in the tort reform story, the *Wall Street Journal*'s Waldholz was limited to information presented by Todd and Habash. That much of it was incomplete or incorrect did not matter because the reporter's methodology—the means by which he met his profession's current institutional and instrumental standards—was limited to information received orally ("Todd said"; "Habash said") without a consideration of antecedent events. The story's event was the "debate," not the issues it pretended to cover. The reporter did not and was not expected to write or consider, for example, malpractice as a class or the resulting cost of multiple injury suits. Thus his instrumental goals of objectivity and completeness could not be met. These limits were largely removed when, through the use of data obtained online, the biases of the debate's participants and the limits of their perspectives became clear. Then the reportage became, or had the potential to be, structural or contextual, not ephemeral and perhaps even misleading.

As the example of the drug story research made clear, news is affected by historical, social, and economic patterns that influence what is printed or broadcast in individual cities. Stories must still be passed by editorial gatekeepers and be accepted as relevant to the degree that they are not only placed on the media's agenda but placed there prominently. Concern over traditional sources, distrust of "eggheads," worry over the possible offense of other sources, and a disposition to interpret stories through their overt, economic relevance all affect what is written and, of course, what will be researched. But that story did run, despite the reservations of the newspaper's editorial staff. To the extent one can speak of journalism as divorced from these restraints and argue solely to the instrumental and institutional myths, it seems clear that these technologies have the potential to forge a new and perhaps more complete news.

NOTES

1. Tim Miller, "Databases: Finding Your World in the Electronic Newspaper," *Editor and Publisher*, September 10, 1988, 35.

2. The "one-in-a-million" death is usually part of a pattern of preventable injury amenable to electronic research. For example, see the analysis of the death of Marvin Loewen in Tom Koch, *The News as Myth: Fact and Context in Journalism* (Westport, Conn.: Greenwood Press, 1990), chapter 4.

3. My first experience with online databases came in the early 1980s during research on a type of anesthetic death in Vancouver that authorities dismissed as atypical and unique. Since that time, the majority of my online research and writing has centered on medical issues. That personal familiarity accounts for this book's emphasis on medical examples.

4. Alvin Kernan, *Printing Technology, Letters and Samuel Johnson* (Princeton: Princeton University Press, 1987), 49.

5. Kernan, *Printing,* 125.

6. Marshall McLuhan, *The Gutenberg Galaxy* (Toronto: University of Toronto Press, 1962), 250.

7. Kernan, *Printing*, 250.

8. This is not meant in any way to dismiss the historical analysis of others who have studied the complex of forces that shaped the press in the nineteenth and twentieth centuries. Herman and Chomsky, for example, refer to the economic forces that spelled the death of a radical working press in nineteenth century Britian and how similar forces limited the growth of an opposition press in the United States. They, in turn, cite the work of Curran and Seaton. See Edward S. Herman and Noam Chomsky, *Manufacturing Consent: The Political Economy of the Mass Media* (New York: Pantheon Press, 1988), 19. Also, James Curran and Jean Seaton, *Power without Responsibility: The Press and Broadcasting in Britain*, 2d ed. (London: Methuen, 1985), 24.

9. Walter Lippmann, *Public Opinion* (1920; reprint, New York: Free Press, 1965), 157.

10. Leon V. Sigal, "Sources Make the News," in Robert Karl Manoff and Michael Schudson, eds., *Reading the News,* (New York: Pantheon, 1986), 20.

11. Miller, "Databases," 34.

12. Michael Waldholz, "Malpractice Liability: Can the Law Serve Both Doctors and Patients?" *Wall Street Journal*, April 4, 1986, 23. The *Wall Street Journal* is available online through the Dow Jones News Retrieval Service and indexed on a variety of electronic databases, including *Public Affairs Information Bulletin* (PAIS), *Banking Limited, Index,* and *Fanatic Reader.*

13. The use of parenthetic phrases in a search phrase and the means by which an electronic search phrase is constructed will be covered in Chapter 4.

14. This search was carried out under a 1988 grant from Vu/Text, whose support is gratefully acknowledged here. At that time there were about forty newspapers available online. By late 1990, the number was over sixty.

15. "Protopappas Loses Bid for Hearing in Multiple Murders," *Los Angeles Times*, July 21, 1988, 3. Also see, as an example, "3 Lawsuits in 5 Years Result in Investigation of Texas Physicians," *Houston Post*, May 15, 1988, B1. Both the *Los Angeles Times* and the *Houston Post* are searchable, electronically, through Vu/Text Information Services.

16. "Jury Awards Man $28 M in HHC Suit," *Newsday,* May 13, 1988. Again, *Newsday* is available online through Vu/Text, as are all other U.S. newspapers cited in this chapter, excepting those published in Hawaii.

17. "Court Allows $250,000 Limit For Pain, Suffering: Ceiling on Malpractice Award Upheld," *Los Angeles Times*, November 30, 1987, 2. The story quotes Cassandra Green, who was left a quadriplegic following a gynecological operation.

18. Harry Franken, "Suit in Coma Case Settled," *Columbus Dispatch*, September 19, 1987, B1.

19. Franken, "Suit," B1.

20. "Move to Save Lives in Operating Room: Researchers Urge Anesthesia Standards," *Sacramento Bee*, August 22, 1986, A24.

21. J.H. Eichorn et al., "Standards for Patient Monitoring during Anesthesia at Harvard Medical School," *Journal of the American Medical Association* 256 (1986), 1017-20. This and all other medical articles cited in this chapter are accessible on the database *Medline* and through Paper-Chase, a Beth Israel Hospital, Boston, program that simplifies searches of *Medline*.

22. C. Whitcher et al., "Anesthetic Mishaps and the Cost of Monitoring: A Proposed Standard for Monitoring Equipment," *Journal of Clinical Monitoring* 4 (January 1988), 15.

23. See, for example, W.K. Hamilton, "Unexpected Deaths during Anesthesia: Wherein Lies the Cause?" *Anesthesiology* 50 (1979), 381-83.

24. Franken, "Suit," B1.

25. "Re-Examining the 36-Hour Day,"*Time* , August 31, 1987, 54. *Time* magazine is available on Information Access Company's *Magazine Index* and *Magazine ASAP*. Both databases are distributed by various vendors, including CompuServe Information Services and Dialogue.

26. Associated Press, "Report Sees Greater Nurses' Shortage," *Buffalo News*, May 18, 1990, A4. In fact, many physicians did leave the profession in the 1980s, but the relation between those departures and confusion over a poorly understood system is unclear.

27. L. Masnerus and K. Roberts, "AMA Takes On Inept Doctors," *New York Times*, July 6, 1986, E7. As these stories must, the *New York Times* story quoted physicians on what they were doing to police their own. The news piece did not really examine the proposition that doctors might by definition be biased and unable to adequately evaluate and discipline their peers.

28. "Doctors Seldom Tell On Doctors," *Detroit Free Press*, April 6, 1984, A12. Quoted in Charles B. Inlander, Lowell S. Levin, and Ed Weiner, *Medicine on Trial: The Appalling Story of Medical Ineptitude and the Arrogance That Overlooks It* (New York: Pantheon Books, 1988), 179-80. For this story I used the search phrase: (doctors or physicians) and (incompetent or impaired). The story was also found through

a companion search using the extended phrase: (doctors or physicians) and (alcohol or drug) or (impaired or incompetent). The elements of a search phrase and the function of parentheses, slashes, etc., in them will be discussed in Chapter 4.

29. Richard Jay Feinstein, "Special Report," *New England Journal of Medicine*, 312:12 (March 21, 1985), 803-4. The report was from data supplied by the Federation of State Medical Boards, the agencies which, in each state, discipline their physician members.

30. Dean Edell, "Doctors and Drugs," *Province*, August 13, 1987. Dr. Edell is a syndicated columnist who quoted in this column a 1987 study published in the *Journal of the American Medical Association*.

31. Joel Brinkley, "28,000 'Doctors' Are Feared Unfit," *New York Times*, May 5, 1986, 15.

32. Brinkley, "28,000 'Doctors'," 17.

33. See, for example, "3 Lawsuits in 5 Years," B1; Susan Schmidt, "Review of Complaint Delayed Despite Court Request," *Washington Post*, January 12, 1988, 17. The *Washington Post* can be searched electronically through both Dow Jones News Retrieval and Vu/Text.

34. To see how in error such an assumption can be, see the analysis of Honolulu police official's investigation into injuries sustained by Circuit Court Judge Harold Y. Shintaku. Koch, *News as Myth,* chapter 3.

35. Canada's socialized system provides good patient care and results in a health bill of under 10 percent of that nation's gross national product (GNP) while the United States pays over 12 percent of its GNP, in an average year, for health care. New Zealand's system is, some argue, even more efficient and more equitable than Canada's. Dr. William McArthur, personal communication, February 8, 1990.

36. In 1983-1984, nosocomial infections accounted for 15 percent of all hospital charges adding an estimated $1.5 billion to the U.S. health care bill. The death toll directly attributed to hospital-engendered infections was estimated at "no fewer than" 100,000 deaths and accounted for two million hospitalizations a year—between 5 and 10 percent of the total hospital population. See Charles B. Inlander, Lowell S. Levin and Ed Weiner, *Medicine on Trial* New York: Pan-

theon Books, 1988), 124-25. Articles on nosocomial illness can be found by searching medical databases like *PaperChase* and *Medline* with the phrase: nosocomi/ or (hospital and infection).

37. See, for example, N.M. Davis and M.R. Cohen, *Medication Errors: Cause and Prevention* (Philadelphia: George F. Stickley, 1981), a text cited in other works and popular articles on this class of problems.

38. The general approach used here is an attempt to apply Barthes' semiology to the analysis of news. For an introduction to his system, see Roland Barthes, "Myth To-day," "The Imagination of the Sign," and "Introduction to the Structural Analysis of Narratives" in Susan Sontag, ed., *A Barthes Reader* (New York: Hill and Wang, 1982). For Barthes' analysis of cultural signs and artifacts, see Roland Barthes, *The Eiffel Tower and Other Mythologies* (New York: Hill and Wang, 1979). This approach extends my earlier attempt to integrate semiology into an analysis of the North American news system in Koch, *News as Myth*, 23-27.

39. Had he been less skillful or more argumentative, Habash could have savaged Todd's suggestion that only physicians should sit on juries involving malpractice. After all, if physicians are so befuddled by the malpractice insurance "crisis," are they, in fact, sufficiently capable to speak on this issue at all? If only doctors can judge members of the profession, how embarrassing to have so many bogus physicians in practice and as members of the American Medical Association. The whole history of the ideal of a jury of peers, of course, works against the professional elitism Todd seems to advocate.

40. In Bush's first year as president, he created a cabinet-level post for an antidrug coordinator, popularly referred to as the Drug Czar; asked Congress for more than $9 million to pursue a war on drugs; and used the issue of cocaine supplies as an excuse to invade the country of Panama, bomb Panama City, and kill a still unknown number of Panamanian citizens—all in the hunt for that country's leader, General Manuel Noriega, whom American officials wanted to bring to trial on drug smuggling charges.

41. Andrew J. Glass, "Why Drug Crisis Is Spinning Out of Control," *Honolulu Star-Bulletin*, March 10, 1988. Glass is a syndicated news columnist.

42. Jeff Greenfield, "'Pack Journalism': Horde Copy," *Nightline*, September 27, 1989. In the body of Greenfield's report, he makes clear that most of these stories, without any critical thought or objective consideration, promulgated the government's official position on drugs..

43. Al Giordano, "The War on Drugs: Who Drafted the Press?" *Washington Journalism Review* 43 (January 1990), 23.

44. Giordano, "The War on Drugs," 21. The answer is, of course, nobody drafted them. Their participation was volunteered through the reflexive reportage of press conferences called by officials ranging from the president or prime minister to the local police chief.

45. Scripps Howard News Service syndicated columnist B.J. Cutler objected to this participation by Brokaw in the docudrama as a "foreign policy disaster" because of its unfair treatment of Mexico. Its quality as "objective" journalism or as anything but propoganda was not questioned, however. See B.J. Cutler, "TV Drug-War Series Was Foreign Policy Disaster," *Honolulu Star-Bulletin*, January 23, 1990, B3.

46. "Drugs Thwart Justice, Lawyers Find," *Columbus Dispatch*, December 1, 1988.

47. Greenfield, "Pack Journalism." Greenfield is an ABC reporter who often presents reports on *Nightline*. The suggestion here is that, through use of electronic databases, these questions can be not only asked but answered as well.

48. "Poverty/Drugs Factor Ignored, Jackson Says," *Honolulu Star-Bulletin*, September 16, 1988, C1. This was a wire report with a Washington dateline and no byline.

49. Jane Mayer, "Street Urchins: In the War on Drugs, Toughest Foe May Be the Alienated Youth," *Wall Street Journal*, September 18, 1989, 1.

50. Mayer, "Street Urchins," 1.

51. Lewis P. Lapham, "A Political Opiate," *Harper's Magazine*, December 1989, 43-47. *Harper's* and the *Atlantic* can both be searched through either the *Magazine Index* or *Magazine ASAP* databases.

52. Lapham, "Political Opiate," 45.

53. Salmon reviews the work of Craig Reinarman and Henry Levine within the context of a broader argument which suggests that the manufacturing of stories and editorial postures is a structural problem of which this is simply an example. See Charles T. Salmon, "God Understands when the Cause is Noble," *Gannett Center Journal* 4:2 (Summer 1990), 26-27.

54. I first researched this issue in 1979, when, as a reporter at the *Province* newspaper in Vancouver, Canada, I was introduced to Barry Beyerstein, a leading researcher in the field of addiction.

55. Lee N. Robins and John E. Helzer, "Drug Use among Vietnam Veterans—Three Years Later," *Health World News* (October 27, 1975), 44-49.

56. The work of Canadian drug researchers Bruce Alexander and Barry Beyerstein has been conclusive in this area. See, for example, Bruce K. Alexander, Barry L. Beyerstein, and Patricia F. Hadaway, "Effect of Early and Later Colony Housing on Oral Ingestion of Morphine in Rats," *Pharmacology and Biochemical Behavior* 154 (October 1981), 571-6; Bruce K. Alexander, Patricia F. Hadaway and Barry L. Beyerstein, "Rat Park Chronicle," *B.C. Medical Journal* 22:2 (February 1980), 54-56; Patricia F. Hadaway, Bruce K. Alexander, R.B. Coambs, and Barry L. Beyerstein, "The Effect of Housing and Gender on Preference for Morphine-Sucrose Solutions in Rats," *Psychopharmacology* 66:1 (1979), 87-91.

57. This is noted cheerfully and in passing by a shallow *Newsweek* cover story on the number, kind, and success of support groups in the United States. See "Unite and Conquer," *Newsweek*, February 5, 1990, 50-55. The magazine's writers describe and discuss self-help groups for those addicted to, among other things, gambling, cocaine, and alcohol. But they see no relation between the ability of these addicts to wean themselves from their dependencies and the possibility the war on drugs—supposedly a war on addictive substances—may be based on unsupportable premises. *Newsweek* is a major reporter of the drug war on all its myriad fronts. *Newsweek* is accessible through *Magazine ASAP*

and *Magazine Index* databases.

58. That is to say that young adults who use drugs tend to voluntarily cease that use as they become settled in work, graduate school, marriages, etc. See, for example, V.H. Ravis and D. B. Kanel, "Changes in Drug Behavior from the Middle to the Late Twenties: Initiation, Persistence, and Cessation of Use," *American Journal of Public Health* 77:5 (May 1987), 607-11. Also Kanel and Ravis, "Cessation of Illicit Drug Use in Young Adulthood," *Archive General Psychiatry* 46:2 (February 1989), 109-116.

59. Richard Bennett et al., "Morphine Titration in Postoperative Laparotomy Patients Using Patient-Controlled Analgesia," *Current Therapeutic Research* 32:1 (July 1982), 45-51. This study repeated earlier tests by other medical researchers interested in patient-controlled analgesia.

60. Thus, in late 1989 and early 1990 cocaine and crack cocaine were being supplanted in the public imagination by crystal methamphetamine, a new synthetic that attracted media attention and antidrug dollars. See, for example, Michael A. Lerner, "The Fire of 'Ice'," *Newsweek*, November 27, 1989, 37. It would be an interesting exercise to track, year by year, coverage on TV and in representative newspapers or magazines of the drug problem, drug war, and, now, drug crisis, and then correlate that timeline with monies requested and granted at federal, state, and local enforcement levels. This could then be compared with news coverage of the findings of, and funding for, researchers in psychology and pharmacology who have explored the root causes of addiction and habituation.

61. This was an open letter by Friedman to the Bush administration's then newly appointed drug czar. It is also quoted in Giordano, "War on Drugs," 21.

62. Three stories were published in a takeout based on the Simon Fraser University researchers' work and its implications to the then growing antidrug crusade. See (Vancouver) *Province*, October 17, 1982, A1, A4.

3

Transformations: Scale and Focus

One result of increased use of electronic databases in news and public affairs writing will be a change in the narrative form currently accepted without thought by the contemporary newswriter and editor. If one thinks of news as a social system for the relay of information, then the rules by which news stories are written—their narrative form—are the mechanism by which data are sifted and arranged in intelligent form. In both training texts[1] and specialized news manuals,[2] that form is typically defined today, as it has been for a century, by the "5W's": who, what, when, where, why, and how. First formally articulated by Rudyard Kipling,[3] the 5W's have been accepted as the narrative norm by news organizations throughout the English-speaking world and remain the basis of practical instruction in contemporary schools of journalism in both the United States and Canada.

Whether the story to be written is a simple police report ("Police blamed Thursday's heavy rain and strong winds for three accidents that claimed two lives and seriously injured two other people.") or a political story at the national level ("President Bush demanded Thursday that Congress appropriate $9.4 billion to fund his administration's 'all-out' war on drugs."), the elements are the same. "Who" describes a single person (the president) or official group (the police) concerned with "what," a narrowly prescribed but recently past event. That subject may be a plea to Congress for money or a policeman's explanation of a death on the highway, but whatever its focus, that subject is narrowly bounded in its definition of "where" and "when."

This reliance on the 5W's has elsewhere been defined as the narrative form's emphasis on the journalistic event, the statement at a press conference, in an interview, or through a press release of an official's interpretation or explanation of a prior occurrence.[4] That level of report may have no logical or direct relation to the occurrences of the boundary event, the use of cocaine by an individual, the death of a motorist in a specific highway crash, or the injury of a patient on a surgeon's table. Information at this level of the boundary is naive, without interpretation. At the level of the boundary, a person ceased breathing at a specific time and place while under surgery. Pronouncement of death and an assignment of causes for that demise are official interpretations of prior events based, one presumes, on adequate investigation. The journalistic event gives public authority to those conclusions, although the relation between an official interpretation of the boundary event and objective, verifiable "facts" relating to it need be nothing but accidental.

Somebody died last night in the rain, and even if hundreds have perished in recent years at that same traffic intersection, today's story will state as fact the police sergeant's opinion that rain and wind were the immediate culprits. Bush's war on drugs may have been a sham and a failure for a decade, but noting the widely acknowledged impossibility of controlling through prohibition and interdiction what scientists define as a response to social and environmental problems has no place in the news form as it stands. "President Bush said" or "Speaker of the House Tip O'Neill responded"—the news is traditionally limited in time and space by its function as an official relay of oral statement through reporters and public relations channels for dissemination to modes of print or broadcast production. No matter how silly or foolish those statements may be upon examination, the narrative necessity of "who said precisely what at a specific time and place" has restricted the reporter's job to that of official transcriber. At best, the reporter becomes a translator who transforms officialdom's often factually questionable and grammatically garbled statements into seemingly coherent and authoritative news quotes.

To the extent that the official's statement is the daily newswriter's primary source of information, this result is perhaps inevitable. It is necessary because oral speech, the medium that reporters quote and transform, is typically vague and circumlocutious, allowing the speaker to state as fact what has yet to be determined. As H. Garfinkel summarized in describing the problems of analyzing and understanding orally delivered statements: "The anticipation that persons will understand, the occasionality of expressions, the specific vagueness of references, the retrospective-prospective sense of present occurrence, waiting for something later in order to see what was meant before, are sanctioned properties of common discourse."[5]

The oral statement's characteristic vagueness has typically required news reporters quoting officials to be active participants in the creation of their own quotes and thus unpaid assistants for the officials they covered. *Newsweek* called this the "age-old practice of cleaning up (subject's) quotes."[6] Presidents like Lyndon B. Johnson, whose speech was typically filled with the earthy and profane, was always quoted with his vocabulary edited to approximate the newswire's ideal of nonvolatile speech. Grammarians who attempted to diagram the extemporaneous statements of President Ronald Reagan ended with unintelligible, garbled, convoluted sentences that somehow gained the chimera of intelligence and authority in a five-second television clip or editorial rewrite.[7]

The form of the news is the perfect vehicle of assistance to officials or experts who wish their opinion to be placed in the public forum as fact—whatever the independently verifiable validity of those views. The narrative form of the news is itself simple, with short paragraphs and a single focus: what "X" said last night or this morning at a single place about a narrowly defined subject. It does not admit complexity of thought or statements filled with subordinate clauses. Officials who speak circumlocutiously are automatically edited until their speech conforms to the narrative necessities of the news form. There is, at present, little

the form or in the news process—for the translator
)ral to print report or broadcast clip to question the
f the subject's words. News in its current form thus
,-------- a profoundly unary transformation, a system by
which statements or ideas are presented without allowing
for questioning or discussion of context or underlying fact.
This class of transformation limits the range of discussion by
stating as fact but without respect to content or context the
conclusions of subjects about antecedent events. The term
unary originates in structural linguistics and has been used
by semiologist Roland Barthes in his analysis of news images:

> A transformation is unary if, through it, a single
> series is generated by the base: such as the pas-
> sive, negative, interrogative and emphatic trans-
> formations. The photograph is unary when it
> emphatically transforms "reality" without dou-
> bling it; without making it vacillate (emphasis is
> a power of cohesion): no duality, no indirection,
> no disturbance. The unary photograph has every
> reason to be banal. . . . "The subject," says one
> handbook for amateur photographers, "must be
> simple, free of useless accessories; this is called
> the search for unity."[8]

The single series of the contemporary news story is the
official interpretation of a boundary event. That is what
reporters present, in attributed quotes, as reality: "no dis-
turbance."

Doubling, in this context, means adding a level of reportage in which the assertions of actors in any prior event
are tested against available data in the printed literature for
a story that combines both official assertion and a context for
those "facts." This doubling of the information base alters
the focus by inserting a duality. The "what" is not only what
an official said but, simultaneously, what others uninvolved
in the immediate press event may have written on the
problem. The reportorial event itself is at least doubled from
"President Bush said last night in a televised address to the
nation" to a comparison of his statements last night to the

body of statements by others in recent years on the issue of drugs. The opinions of a speaker (Todd, Habash, Reagan, Coroner McKey, etc.) are reported as assumptions to be tested against the yardstick of available information on one or more prior boundary events.

Semiologists distinguish between the "signifier" and the "signified," between the bare data of an event (a body ceased respiration at 5.53 P.M. during surgery at St. Luke's Hospital, Seattle, Washington) and the conclusion that Mr. Jones died yesterday of natural causes. At a more complex level, the signifier might be that Jones, 83, received treble the accepted dosage of anesthetic gas in one-half the time such gas should be administered. What this statement might signify to a physician—that Jones was killed by an overdose— is not a conclusion reporters are able to make. If the attending physician says at the inquest, "Mr. Jones died of old age," the reporter must, as nothing more than a translator from the oral to the written, accept that statement on faith as a fact. Doubling or disturbing the transformation is, simply, using information resources to recapture for the writer the ability to state what is signified. At the very least it assures that the writer, reporter, or researcher can appropriately question the interpretation of experts and officials who may blithely and inaccurately, for personal reasons, define what is signified with little reference to the broad range of context and the specific details of a prior event.

What was earlier called a "trivial story" can be seen from this perspective as a unary narrative transformation. It was trivial or ephemeral to the degree that its transformation from oral to print was singular and thus lacked the doubling effect of an objective context. The "who" was based solely on what an official said to the press, and no room was allowed for the reporter to balance that official statement against the weight of other, nonoral information. The official defines the signifier, the parameters of the prior event, and assigns it a conclusion, thus giving it meaning. Structural stories were doubled through a comparison of the facts of other, structurally similar events with information provided by officials in the context of press release or news statement. Contextual stories, to continue the analogy, were disturbed by addressing the issues of a prior event and focusing reportorial inquiries on the antecedent context, often provided by structurally similar, antecedent occurrences, to seek root or systemic causes for what may be blamed, by "experts," on nonactive causes. They reject the official's limited signifier for a broader class of event, allowing the writer independently to focus on social issues, trends, or principles in what is signified. Thus reports concerning the war on drugs are doubled by focusing on the unending requests by politicians and police officials for more money while simultaneously demonstrating how little effect the interdiction programs have had. The official focus is disturbed by what is signified, that drug use is a symptom of poverty and the failure of social assistance programs, precisely those areas upon which successive administrations have refused to focus their energies.

Simply put, increasing reliance on electronic databases is likely to alter the narrative form by changing the level of transformation from unary to dual or multiple exchanges. As the examples in Chapter 2 demonstrated, this transformation, which also can be described as a change from the ephemeral or trivial to the contextual story, necessarily makes overt the degree to which actors in a drama may have biases or perspectives that define the partiality of their views. A dual transformation means that one not only can say "Mr. Bush said last night" but can ask, as part of the story, "Is the statement verifiable?" The result is a change in focus from acceptance of what *was* said to a focus on "why" (the causal factors), "how" precisely did "x" happen, and "who" or "what" is responsible for a given situation? Balancing official statements and printed reports will allow daily newswriters to insert into stories the "why" and "how" that Kipling's poem promised but news rarely delivers. Through this process, control of the signifier and conclusions about what it might mean—what is signified—are transferred from offical control to the writer's domain.

Another way of stating this is to say that unary transformations based on a single, official point of view have no perspective. Doubling the narrative adds perspective by juxtaposing the expert's or representative's view with information derived from another information base. In tradi-

tional stories, the expert's agenda is still in the foreground
but, in contextual stories, it becomes background. If a statement by President Bush about the war on drugs is placed
within the context of academic research on addiction and
habituation, then two levels of information—oral and written—are balanced, and opinion is stacked against the body
of longer term research. If Todd asserts that avaricious
lawyers are the cause of rising malpractice insurance premiums but medical literature suggests the problem is with
physician techniques, then the immediate event is placed in
perspective when viewed from the scale of the medical and
legal literature.

Treating stories with attention to their duality and
scale will change the relation between a subject and the
reporter, who becomes not merely interpreter and translator
but, perhaps for the first time, approaches the potential of
the profession's instrumental goal. Objectivity is based on
the promise of disinterested and verifiable hypothesis. But
as a system of translation from the oral to the printed, daily
news has no method of verification. At best, it presents what
logicians call "weakly verified statements," which, while
true in a limited sense (Bush really said "x" last night), must
be subjected to further examination if they are to stand
objectively on their own.[9] In the discussion of the *Wall Street
Journal's* story on tort reform, for example, we saw that the
statements of Todd, while perhaps true representations of
what he said to the *Journal*, were questionable within the
broader context of the medical-legal literature. Electronic
information resources offer at least the possibility for the
verification or rejection of oral statements by the reporter
and thus promise the potential of fulfilling the professional's
instrumental goal.

At the least, this technology will allow the newsperson to
place the often vague, contradictory, and circumlocutious
public statement in a context where it can be first measured
and then transformed beyond the unary level. As the information base changes so, we suspect, will the narrative rules
that govern the writing of news stories in broadcast and
print media.

A UNARY EXAMPLE

The difference between unary and multiple transformations, between official statement and contextual fact, is demonstrated in the following example of reportage resulting from testimony at a British Columbia, Canada, coroner's jury. The story was published in the next day's *Province* newspaper:[10]

Fatal Slip Unnoticed

By HOLLY HORWOOD
Staff Reporter

The life-giving oxygen tube accidentally "came out."

But it wasn't until 15 minutes later that hospital staff discovered the mishap, which cost a retired Cloverdale music teacher his life.

A coroner's jury was given that evidence yesterday at an inquest in the death of Robert Graham, 64, at Peace Arch Hospital in White Rock.

Graham died two weeks after undergoing a routine operation for varicose veins last Sept. 20.

Anesthetist Dr. Robert Barnbrook said that, by the time it was discovered that the tube had come out, Graham was already brain dead.

Barnbrook told the inquest that, "in 20/20 hindsight . . . it's my belief that the patient extricated the tube when we turned him over."

He said the oxygen tube slipped out between Graham's vocal cords and became lodged in the esophagus which leads to the stomach.

The mishap occurred when the overweight, anesthetized Graham was turned over onto his stomach in preparation for the operation.

Barnbrook said there was no indication of any problem.

He said the congested, bluish hue of Graham's skin resulted from the face-down position of the patient.

Witness Dr. Rinz Dykstra said he first pointed out a bluish color in Graham's complexion to Barnbrook when the tube was first inserted.

Barnbrook replied that the color was normal under the circumstances.

When Graham's leg was cut open, and the blood was a purplish color, doctors realized they had a crisis.

Two minutes later, Graham's heart rate dropped to zero and he went into full cardiac arrest.[11]

This story is an excellent example of a unary transformation in which the contextually sanctioned, official statement of an expert is transcribed for a news publication without thought or consideration. Horwood quotes the physician, Barnbrook, who insists to an inquest jury that an unconscious Graham "extricated the tube when we turned him over." This writing makes of the unconscious patient an active suicide, and the "overweight, anesthetized Graham" becomes a participant in his own demise. The active tense and simple paragraphing underlines Graham's culpability. In the final paragraph we are told that, after doctors realized a crisis had developed, "Graham's heart rate dropped to zero and he went into full cardiac arrest." But the patient did not go willingly or of his own volition. Cardiac arrest was the result of a series of operating-room events that happened to the unconscious patient, not an act of free will.

The caution by Dykstra to Barnbrook concerning the increasingly cyanotic color of the patient is noted in the story without comment or investigation. The only context of this very traditional piece of reportage is what was said at the inquest. The virtual impossibility of those statements (e.g., "the [unconscious] patient extricated the tube when we rolled him over"), and any possible relation of Graham's death to a broader pattern of malpractice, are also ignored. Textbooks for anesthesiologists and scores of articles in the medical literature uniformly warn of the results of failure by anesthetists to note signs of respiratory difficulty and this literature places the responsibility for monitoring oxygenation (the absence of which does present a change in coloration) on the attending physicians. Further, several days earlier the same newspaper carried a national wire story about other patients dying in other Canadian cities because similar gastrointestinal tubes had buckled during surgery, causing oxygen starvation.[12] The possible relation of those deaths to Graham's is obvious in retrospect, but in Horwood's story it is never addressed.

As presented, the copy raises no questions and presents no perspective, other than that of inquest statement. It does not question Barnbrook's testimony as an interested if official witness in the journalistic event or test his conclusions about the boundary event against a wider frame of information. Nor does it question, with reference to the literature or common sense, even the most blatantly inane statements made by him. Indeed, it contributes to the impression that nobody was responsible for this death except, perhaps, the patient himself. The reporter does not ask why it took the surgeon fifteen minutes to notice that his patient was receiving no oxygen; makes of the surgeon an almost disinterested bystander ("by the time it was discovered that the tube had come out"—who is supposed to watch this?); and makes no connections, paragraph to paragraph, between the "15 minutes" and the fact that within that time Barnbrook was, in fact, warned by Dykstra that his patient was turning blue. That this death was not a freak "mishap" but more likely a textbook example of physician failure adequately to monitor a patient during surgery and react to those monitoring signs was not an issue raised by the coroner and therefore one ignored by the reporter, who diligently translated the oral inquest testimony for a media report.

This story was unary to the degree it admitted no real knowledge about the boundary event of Graham's failure to breathe while on the respirator and his subsequent expiration. Barnbrook's interpretation of Graham's death, not the boundary event of the demise itself, is the story here. In the narrative's parade, quick quotes are presented in short paragraphs balanced by general, summary statements. The whole story presents as fact, without reflection or consideration, Barnbrook's interpretation of Graham's death. But Barnbrook was involved and certainly cannot be considered an objective witness. To transform this short news story—to double it, in Barthes' phrase—would require only that the "facts" of Barnbrook's and Dykstra's statements be examined within a broader, less partial context. A search of the *Province*'s newspaper files on previous, anesthetic-related deaths would show that a systematic failure of physicians in that region to monitor their patients during surgery often led to oxygen starvation and expiration—by brain death or heart attack. A search of the medical literature on anesthesia, the same literature reviewed here in the discussion of tort reform, would describe other cases where patients had, like Graham, had their oxygen supplies cut off during surgery with similarly disastrous results.

Some of these cases could also have been found by electronically searching U.S. newspaper files. A search of thirty-five U.S. newspapers published in 1987 found a number of cases in which disruption of oxygen during surgery caused death or permanent disability.[13] Several dealt specifically with problems of intubation similar to Graham's. In New York, for example, a jury awarded nearly $28 million to a Bronx man who entered a city-run hospital with a broken leg and emerged with profound brain damage. Court testimony, reported by *Newsday*, showed that surgical attendants at North Central Bronx Hospital improperly placed a breathing tube when twenty-four-year-old Djon Pjetri was operated on and, in part because they did not monitor his breathing, he suffered brain damage from lack of oxygen.[14] In a similar case Humana, Inc. and the University of Louisville were sued following the death of a patient during operation on his thigh. Dwight Wise died when his anesthesia began to wear off and he began, according to Coroner Richard Greathouse, "bucking the tube down his throat." The suit, asking for compensatory and punitive damages, charged that the university lacked a protocol for emergencies during surgery, that the operating room was insufficiently staffed and had insufficient monitoring equipment.[15] In most cases found in online research, failure adequately to monitor the patient during surgery was described as a major factor in anesthesia-related injury or death.

Any reportorial investigation of the circumstances at the boundary level of Graham's death would have created a second order of reportage, a doubling that questioned the competence of Barnbrook's refusal to consider his patient's coloration. Contextually, the signifier would then have been not simply a man's expiration but the complex of specific medical procedures followed or ignored during surgery. Such a treatment would have raised structural issues regarding the efficacy of the provincial medical review system (and that of the coroner's inquest system) because, after all, it is that system that supervises the actions of B.C. physicians. Why was this death allowed to happen? If inadequate monitoring of anesthesia had caused previous deaths or permanent injuries elsewere, as a search of the newspaper's own files assures us occurred, don't the coroner's service, the provincial ministry of health, and the College of Physicians and Surgeons bear some responsibility for a failure to assure that regional physicians follow appropriate procedures? The story, thus grounded in a broader written record, would begin to resonate with allegations and questions stemming from a specific boundary event—one now placed not in Barnbrook's context but in that of an independent and technically informed questioner.

Clearly, it is not in Barnbrook's interest for the newspaper to take this approach. Although as a physician he has instrumental and institutional goals of saving lives and curing illness through appropriate medical and surgical techniques, he also has a practice and reputation to protect if he is to continue to earn an income. That final, functional, goal would not be well served by admitting that he not only did not see signs of distress in a patient but ignored them when another physician said, in effect, "your patient is turning blue." Nor is it necessarily in the best interests of the presiding coroner or the B.C. Coroner's Service for a reporter to question independently (and in print) the very limited "facts" allowed into the inquest as evidence. The service, an arm of the government, might be embarrassed if it were shown for years to have been at best impotent to change the conditions and at worst negligent in uncovering cases of death by anesthetic mishap. The coroner service's investigators would be equally ill served if a reporter looked at this case and found that as early as 1980 previous inquests had noted that failure adequately to monitor patients during surgery had caused deaths by delaying prompt action in cases of oxygen failure or anesthetic drug overdose.[16] Such reportage would make them look bad. Their mandate under law is to make public all information concerning an unusual and preventable death, but they clearly did not do so here. All relevant information would have hit hard at the physician's responsibility in such cases, as well as the inability of the provincial coroners—despite a large budget—to keep such medical failures from occurring again and again.

So again we see a conflict between the stated institutional goals of "experts" or politically constituted bodies and the functional concerns of their members. The reportorial transformation is unary and trivial to the extent it allows subjects to choose their level of description and accepts that choice without question, criticism, or complaint. By using databases to examine the distance between the actions or statements of experts and their (or their professions') instrumental or institutional goals, the story is doubled and becomes at least contextual.

The emphasis on functional goals— to safeguard their professional positions and continue to earn income— need not be conscious mendacity and, indeed, it is unlikely that Horwood's story represents a draconian cover-up. One expects, rather, that individuals like Barnbrook or the coroner will choose the posture that puts their actions in the best light. Further, newspeople like Horwood relaying that position in the news are not necessarily conscious participants in a white-wash. They are merely relaying what was said and, as unary translators, are enmeshed in a conflict of goals and myths as complex as that of their subjects. The whole represents the acceptance of established parameters by officials and the reflexive endorsement of them by newspeople.

Horwood did her best. Presumably, Barnbrook and his operating staff did theirs. Just as we will see, in our discussion of search phrases, how conjunctions can keep search information apart (using the word *not*) or bring data together (using the word *and*), so too do unary transformations prevent questioning and associations ("at the inquest Dr. Barnbrook said"), while double and multiple transformations bring in other perspectives ("In the thirtieth such death in Canada over the last five years, physician failure adequately to monitor a patient contributed to a B.C. man's death."). A regional story based on data from sources other than the inquest might have begun with: "A Surrey man died unnecessarily during surgery at a local hospital, according to a *Province* investigation based on inquest testimony into the death of Cloverdale music teacher Kenneth Graham. This was the fourth case in Canada this year related to problems resulting from anesthetic breathing tubes. It was at least the eleventh in B.C. since 1980 to result from physician failure to adequately monitor their patients."

Changing from unary to multiple transformations is a matter of searching an electronic database for conjunctions that will link occurrences at the level of the boundary event—Graham's death during surgery—with other, similar occurrences. This deeper narrative focus requires the crafting of search phrases that can be applied to one or another database (from the newspaper's own published records to review articles in medical journals) and placing the death in a context where the statements of boundary participants and investigating officials can be considered objectively by newspeople and their client readers, viewers, or listeners.

SCALE AND FOCUS

Data is available at a variety of levels and at various scales for those who wish to pursue an active examination of a specific event. Graham's death, for example, could have been examined at a provincial scale over time, a North American scale through the medical literature, or nationally through attention to Canadian deaths blamed in part on breathing tubes used to provide patients with oxygen. Changing the scale of reportage from the journalistic event—where information is orally transmitted—to a broader examination of the prior, boundary event can occur only through reference to prior documents that place the apparently trivial, local occurrence within the context of a general pattern. The death of an overweight man during surgery becomes, in this manner, a part of the mosaic of anesthetic misapplication and an element in the debate over medical insurance, tort reform, or physician review.

The next two chapters describe in some detail practical aspects by which an event is examined through searching of various levels of information (technical, popular news, primary data) at varying scales of publication (local, regional, national, or international). At this point in the argument it is necessary only to acknowledge that those scales exist and may be of varying use, depending on the general events to be reported, the time writers have to pursue the story, and the restraints under which they may work. For a narrative's transformation to be doubled (or trebled or quadrupled) and for a story to be expanded from the ephemeral to a contextual or structural framework, it must be taken from the narrowly defined official context and placed in a broader perspective. Research at a different scale will force what Horwood's traditional reportage did not allow—the consideration of a speaker's testimony within a broader context.

Illustration 3.1 provides in graphic form three distinct levels of information and four separate categories of print information currently available from online libraries. It describes a series of pertinent but more general information sources originating at local, regional, and national levels. Reportage or discussion can be at the local level, describing specific events, at the regional level in which state or provincial jurisdictions apply, and, finally, at the national level. For newspapers, these levels correspond to the "local" newspaper (e.g., *Buffalo News*), the principal daily publication in any state (the *Boston Globe*, for example, may be considered the critical New England newspaper), and a small number of "national" newspapers. In Canada, for example, only the *Globe and Mail* would qualify for the latter category while, in the United States, several newspapers vie for the title of "national" paper (e.g., *USA Today*, the *Washington Post,* and the *New York Times).*[17]

Illustration 3.1
Library Categories: Scale

	Newspapers	Magazines	Newsletters & Journals	Documents
	1	2	3	4
A.	Local	City	Advocacy	Scientific
B.	Regional	State or Provincial	Professional	Corporate
C.	National	National	Special Interest	Governmental

THE MIRACLE COLLAPSE

A brief example may help in understanding how the choice of library scale makes searching these databases more efficient, facilitating retrieval of appropriate information. Consider the following scenario: In Middleweight, Arkansas, a new and huge supermarket collapses on the day of its official opening.[18] During the festivities celebrating the technical triumph of its construction—a huge party in which success for the supermarket is predicted and the skills of architects, engineers, and construction workers are praised—the building begins to rumble and, as the guests exit hastily, collapses. The multimillion-dollar beauty is now nothing but a very embarrassing piece of scrap seen on the evening news around North America as a miracle only because its collapse did not result in a vast loss of life. Immediately, state officials promise an inquiry into the causes of the collapse, and, as immediately, all those involved in its construction begin to deny they were in any way responsible for the disaster, which has become the focus of five official investigations and ten conflicting lawsuits.

How would this event be reported? The first day's story is "The Miracle Collapse," with local TV stations dedicating eight minutes of airtime (and newspapers pushing out an extra six pages) to eyewitness descriptions, praise for rescue workers, and statements by market owners and state investigators rushed to the scene. "Government Investigation Promised" is the second day's story focus, and, for a few more days, denials of responsibility by the construction company that built the supermarket, the building inspectors who supervised its construction, and the architecture firm that designed it all are paraded across the news. Then official investigators promise a full report on the causes of the collapse at some future date, and the next one hears of the miracle collapse is when the market owners sue the principal contractors for $14 million as they in turn sue their various subcontractors, who, for their part, file suit against the concrete suppliers and, perhaps, the architecture firm that designed the building. The cases will be in court for years, and the state investigator's report will become not public revelation but ammunition for one or another faction in the court fight. The story has passed from police reporter (who fielded the first call) to general assignment staff (which covered the general collapse) to the business reporter (how much money did it all cost?) to the person who holds the courtroom beat. Perhaps, six months down the road, a building inspector resigns quietly, and nothing more is heard about the man who was, not coincidentally, inspector on the collapsed site.

For reporters with no knowledge of building construction, architecture, or engineering, what else is there to do? They can't read blueprints, do not understand structural engineering, and have designed nothing more complex in their life than a paper airplane. Newspapers would have no reason and no authority to investigate the personal finances of the building inspector, although the police might if a judge could be convinced sufficient cause existed to subpoena that individual's bank records. Interviews with participants in the construction of the supermarket will be worse than useless. Everyone involved has a vested interest in denying responsibility, and it is entirely possible that none will know, in fact, if they were or were not responsible. Insurance investigators are about as forthcoming as police sergeants and, at best, usually will only say that their "investigation is continuing."

Beyond the reflexive and unary assurances immediately available in these situations from concerned officials, what can a general assignment reporter say, using electronic databases? Official assurances are typically promises that: "We will determine what happened and, I promise you, will make sure that such a disaster never happens again in this county/state/province/region or the world." But what, in fact, happened? All that is known, really, is the signifier (a building collapsed) and the category of that event (structural collapse). The principal question is: Who or what was responsible? To gain perspective, we could ask what claims have been asserted in previous court cases of building collapse, using a legal database to search for past cases involving "structural collapse." But legal judgments are a very technical place to start a search, and it is hard to know, at the beginning, if cases from elsewhere would be pertinent. There are a number of specialized and general engineering databases, but the articles they contain deal with very specific types of structural problems and issues that, at the moment, may mean absolutely nothing to the reporter. What we need to know, first, is whether this is a truly unique event, like the Stuart case, or one of a series of structurally similar events, like those involving deaths as a result of anesthesia administration? If the collapse of a huge structure is not unique, then we really want to know where this type of failure has occurred in the past and what, in general, are the categories of problems that have caused other structures to suddenly crumble?

What is needed is a handle, some ideas on which to work, a context at the broadest scale in which to examine this local event. Searching a general, national database for references involving building (built), structure (structural), or bridge and collapse (collapsed, collapsing)—will retrieve a number of potentially pertinent stories. All these possibilities are included in the Boolean phrase: collap/ and (buil/ or struct/). By applying the search phrase to a "titles only" database of national publications, one in which a pertinent story's title, author, and source is returned but not the text of the piece itself, one is searching for background material. *Magazine Index*, for example, catalogues a huge number of popular U.S. magazines, ranging from *Time* and *Newsweek* weekly magazines, which may briefly describe individual cases, to national publications and legal journals. Titles returned by this search range from a 1979 *Fortune* magazine article, "Why All Those Buildings Are Collapsing,"[19] to the *Smithsonian*'s 1988 piece, "A New Science can Diagnose Sick Buildings—Before They Collapse."[20]

The reason for the truncation marks (/) in the search phrase is now clear. One wants to allow for both plural and singular of a noun and different tenses of a verb (i.e.,for stories on collapsed (collapsing, collapsed) and building(s)). The slash tells the computer library to look for the root word with any suffix or ending. It thus brings forth stories about structures and about structural issues. In this search, several more technical articles are also uncovered from engineering and legal journals, but they can be set aside for the moment. Both *Smithsonian* and *Fortune* magazines are written for the general reader and, before one can use the technical information, it is necessary to understand the general issues. The first question is: How common is this type of collapse? Is the local event part of a larger pattern?

This search is precisely the type of "fishing expedition" that traditional news librarians dislike, but the benefits of a general first search cannot be dismissed. A preliminary overview search for general or review articles often allows later searches to be targeted with real specificity. In general searches, it is usually most efficient to read the most recent article first. A good review article will typically include information from past articles, and the *Smithsonian* article is likely to contain information from the *Fortune* publication of almost a decade earlier.

At the library (or on a full-text database) one finds the *Smithsonian* article, whose text includes a chronology of past collapses of all sorts of buildings in the United States: in June 1979, the roof collapsed of the Kemper Arena in Kansas City; the roof collapsed several years later of the Hartford Civic Center Coliseum in Hartford, Connecticut; in 1973 a collapse occurred during construction of the Skyline Plaza, Fairfax County, Virginia; in Bridgeport, Connecticut, in 1987 a collapse occurred during construction of the L'Ambiance Plaza; a Hyatt Regency hotel walkway collapsed in July 1981, and so on. We have, indeed, a category of events (building collapse) and a subcategory that includes roofs.

The story includes extensive quotes from structural engineers whose job it is to inspect buildings and investigate collapses. These are the type of independent investigators who, when called, are often willing to provide a newsperson with general guidance and background. James Stratt, for example, is an Atherton, California, engineer who investigated the collapse of the Kemper Arena in Kansas City and found it was caused by the improper use of a type of bolt named the A490. Were these bolts used in the local disaster? How were they used? Here is a real, meaty question one can ask in the next interview with the architect or with construction company officials. David J. Bonneville, a structural engineer based in San Francisco, says in the *Smithsonian* article that it is quite common for people to employ experts like him during a building's construction because "there's so much potential for litigation now, people want to know a lot more about their buildings than they used to."[21] Would a good structural engineer have been able to predict this type of collapse before it spoiled a great party (and nearly killed several hundred corporate guests)? Was a structural engineer employed on the Arkansas site? If so, who was the engineer and what were this person's qualifications?

At the level of C2 in Illustration 3.1—national magazines—one has developed a context in which local reportage of the specific event (A1) can begin. Even on the sole basis of this article, questions can be formulated: Was a structural engineer running tests during construction? Were these A490 bolts used? What expert is being called in by the insurers? Bonneville? You don't say! With all involved parties issuing statements while scrambling for legal cover, the reporter has questions to ask and the names of independent experts who can guide the writer's or researcher's quest for an objective portrait of the context of the building's collapse.

The *Smithsonian* article states that "most catastrophic failures have more than one cause; usually errors compounded by other errors: a designer's mistake, made worse by a worker's mistake, made worse by lax inspection."[22]

Design, construction, and inspection, then, apparently are the three keys. Now one can look at the national level for specific documents (C4 in our diagram) related to these issues. Have there been judgments rendered in court cases stemming from past collapses in other cities? Legal databases will carry this information, as may local newspaper files, which often report on such decisions. The same sources can be searched for evidence of legislation passed in the wake of other disasters to tighten building inspection procedures or construction standards. Has similar legislation been proposed in the Arkansas region? More detailed information is available through national, special interest categories (C3 in the diagram), including books in print on engineering disasters[23] and a number of structural engineering journals that have exhaustively examined the technical aspect of these issues.

Certain documents relating to the Middleweight structure will be matters of public record, and a reporter looking into these issues—design, construction, and inspection— now knows what to look for. What companies were involved in the design? Have they had other collapses? If so, what judgment was rendered by the courts? Who was the state or local inspector? What other collapses have occurred on sites for which this person was responsible? Was a structural engineer testing the building during construction and, if so, what can be learned about this person? The news researcher may be unable to put together a Tinkertoy but, if the A490 bolts mentioned in the *Smithsonian* were also used in the local collapse, the question becomes where else have they contributed to structural disasters. This type of question is best answered in the technical literature.[24] The news writer or researcher can't say "That's the culprit. That's what caused this collapse." But the computer-assisted search has created a suspect, and the reporter can then intelligently question investigators of the boundary event about this aspect of the building's construction and design. He or she can write that "in other cases of building roof collapse, the improper use of this binding bolt was assigned major responsibility for the disasters." One has, in short, a series of hypotheses based not on the vague promises and conflicting statements of individuals involved in and afraid of responsibility for the collapse but on specific data from impartial sources.

These questions are in all likelihood the same ones official experts will be asking. To the extent the writer/ reporter/researcher uses reports from other disasters and articles on engineering, these will be the same background materials informing the insurance and regional investigators. Newspeople thus can stand not simply as translators for the statements of officialdom but also as independent individuals knowledgeable enough to know when they are being duped or used by an involved party whose press conference statements may be mere obfuscation. The resulting stories will not necessarily reflect the perspective that experts, lawyers, or involved officials wish to be disseminated. Those views will be subsumed in a more critical posture that focuses information from multiple sources at varying scales of involvement on a description of the immediate, Middleweight, Arkansas, event.

CANCER AND ELECTRIC POWER SOURCES

The relation between unary and multiple transformations, and the ability of online resources to carry reportage from one to another, can be seen through the review of a story broadcast in British Columbia, Canada, in 1990. On March 12, 1990, the Canadian Broadcasting Corporation's (CBC) Vancouver television station reported on its evening news that twice the normal number of cases of acute childhood leukemia had been reported in the town of Kamloops over the previous decade.[25] The mothers of those affected children were convinced that the occurrence of so many victims of the disease, all living within walking distance of each other, was not normal and had lobbied to have the incidence of the disease investigated by the Cancer Control Agency of British Columbia (CCABC).

In an interview with CBC reporter Catherine Clark, CCABC official Dr. Keith Donaldson, acknowledging the mothers' concerns, said that a study of these illnesses had begun. But he insisted on camera that, although the incidence of acute childhood leukemia in Kamloops was high, there was every likelihood it was just a statistical "cluster" with no single etiology, other than "chance," linking the cases to a specific environmental origin. He thus from the start appeared to discount the possibility of a serious environmental problem. He was aided in this by Clark, who told viewers that "even if there was a cancer-causing problem around, there's no guarantee it's still there."

It is surprising that she would suggest that any environmental factor that could have caused so increased an incidence of a serious illness for more than a decade might have disappeared, not only just when her story went to air, but precisely when an investigation of its presence was about to begin. The power of the press is legendary but not sufficient to erase environmental wrongs simply because a story, even one as good as hers, was broadcast. Clark is, one suspects, relaying to her audience the official's supposedly reassuring words. She thus from the start downplays the possibility that there is, in fact, a problem equal to or greater than, well, a bunch of kids with leukemia. Donaldson said in her story that the incidence of disease was most likely a simple statistical "cluster"—in effect the luck of the draw— with no single cause or epidemiological significance. But can we trust his minimization of the potential seriousness of this cluster of currently unexplained but certainly serious illnesses?

Like Todd, who was a spokesman for the American Medical Association, Donaldson is a representative, the person who speaks for, in this case, a provincial body. He is not a free, scientific agent but a representative of specific authorities and must be circumspect, as was Todd, in what he says. If this situation is not simply a statistical anomaly, what does that fact say about the CCABC? Why did the Cancer Control Agency wait so long to investigate so high an incidence of a specific disease? Doesn't it monitor the incidence of cancer in the population? Shouldn't it have acted before a group of mothers complained so loudly that a Vancouver-based CBC reporter heard them?

Of even more concern is the disturbing but logical next step: If some agent is causing increased incidence of cancer in children in Kamloops, wouldn't that environmental cause lead to higher incidence of other cancer types in the greater population? Is acute childhood leukemia so specific and unusual a disease that its causal agents do not also lead to, say, chronic lymphocytic leukemia in the elderly and, perhaps, other tumors in   adults? Clark noted that investigators would be looking at power lines and local industrial pollution as possible carcinogenic agents. If the latter was the crucial issue, shouldn't it result in higher incidence of other types of cancer, and hadn't the possibility of industrial pollution causing a health risk been considered before by the CCABC? Why were power lines being investigated? How do they relate to the issue of cancer-causing agents in children? What, if anything, was different about the power lines in Kamloops from those used, say, in Vancouver? None of these questions were addressed in the CBC story, which ended with the Cancer Control Agency's announcement that its report on the problem would be finished in perhaps a month.

Clark either asked none of these questions or, if she explored these issues, did not record the responses for her public. Perhaps Donaldson urged her to exercise caution in her reports to prevent a panic before the "facts" were known by his agency and thus before they could be revealed to her. Certainly the CCABC and the CBC do not want to start a panic. Had she gone against Donaldson's wishes, Clark might have alienated him before the completion of a report whose conclusions were promised to her (and thus to her viewers) if only she would be patient.

The Story

As an example of standard TV journalism, this was an excellent and effective piece. There were briefly shown photographs of the obviously diseased, leukemic children, an interview with a mother expressing her concern, photographs of power lines and mills smoking in the Kamloops district, and the reassuring, authoritative statements from Donaldson. The story was "balanced" (a mother's concerns, Dr. Donaldson's assurances), reasonably complete (they're looking at pollution and power lines), and anything but sensational. It raised no questions, really, but chose instead to put its faith in the Cancer Control Agency of British Columbia's investigation (tune in next month) and thus affirmed the network's confidence—and by extension that of the viewers—that the CCA was on the job and would let everyone know if a problem existed. It isolated from the whole a small town in the center of a huge province and made of the mothers' concern an anomaly on the statistical charts of B.C. epidemiology. All the fear, concern, and uncertainty of the issues were transformed, in short, into a reassuring story of officials at work in the field of public health.

Thus this story was another unary transformation in which the official vision (authoritative and reassuring) dominated. Its lead actor was Donaldson, whose statements—that an investigation was under way—were taken as definitive. Clark's story *is* the doctor's public statement of reassurance. He was this story's "who," not the sick children, and the "what" was the official investigation, not the "cluster" of incidences of an uncommon illness. Despite the brief mention of pollution and power lines as possible carcinogenic agents, the story was also not about investigating or discussing the causes of the sickness in these children. The CBC report assumed the CCABC is vigilant and up to the job of first finding and then reporting the answers to all questions (and perhaps announcing them through the CBC) in its own good time. The only issues treated in the story were those acknowledged by Donaldson in his interview. Even the possibility of disease was limited to a few children living near "power lines" or mill pollution in Kamloops. In its own way, the report was authoritative and presented official concerns for the sick children (whose illness was the boundary event) and their families but which focused quickly on the official's announcement of an investigation—the level where news is currently most comfortable.

The story thus obscured what needed to be asked. Are there similar "clusters" (twice the normal incidence!) of acute childhood leukemia elsewhere in British Columbia or in Canada? Had the CCABC been looking into this question before Clark involvement, or was the "investigation" begun after she called them? Why has it taken so long (a decade) to get an investigation going? Could an adequate study be done in one month? Have power lines or pollution been identified as culprits elsewhere when "clusters" of cancer were observed? Why power lines? Why only Kamloops, a not atypical town in western Canada? If it is there, why not elsewhere? Clearly, Clark does not know, and if Donaldson does, he's not saying. His job is, in part, to assure the image and the presence of his agency. Even if he is a great physician, and we have no reason to believe he is not, his role in the interview was as spokesperson for the CCA, and thus his bias was at least partially official. At best, it can be said only that he apparently responded in his official capacity to Clark's questions and does not appear to have volunteered any information. Her job was, in turn, first to interview him and then to relay to the public the information he provided. It was not her job, despite journalism's instrumental and institutional goals, to assure that information was complete, factual, "objective," or sufficient to explain what had caused a high incidence of sick children in a provincial town.

Literature Search

Let us presume that the reporter was determined to go further. Perhaps she didn't trust the CCABC's assurances,[26] or simply was burning with curiosity about the story CBC's editors had given her. How (and where) to look for information on the possible cancer-causing agent affecting children in a small Canadian town? A medical epidemiologist might first turn to the technical literature for known causes of this type of leukemia, which include radiation and specific classes of chemical agents. But searching for specific environmental factors resulting from industrial pollution or simple radiation is beyond most reporters' expertise. There may be hundreds of agents—chemicals used by local industries that would have to be traced to, say, the water table and from there to the drinking water. Without a full research team, there's little hope of finding an answer here. Radiation, unless a nuclear waste dump is located nearby, is problematical as well. What type of radiation, and at what levels of exposure, would cause this incidence of disease? Where would it come from? At this point there is not sufficient information (what type of radiation? what source? what levels of exposure?) to search for appropriate data using the word radiation as the sole criterion. The literature on radiation is just too broad.

An easier question is: Why power lines? Why did Donaldson tell Clark his agency would be looking into the possibility that local power lines were the carcinogen causing double the rate of leukemia in area children? Here is a single, defined element amenable to electronic research. I put the phrase "leukemia and (electric power)" to *Health Database Plus*,[27] a service that offers full text retrieval of medical articles published in both the technical (e.g., *New England Journal of Medicine*) and semipopular (e.g., *Hippocrates*) literatures. Electric power would be the general agent or category by which "power lines" affected health, I reasoned, and a search for the health effects would be more general with "electric power" as a key phrase.

Bingo! Two articles were returned, and I asked for their full text on screen.[28] One, by Linda C. Higgins, was published in September 1989 in *Medical World News*, a journal whose reputation I knew from past stories. It detailed a series of studies showing concern over and a relation between electric power and health problems, including leukemia! Among those cited was a then recent, five-hundred-page report by the California Public Utilities Commission (CPUC), as well as a federal study for the Congressional Office of Technology Assessment. That study, done by a team from Carnegie-Mellon University in Pittsburgh, identified "legitimate reasons for concern about the public health implications of low-frequency fields [power lines]," and recommended "prudent avoidance" of them.[29] Congressional studies are in the public domain and available electronically through U.S. federal databases. Further, the CPUC's full report had probably been written up and analyzed to death by California newspapers like the *Los Angeles Times*.

The rest of the article listed other studies then under way on the health risks of power lines. Further, Higgins' story said that recent public interest in the health effects of power lines stemmed from a series on this type of health risk published in the June 1989 issue of the *New Yorker*.[30] Clearly, a number of people have looked into the relation between cancer and electric power-line emissions. As a piece of background history, her article included the following paragraph: "In 1979, Dr. Nancy Wertheimer, a Colorado epidemiologist, reported that Denver children who died of leukemia, lymphoma, or cancer of the nervous system were two to three times more likely than control group members to have lived in homes with high-current wiring configurations."[31]

Here was the tie between power lines and leukemia in children. Wertheimer's study was also mentioned in the second retrieved article by Junu Kim, as evidence substantiating a relation between cancer and low-frequency electromagnetic emissions (EMF) from power lines and from other sources:

> In 1976, two doctors at the Veterans Administration Hospital in Syracuse, N.Y., showed that the offspring of mice exposed to extremely low frequency EMFs from power lines were born stunted. *Other studies have focused specifically on the suspected connection between EMF exposure and cancer.* In 1979, two University of Colorado researchers, physician Nancy Wertheimer and physicist Ed Leeper, pored through childhood mortality records in the Denver area and correlated long-term exposure to weak EMFs with a higher incidence of cancer. Seven years later, Dr. Lennart Tomenius, a Swedish researcher, *found the same relationship between EMF exposure and cancer rates among children in Stockholm.* And in 1982, Samuel Milham, an occupational health physician in the Washington State Department of Social and Health Services, noted in the *New England Journal of Medicine* that he *found more leukemia-related deaths in men whose work brought them in contact with electrical and magnetic fields, such as employees of utility companies.*
>
> Furthermore, EMFs have been implicated in pregnancy problems. In 1986, Wertheimer and Leeper reported that women who used heated waterbeds or electric blankets, both of which emit EMFs, had longer pregnancies and a higher miscarriage rate. And in 1987, Kurt Salzinger, a psychology professor at the Brooklyn-based

Polytechnic Institute of New York, found that
rats exposed to EMFs for 30 days had more
problems than unexposed rats in learning to
press a bar on command. Their offspring, exposed in the womb and for nine days after birth,
developed permanent learning disabilities.[32]
[italics added]

Kim's article also included a list of U.S. court cases in
which power companies had been sued because of this problem. That means liability, damages, and the issue of reasonable concern had been adjudicated. A summary of those
cases, whose rulings could be searched through a legal
database like *WestLaw* or in *Vu/Text* for summaries published in local newspapers, includes:

- In 1985 a Texas jury ordered the Houston Lighting
  and Power Company to pay a local school district
  $25 million in punitive damages after the utility
  built a transmission line through school property
  without the district's permission.
- In Florida, juries have awarded more than $1 million
  to owners of land next to high-voltage lines.
- Some New York state landowners filed a $60 mil-
  lion suit against the New York Power Authority,
  alleging that a half-completed power line could
  produce a "cancer-phobia corridor," where property
  values would tumble.

These two returned articles together made a strong case
for the relation between higher incidences of cancer, including leukemia in children, and emissions of some types of
electrical power. At the library I asked for the issues of the
New Yorker cited by Higgins. Written by Paul Brodeur,
"Annals of Radiation: The Hazards of Electromagnetic Fields"
begins with how epidemiologist Nancy Wertheimer began
investigating deaths resulting from childhood leukemia in
the four-county Greater Denver, Colorado, area and found
twice the expected rate of acute childhood leukemia in residents living in homes nearest to power-line transformers,
which step down current to household user levels.[33]

The *New Yorker* articles documented, page by page and issue by issue, a series of studies linking cancer-related health risks with emissions from electric power systems and telecommunications facilities. Those articles (moving from the national level of sources [C2] to those of technical documents [C3]) showed not only that high incidence of childhood leukemia has been attributed elsewhere to emissions from power stations and lines, but that adults who worked close to these facilities also were found to have "developed cancer at a significantly higher rate than the population as a whole."[34] After Wertheimer found the correlation between EMF emissions and high incidence of childhood leukemia, other studies showed an equally strong correspondence between these emissions and adult tumors as well. Further, Brodeur reported and documented how the early research in this area was both dismissed and denigrated for almost two decades by the electric utilities industry, and by military agencies whose facilities were major emitters of the EMF identified as a carcinogen.

For a reporter in British Columbia in March 1990, the *Medical World News, Bestways,* and *New Yorker* articles were a gold mine. They showed how deaths from the same type of cancer, acute childhood leukemia, had been traced in other regions to a specific environmental agent. They quoted from technical articles that substantiated the case, listed permissible federal levels of emissions in other countries (but not Canada), and showed a long-term pattern of cover-up of this information in the United States. Even Holden, the *Province* assistant city editor who distrusted academics and eggheads, presumably would accept this wealth of evidence as the reasonable basis for a story. That there had been court cases would, of course, have helped convince him. That reports linking leukemia and electric power had appeared in both the *New England Journal of Medicine*—the only medical journal most editors have heard of—and the prestigious *New Yorker* would have clinched the case for even so hardy a skeptic as he.

Perhaps best of all, the Brodeur articles made clear how easy it would be for a reporter to test the hypothesis that similar levels of emission could be found in the affected neighborhood of Kamloops. When they first appeared in the *New Yorker*, reporter Mike McCardell from BCTV, one of three major Vancouver-based TV stations,[35] showed on air how these potentially dangerous emissions from power lines could be measured by a layperson using a gaussmeter.[36] But when a chance to use that information in a real test case occurred in British Columbia, neither BCTV nor the CBC chose to put that knowledge into practice.

An example of what could have been done, had local newspeople been interested in "objective" and data-based reportage, can be seen in an innovative use of research by a computer magazine. *MacWorld* is a publication serving Macintosh computer users, and, in the July 1990 issue its editors addressed health concerns and fears concerning electromagnetic emissions from the Apple system. The Macintosh, like many other computer systems, uses a cath-ode-ray-tube screen monitor which, like power transform-ers, emits very-low-frequency and extremely-low-frequency electromagnetic radiation. Following the *New Yorker* series, concern about their effect on computer work stations had become an issue within the general community of computer users.

For this issue, *MacWorld* hired Brodeur to write a sum-mary of available information on electromagnetic emissions and their effect on human physiology.[37] This article re-viewed the denials of equipment manufacturers and govern-ment officials, while summarizing the data on the connec-tion between power-line/leukemia studies and other health studies. The magazine's technical staff then measured emis-sions from ten popular Macintosh screens, using an ELF/Power Frequency EMF Survey Meter. The results showed that a number of popular screens, whose manufacturers regularly advertise in *MacWorld*, emitted levels in the low frequency magnetic and electrical bands, which have been found to create health problems in other contexts.[38] Tests were also run to examine performance claims by manufacturers (who advertise in the magazine) of antiglare and antiemission screens for the Macintosh. The results of those tests were summarized and interpreted in a consumer column which noted that, while the screens may affect electrical emissions, they have no effect on extra-low-frequency magnetic emissions, and manufacturer's claims were "not entirely true, according to our testing."[39]

The whole was preceded by a roundup and editorial written by the magazine's editor-in-chief, Jerry Borrell, who summarized the data his magazine had accumulated and concluded that: "This tool, that you've heard about all of these years as the thing that can do so much, may be killing you . . . Extremely-low-frequency magnetic emissions may prove to be one of the most troublesome issues we face with information technology over the next decade, unless standards are established by the government—something that is unlikely to happen without a congressional requirement."[40]

What was perhaps most heartening about *MacWorld*'s stories was that they demonstrated the degree to which journalists can, when they choose, act out instrumental and institutional myths, whatever the potential economic effect of the resulting report. In these articles, after all, *MacWorld* editors and reporters questioned the safety of the machine whose users are their total subscriber base and demonstrated that principal advertisers were making false advertising claims. Further, it did so in an area of evolving and complex research, precisely the type of story which, traditionally, reporters have avoided because of the complexity of its elements. *MacWorld* did all this by particularizing the general subject of electromagnetic research as it related to a range of manufacturer claims about a large class of computer screens, a far more difficult subject than the relation between cancers like leukemia and emissions from power-line systems.

Scale and Focus

The scale of the story has enlarged, and its focus has changed. It is no longer what Donaldson says his agency is doing about a suspected health problem in British Columbia. The issue has doubled and becomes the similarity between a pattern of illness in Kamloops and identical patterns identified elsewhere and attributed to emissions from electric power facilities. The local boundary events have been placed in a context whose scale includes a pattern of events seen again and again over eleven years in locations from Denver, Colorado, to Stockholm, Sweden. References have been taken from the national (technical) literature and from U.S. legal citations (C4) about those past events (and responsibility for them) so that the story could be focused at the local level by a regional media outlet (CBC, BCTV, the *Province*, etc.) at level C2 in Illustration 3.1.

It is unlikely, had Clark pursued her story in this manner, that either provincial officials or Donaldson would have thanked her. Certainly B.C. Hydro, which provides electric power to the province, would not have welcomed her questions about the level of ELF its system presents in Kamloops and, by implication, elsewhere in the province. Remembering that Brodeur's report showed systematic attempts to dismiss the evidence of researchers in this area, Clark might well have been skeptical of assurances from the provincial power authority and thus would have wished to question them closely. What had B.C. Hydro done to test for high levels of electromagnetic emission in Kamloops and other B.C. communities? Knowing about the potential dangers attributed to power lines elsewhere, weren't they morally (and, perhaps, legally) obliged to have investigated these hazards and changed their lines long before? Were they aware of the work of Wertheimer and the rest? Were they aware of U.S. court cases assigning responsibility to power authorities in this type of case in the states of Texas, New York, and Florida? Were they concerned about the health effect of their lines and systems on the customer? Where else are the same line systems found in Kamloops used in British Columbia?

Using the information from these databases, Clark—or another reporter interested in the story—would be empowered with knowledge sufficient to ask probing and powerful questions.

It is equally unlikely that the Cancer Control Agency would welcome a fully briefed layperson asking similarly uncomfortable questions. The probability, based on these reports, is now not simply that there is a random "cluster" of illnesses but that Kamloops represents another case in the growing North American and industrial pattern of cancer whose etiology originates in "power-line" emissions. What other geographic areas in British Columbia (or Canada) had these "clusters" of childhood leukemia, and what further studies were being done to assess the level of other cancers in British Columbia communities with similar power facilities? Had a reporter gone to Kamloops and found high readings on a rented gaussmeter, the link between emissions and cancers would have been a truly independent "fact." But even without that, the reporter is armed with a rather impressive array of knowledge to create a hypothesis which can be tested and with which the eventual CCABC report and its performance, as well as that of the provincial power authority, could be critically judged.

The Cancer Control Agency's preliminary report on the Kamloops problem was that a link between electromagnetic emissions and the unusual levels of leukemia in that community was inconclusive. A few months later, in June of 1990, the Cancer Control Agency of British Columbia also announced a "ground-breaking study into a possible link between electromagnetic fields and leukemia."[41] The CCABC had been awarded $900,000 to measure the electromagnetic field in a child's living environment, not just his or her home, the study's co-principal investigator, Mary McBride, told reporters.

The expenditure of such monies was not, however, to be seen as an indication of significant health problems resulting from power-line emissions, she said. "We know if there is an effect," McBride told local reporters, "it's not a large one." One B.C. Hydro official, who admitted his office received between thirty and forty telephone calls a month from residents concerned about their homes' proximity to power lines, echoed her sentiments when called for a comment. "We know the risk—if it exists at all— is quite small in a public health sense," B.C. Hydro project manager Killy Gibey told the *Province*.[42] McBride's co-investigator, Richard Gallagher, made the subject of these emissions sound like virgin research territory. He told reporters that "We really have no idea what a dangerous level (of emission) is. . . . It's equally likely we will find nothing as we will find something."

It is hard to believe that provincial reporters remained totally unaware of the mass of information on this subject that was available by June 1990. The *New Yorker* articles,

Brodeur's book, and publicity about them both had been a major news story over the previous seven months. And yet, apparently, nobody thought to seriously question either Gibey's assertion that risk—if it existed—was certainly very small or McBride's cheerful assurance, prior to the beginning of her five-year study, that "if there is an effect [on health], it's not a large one." The skeptical reader might wonder if, had the Kamloops study actually found a clear link between leukemia and power-line emissions—the same connection demonstrated in many other environments— would that have affected approval of the McBride grant? A careful reader might ask, if researchers had examined the Kamloops environment with diligence, would the CCABC report on the high incidence of childhood leukemia in Kamloops still have been inconclusive?

It is easy to argue that, at a political level, the CBC report and then later coverage of the CCABC's study served a number of officially sanctioned functions. Both underlined the legitimacy of the provincial Cancer Control Agency. The CBC story informed people of the mothers' concern, and, through its narrow focus and reliance on Donaldson, solidified the practical relationship between the CBC (in the person of its reporter) and officialdom. To have charged in aggressively, armed with this print-based research, would have alienated officials and certainly would have caused real concern among members of the resident population. Thus the CBC story fulfilled a public relations function by reassuring the B.C. population at large, and that of Kamloops in specific (Clark said that even if an environmental problem had existed, it may have ceased on its own), while giving officials an omnipotent voice when faced with the concerns of a few mothers.

After all, reporters are not investigators or clinicians. Rather, they are relays for what is said by officials or groups to the greater population. The mothers expressed their concern, and Donaldson promised to look into the matter. Everyone is reassured. What the CBC and other news agencies lost in this approach was control of the story and the right "objectively" and "skeptically" to examine the "facts" of a potentially serious health problem. The "fact" of a few kids with acute childhood leukemia in a single city or neighborhood takes on meaning only within the context of the broad relation, shown in many other areas and literatures, of that disease to a specific environmental cause. The announcement of a new grant is ephemeral, except where it impacts on current problems and issues.

Donaldson and other members of the CCA won in the CBC story both time and the ability to dictate future news because in a month (or whenever the report is ultimately released) newspeople will be allowed to hear what experts have found out about a study of the "cluster" of acute childhood leukemia cases in Kamloops. The greater issue of danger from emissions across the province will have been either totally silenced or, as it turned out, transformed into a grant for non-critical research. Although the Kamloops power system is not unique, questions about other areas of the province that may have been affected by their own power systems have also been finessed. Likewise eliminated are questions concerning the incidence of this and other types of cancer in not only Kamloops but in the province and the nation at large. Researchers elsewhere have found a whole class of service people—line workers, electricians, and other electric-power trade professionals—with higher than expected cancer rates, presumably because of sustained exposure to the same emissions that created double the number of childhood leukemia victims in the Colorado study. The scale of the story, in short, has been set by officials at the narrowest and most benign level. Use of electronic databases increases it to one in which the news agency and its reporter can act.

Finally, the issue of the vigilance or inactivity of precisely those agencies and officials who are supposed to guard the public health has been effectively shut off by the deal. Why did this whole thing have to wait for a bunch of mothers with deathly sick children to do some backyard research (maybe even using the *New Yorker* as their guide) before the issue was accepted as an even marginally legitimate concern by the CCA and, simultaneously, the Canadian Broadcasting Corporation? If this problem has been so well studied for so long, if risks are known to be minimal, why was a new study being launched? Years before Clark's story went to air, as evidence mounted of potential risks elsewhere, shouldn't the Cancer Control Agency, the provincial hydroelectric agency, the B.C. Ministry of Health, or federal officials have begun a systematic study of the relation of cancer to these emissions in the province or the nation?

Politically one can argue that the answer is simple. Officials whose institutional goal is to protect the health of citizens have a functional need for positive publicity. Officials whose instrumental goal is to find and remove dangerous health situations have a functional goal of protecting their jobs and raising money through research. Those functional goals are not necessarily well served by an independent, informed, and aggressive writer who questions the agency's decisions and actions. Those functional necessities will not be advanced by a reporter's suggestion that tests so simple they're described in a popular magazine have yet to be carried out. It is easier to use reporters to disseminate the information that officials want broadcast within the levels, in Chomsky's words, of "permissible dissent."

Traditionally, reporters have had little choice but to accept an official's scenario because the reports and papers, the knowledge and expertise were, in fact, all in the official's hands. Now it is otherwise. Why didn't CBC, BCTV, or print reporters attack this story with a vengeance? One answer is simply that B.C. newspeople have yet to gain proficiency in the use of electronic databases. Reporters at both BCTV and the Vancouver *Province* said that while their respective agencies have online capabilities, they were reserved for use by editors or librarians. Further, those reporters admitted ignorance of database usage.[43] They, like newspeople interviewed elsewhere, were intrigued with the potential of online information technologies but frustrated by both a lack of training in database use and a lack of access to the tools.

While cost has traditionally been given as the reason for limiting access to database technologies in a newsroom, it is less and less of a real issue. The total bill for the full text search on *Health Database Plus,* including cost of the CompuServe access lines, was $6.50, roughly the price of a movie at a first-run theater in Vancouver in 1990. Clearly, the potential for stories so researched outweighs what was, in this case, a minimal online cost. This does not mean that reporters will immediately adopt a narrative style of doubled or trebled transformation in which official statements are reflexively examined at varying scales of data. It does mean that, to the extent that news organizations retain a fundamentally unary, narrative style relaying official statements into print or broadcast form, issues of cost can no longer excuse that choice. It also means that, where competition for stories exists, one or another competing journalist or news agency can, at little expense, use these technologies to change a story's scale from that of the isolated, local event to one of regional or national information. This ability allows the reporter or public affairs writer to examine issues resulting from a boundary event without relying absolutely on information provided only at the level of the officially sanctioned, journalistic event.

INTERNATIONAL AFFAIRS

The distance between reportorial and boundary events, on the one hand, and the relation between print information and oral statement, on the other hand, is nowhere clearer than in an analysis of international reportage. Nowhere are the critics of U.S. journalism so strong as in their analysis of U.S. newspaper and television reportage purporting to describe with even minimal objectivity their nation's actions in the arena of world events. The degree to which online technologies may affect coverage of national affairs can be seen through a review of reportage following the destruction of Korean Airlines Passenger Flight 007 by the Soviet military in August 1983.

Alan Rachlin has studied the coverage in U.S. newspapers and magazines and compared information found in those publications with that available in other sources, including Canadian newspapers.[44] The absolute reliance on official U.S. interpretation of the events leading up to and immediately following the downing of Flight 007 was, in his analysis, a superb demonstration of the legitimizing function of the media in the national arena as well as demonstration of the degree to which newspeople follow their leader's interpretation of external events. Certainly, on the face of it this analysis is true. President Reagan and other officials set the line followed, editorially, by all major newspaper and broadcast outlets when they suggested that the shooting down of a civilian airliner "points out Soviet disregard for loss of life."[45]

For their part, Soviet officials had a very different version. Acknowledging the destruction of the airplane, the U.S.S.R. insisted that Korean Flight 007 was on a spy mission over their territory, flying in consort with a U.S. RC-135 spy plane; that the plane's lights were not visible, making identification of its shape and civilian cargo almost impossible; and that attempts at radio contact were tried and no response was gained. The shooting occurred during a very sensitive military test over a Russian military test site. The Soviets argued they shot down an unidentified invader that refused to identify itself while flying over a militarily sensitive region. Further, they noted this was not the first time their airspace had been invaded by spy planes and that under international law they were within their rights to do so. The event was thus, in their view, a "regrettable" but understandable and justifiable occurrence. That posture was dismissed almost out of hand by U.S. newspeople. The facts seemed to be, as President Reagan had alleged all along, that Russians don't value life and the downing of a civilian airlines flight that had wandered off course was simply another example of this official truth.

A year after the shooting, David Pearson began what was to become a series of articles based on information in the public record, which showed that a major Soviet missile test was to take place at the time of the Korean airplane's destruction; that the U.S. military knew the civilian flight was off course in the Soviet test site area but did nothing to avert the disaster; and that the Russian allegations concerning the RC-135 spy plane had substantial foundation. His conclusions were, in brief, "that a conscious policy decision was made by the U.S. government—at what level it is not clear—to risk the lives of 269 innocent people on the assumption that an extraordinary opportunity for gleaning intelligence information should not be missed."[46]

Pearson's first article appeared a year after the boundary event and was the result of a careful combing of the public record and subsequent analysis of it, informed by his personal expertise in areas of U.S. defense intelligence. But what could a reporter have found in 1983, had databases then been ubiquitous, to establish at least minimum objectivity in weighing the conflicting interpretations of U.S. and Soviet officials speaking about the specific event? Had such an event happened before? A quick search of national newspaper files (*New York Times, Washington Post,* etc.) finds that on April 20, 1978, Korean Airlines Flight 902 was shot down while flying over Soviet military installations that were more than one thousand miles off its flight course. On June 30, 1968, a non-Korean plane flying from South Vietnam to Seattle, and two accompanying U.S. military aircraft, entered Soviet airspace over the Kuril Islands and were forced down by Soviet MIG fighters. In all, at least twenty-seven aircraft belonging to the United States or its allies have been forced or shot down and sixty others attacked while on electronic or photographic reconnaissance missions over the Soviet Union.[47]

Thus the Soviets were not unreasonable in assuming that this flight, well inside their airspace during a critical and sensitive military test period—a flight whose pilots did not answer radio requests that they identify themselves—might be other than a friendly but lost airplane. There is a pattern of illegal U.S. overflights of their facilities stretching back to the reign of President Eisenhower, and there is some reason to believe that some commercial flights—like KAL Flight 902—had been used in the past as part of the U.S. surveillance program. After the destruction of KAL Flight 007, however, U.S. officials dismissed out of hand what was in fact a pattern evident to anyone searching the published record for information on "Soviet (shooting or downing) and airplane." Civilian and military planes frequently overflew Soviet airspace in violation of international law. Further, U.S. officials dismissed as nonsense the Soviet insistence that KAL 007 was flying in conjunction with a U.S. spy plane before it was shot down. But Pearson, using data from a number of official U.S. and Japanese statements published within at most two weeks of the event, reconstructed the flight patterns of both KAL 007 and USAF spy plane RC-135 to show that the Soviet view was not only possible but likely.[48]

Even more damning would have been a search for information on radar and Soviet surveillance. Only later was the issue raised of prior U.S. knowledge of the KAL flight path and with it the possibility of U.S. complicity, if only by its silence, in the disaster. Pearson collected and presented information virtually proving that, despite assurances by President Ronald Reagan to the contrary, U.S. intelligence officials—even if they were not consciously using the civilian flight for spying—knew it was going off course and made no move to warn it. The interlocking radar and surveillance network created by the United States and its allies virtually blankets the world, and both track flights over and keep track of activities on and above Soviet military sites like Sakhalin Island. The use of the RC-135 spy plane for surveillance had been acknowledged and written about in both the aerospace literature and, less frequently, the general press.

The most interesting thing about the coverage of the Russian downing of the Korean Airlines flight is that within four to six weeks of the disaster, evidence strongly substantiating the Russian position and invalidating that of the United States was available in the public literature. Evidence was available in September 1983 that the plane's pilots may have deliberately steered their plane over the Soviet's test site in a pattern which was both not random but also converged with that of the RC-135.[49]

All this suggested to Rachlin that the function of U.S. reporters in covering the KAL 007 disaster was not an objective description of the antecedents leading to the disaster but, rather, the dissemination of a U.S. interpretation of that boundary event. If the purpose of news is, socially, to legitimize the official posture, then this news coverage was, in retrospect, extremely comprehensive if biased reportage. Similarly, the whole could be used by Edward Herman and Noam Chomsky to substantiate their thesis that anti-communism is an absolute bias in U.S. reportage, a filter through which all information, no matter how blatant, must be sifted.[50]

It is unclear the degree to which this nationalistic bias is a conscious distortion of events, as some believe, or, as I believe, a symptom of the absolute reliance of newswriters on official statements. To manually search for a chronology of all news reports describing the invasion of Soviet airspace by foreign aircraft would have been, in 1983 when online resources were minimal, an arduous and time-consuming task. To manually search for technical journals like *Aviation Week and Space Technology* one would have needed to know first of their existence and then have access to the physical text. Important information concerning the investigation of Flight 007 was found by Pearson, Rachlin, and others in the foreign press. But without a person in Tokyo searching the Japanese newspapers for their summary of that country's defense reports, that information remained unavailable unless one subscribed to a clipping service that monitored foreign newspapers and newswires.[51] Even the information contained in *The Nation*'s articles, which were published well after the fact, was unavailable to those who were not regular subscribers or lacked electronic resources to track through magazine publications for information on the air disaster. The majority of reporters and editorial writers in 1983 had, in short, little information except that which Soviet and U.S. officials presented to them in press conference and news release.

Thus the bias was at least as likely the fault of ignorance as the result of patriotism, cupidity, or complacency. Reporters and editorial writers with no real sources of independent information relayed as translators what was said by their elected officials, "balancing" those stories *pro forma* with Soviet denials. The stories were unary, based on the U.S. position and thus not even minimally objective despite attempts, in one editor's words, to investigate "the flight of KAL 007 [to] within an inch of its life."[52] Certainly one can argue that reporters should have searched the files for examples of past incidents of a similar nature (like the earlier downing of KAL 902), but without better, more pertinent information on Korean Flight 007, that search would have done little good. The result was propaganda, legitimizing copy that lacked both objectivity and even a minimal skepticism in its presentation of President Reagan's views. Failing information that could have changed the story's scale, the focus of daily journalism was limited to what was said by an official on a particular day or at a specific time and did not include any broader context where more information might have been available.

Were a similar event to occur in the 1990s, it would be interesting to compare that news coverage with the reportage of KAL 007 and, perhaps, of the earlier shooting of KAL 902. Current databases (magazine, newspaper, technical journal) carry a wealth of historical and pertinent information about previous overflights, about the radar and surveillance systems employed by the United States and its allies; about U.S. spy planes and their flight paths; about obvious disinformation disseminated by U.S. State Department officials and so on. Were all this information again ignored despite its availability to the general reporter, then Chomsky's insistence that information bias is often conscious and done with full awareness of its function would be substantiated. On the other hand, were public information writers to use available databases to balance official assertions or competing claims through reference to widely available historical and technical data, then the role of the news, historically defined by its method of information transferral from oral statement to print storage, would be seen to be changing as rapid availability of electronically stored data became the basis for an increasing objectivity in the news.

BUSINESS REPORTAGE

Perhaps no subject area has more information available online than that relating to corporate and financial affairs. Thus, to see the degree to which availability of electronic information sources is changing news transformation and narrative form, a brief examination of the use of databases in business reportage is warranted. Coverage by the Akron *Beacon Journal* of the takeover fight for a local employer, Goodyear, will be described in Chapter 5. Where else can one see the effect of these information sources on information presented by the media to their constituent viewers or readers?

Information available daily on contemporary business-related television shows is based on a use of computerized stock price listings, the *PR Newswire*, and other similar sources widely available from various packagers and distributors. This information is essentially trivial, presenting a unary transformation, but it is still instructive. Public television's *Nightly Business Report*, for example, provides the closing stock prices on the three major U.S. exchanges, including the performance of both widely held stocks and those with a large percentage gain or loss each day. With the basic closing figures, available on Dow Jones and other services, corporate explanations of those changes are discussed by the announcer, whose information may come either from a call to the company or from information pulled from one or another database.

Conflict of Interest

More interesting, if rarer, is the use of electronic research tools to go beyond the unary and trivial to the structural or contextual story through a more complex transformation. In the mid-1980s, for example, *Newsday* used a complex of electronic databases to examine possible conflicts of interest on the part of companies participating in a then widely touted federal synthetic fuel program whose general intent was to lessen U.S. dependence on foreign fuels. "Prior to the database research system, we would have had to find other libraries with back issues of trade journals that we didn't have at *Newsday* and also contact many out-of-town newspaper libraries to obtain copies of their clippings. . . . Because we had access to databases, the job of basic research was given entirely to the library."[53]

The Long Island newspaper's librarians first located technical data on synthetic fuels from the *National Technical Information Service* database and then used *Congressional Information Service* databases for documentation of federal hearings on the program.[54] *PR Newswire* provided corporate statements on the fuel program to bridge the gap between public and corporate declarations. By using databases like *Disclosure*, librarians were then able to compare those public statements with the economic gains or projected gains of participating companies. Financial statistics were gleaned from yet another database, the *I.P. Sharp* system.

What this complex of data searches provided was a reasonably objective perspective balancing the publicly stated, national goals of the program and the private gains that might result from national research funding. The search balanced the typically patriotic agenda enunciated in both public relations releases and the rhetoric of Congressional hearings with real financial data filed in annual corporate financial records on record at the federal Securities and Exchange Commission. That the search was organized through the *Newsday* library follows a pattern noted elsewhere, and discussed in Chapter 4, of leaving control of databases in the hands of bibliographically trained researchers rather than giving control of information retrieval to reporters. What differs in this case is that the newspaper's librarians seem to have been full partners in story generation and that control was not simply a cost-control measure but a decision to utilize fully the specific data-searching skills of the best-trained researchers as part of a journalistic team effort.

Corporate Ratings

Another, less complex example occurred in a 1990 column by Bud Jorgensen in the Toronto *Globe and Mail*'s business section after the Canadian-based Royal Trust proudly advertised a triple-A credit rating for its senior debt. Jorgensen pointed out, however, that the "triple A" rating is used only by Moody's of New York (Aaa) and Standard and Poor's (S&P), also of New York (AAA). But the former had given Royal Trust a single A credit rating, while the later awarded the company a "single A plus." The Dominon Bond Rating Service of Toronto, on the other hand, gave the company a "double A" rating, and only the Canadian Bond Rating Service of Montreal (CBRS) gave the company the "triple A" announced in the advertisement. But, in fact, the CBRS's "triple A" is written by that company as an "A++" and not as "triple A" at all.

This was not a simple quibble, a mere matter of different symbols for the same thing. Jorgensen argued that Royal Trust's advertisement was clearly misleading. "When promotional material is aimed at an overseas audience, for example, the targets of such ads are more likely to know about the big U.S. rating agencies and assume the triple A is either from S&P or Moody's."[55] But the big U.S. rating companies, the ones that use the AAA signature, had rated Royal Trust at a lower level. The "fact" of the triple A was not really a fact at all. When placed in the context of varying international rating services it was seen as technically incorrect (AAA is not A++), and perhaps misleading.

Using ownership data available as part of the public record, Jorgensen then asked (and answered) the next logical question: if the rating was higher from the CBRS than from S&P or Moody's, what relation—if any—exists between the CBRS and Royal Trust? Thus Jorgensen questioned not only Royal Trust's credit rating but also the relation between the CBRS (the rater) and its subject, Royal Trust. Is the determination of credit worthiness free of any taint? "The more delicate point in this," Jorgensen argued, "is because the CBRS relies [for income] more heavily on subscription sales than other North American rating agencies, which get the major portion of their revenues from companies and governments whose securities they rate." Thus the Canadian bond rating service must rely for its income on continued use by the companies it examines. Royal Trust is a part of the larger Bronfman group of companies, which make up 10 percent of the total capitalization of companies in the Toronto Stock Exchange 300 index. From this one might conclude that the CBRS must rely for a significant part of its capital on subscriptions from Bronfman group members. While this does not mean they fudged their rating, it does put their triple A and the less stellar ratings of U.S. agencies into an interesting perspective. Just as the reliance on advertisers and supporters is seen as possibly compromising the "objectivity" of the news, so here one might question whether the reliance on subscription sales by the CBRS could not affect the rater's absolute objectivity.

What Jorgensen did was not difficult. He placed a single datum trumpeted by a company as a "fact," its credit rating, within the context of other ratings issued by different companies. Triple A is usually thought of as an American-issued rating but, in fact, U.S. analysts had given the company lower, if still very respectable marks. Then he looked for a possible relation between rater and subject to see whether reasons for these observed anomalies might be uncovered. All this can be done through a series of telephone calls (to brokers or the rating services themselves), but it is faster and easier to do online. Bond ratings from Moody's and Standard and Poor's are both easily accessed electronically through a number of companies (e.g., Dow Jones News Service, CompuServe), as are descriptions of company performance and ownership.

Census Data

Increasing availability online of census data has also become a business reportage tool. As early as January of 1982, for example, the *St. Petersburg Times* was using national census data to write about changing age structure and housing patterns in its Florida circulation region while, in Memphis, Tennessee, the *Commercial Appeal* used similar data in the early 1980s to describe racial shifts and housing patterns in that city.[56] These cases are examples of structural reportage in which specific urban problems were placed within the context of national and regional statistics based on 1980 census data. In the early 1980s, utilization of this type of census-based reportage was dependent on a newspaper's soliciting the computer tapes of census data, running them on a publication's mainframe, and then interpreting the data. More recently, census data has become available online through the *Cendata* database or through private companies like CACIS that use that same raw data and specialized software automatically to configure business and life-style data by county, state, or zip code. Thus for a story on the economic effects of bicycling in Honolulu County, I searched for the number of bicycle shops on the Hawaiian island of Oahu and the number of employees per shop, and used that information as part of a story that showed that bicycling was a more than $20 million retail industry in greater Honolulu.[57]

That some of the earliest and most complex computer-assisted stories have been business-oriented is, perhaps, not surprising in a nation that takes pride in the dictum that "the business of America is business." That use of computers and online libraries has become commonplace for shows like the *Nightly Business Report*, a program whose audience is largely small investors anxious to follow their investments and understand the market, might have been expected. Nor is it surprising, perhaps, that the program's corporate sponsors include a brokerage firm, a computer manufacturer, and an online data company.[58] North American news is itself first and foremost a commodity, and those programs that provide product information are likely to have the best funding and a secure audience whose interest is in corporate growth and news.

But within this context it is clear that electronic databases provide a critical and perhaps unexpected function. By making available to a newswriter or editor the written work of other journalists, technical experts, and general writers on almost every issue, they create a context in which the statements of news subjects can be evaluated objectively and critically by the reporter or layperson. This occurs when specific and often local events are placed, practically, within a regional or national context of prior occurrence and data. Tension among an individual's often conflicting institutional goals, instrumental aims, and functional goals may influence actual statement but be hidden to the oral-based, reportorial translator. They become manifest, however, when the journalist or other public affairs writer using electronic data resources places a subject's testimony in context. The end result of these transformations is a story that is less ephemeral, more contextual, and focuses, ultimately, on the "why" or "how" of any news event. From the perspective of the narrative, the result is not a translation but, rather, a transformation that is not unary but doubled or trebled, one in which the story's focus ultimately returns to the boundary event without necessarily accepting the interpretation of those who, although officially charged with its explanation, may be hampered by personal interest or professional allegiance in that duty.

NOTES

1. See, for example, Brian S. Brooks et al., *News Reporting and Writing,* 3d ed. (New York: St. Martin's Press,

1988), 155. The 5W's rule is subsumed in the story lead. See especially the section on "Basic Obituary Information and Style."

2. See, for example, John Ullmann and Steve Honeyman, *The Reporter's Handbook* (New York: St. Martin's Press, 1983), 4. "We ask only *whowhatwherewhenhowandwhy*, confident that people will tell us the truth and tell it completely."

3. The lines from Kipling are: "I keep six honest serving men/ (they taught me all I knew);/ Their names are What and Why and When/And How and Where and Who." Quoted in Ullmann and Honeyman, *Reporter's Handbook*, 1.

4. Tom Koch, *The News as Myth: Fact and Context in Journalism* (Westport, Conn.: Greenwood Press, 1990). A discussion of both the "narrative form" of daily journalism and its resulting effect on information levels is described extensively in chapters 2 and 3.

5. H. Garfinkel, *Studies in Ethnomethodology* (Englewood Cliffs, N.J.: Prentice Hall, 1967), 41. It may be worth noting here that the problems of verification faced by anthropologists and ethnographers are not dissimilar from those faced by news reporters. The difference, besides one of audience, is that the former understand the limitations of reportage and thus take the oral as a starting point.

6. Jonathan Alter, "The Art of the Profile," *Newsweek*, January 22, 1990, 54.

7. *Roll Call* magazine published these exercises periodically. One especially memorable example was a grammarian's attempt to unravel Reagan's oral response to questions concerning his knowledge of the Iran-Contra arms-for-hostages deal.

8. Roland Barthes, *Camera Lucida*, translated by Richard Howard (New York: Hill and Wang, 1981), 40-42.

9. For a discussion of the issues of verification and objectivity separated from the context of news, see A.J. Ayer, *Language, Truth and Logic*, 2d ed. (London: Victor Golancz), 9. Also quoted in R.J. Johnston, *Philosophy and Human Geography: An Introduction to Contemporary Approaches*, 2d ed. (London: Edward Arnold, 1986), 9.

10. The following example was discussed extensively in a previous work describing the limits of the traditional

narrative form and the resulting truncation of information at varying levels. The following is excerpted from that discussion. See Tom Koch, *The News as Myth*, chapter 2.

11. Holly Horwood, "Fatal Slip Unnoticed," *Province*, February 11, 1986, 4.

12. "Death Sets Off Alarm," *Province*, February 3, 1987, 9.

13. Twenty-three separate stories were returned for the 1987 search on *Vu / Text* of stories describing "anesth/ and (injury or death)." See, for example, "Raymie Zahn, Coma Victim, Dies," *News Sun Sentinel* (Florida), January 4, 1987. (Zahn's coma was caused by lack of oxygen while under anesthesia during surgery); Harry Franken, "Suit in Coma Case Settled," *Columbus Dispatch* (Ohio), September 19, 1987, 1B. The award was for Jerome Morgan, who had, at the time of the story, been in a coma since August 3, 1978, following a period of oxygen deprivation that occurred during surgery.

14. "Jury Awards Man $28M in HHC Suit," *Newsday*, May 13, 1987, 18.

15. "Woman Sues after Son Dies during Surgery," *Lexington Herald-Leader*, July 13, 1987, B1. Another story from Texas detailed a potentially similar case, but the news story provided insufficient data to include in any regional wrap-up.

16. One B.C. coroner's inquest into the February 19, 1980, death of four-year-old Darcey Leo found that failure to monitor a patient or to be adequately prepared should an emergency arise resulted in the boy's death.

17. These newspapers are included in the *National News-paper Index* and include the full text of the *Christian Science Monitor*, the *New York Times*, and the *Wall Street Journal,* and indexes from the *Los Angeles Times* and the *Washington Post.*

18. In the 1980s a new and enormous supermarket complex did collapse in Vancouver, B.C., and this scenario is broadly based on that incident. I was not involved in the reportage of the incident or in the inquiries into the collapse, and the general parameters of this story are used for illustrative purposes only.

19. Walter McQuade, "Why All Those Buildings Are Collapsing," *Fortune*, November 19, 1979.

20. Erik Larson, "A New Science Can Diagnose Sick Buildings—Before They Collapse," *Smithsonian* 19:2 (May 1988), 116-29.

21. Larson, "New Science," 118.

22. Larson, "New Science," 119.

23. For example, Steven S. Ross, *Construction Disasters: Design Failures, Causes, and Prevention* (New York: McGraw-Hill, 1984).

24. Print researchers faced with this type of question might use the *Engineering Index*, whose abstracts attempt to cover the broad range of technical engineering literature. *Compendex* is the electronic equivalent available through Dialog Information Services and related gateways. Also available online is *Engineering News Record*, packaged by McGraw-Hill Publications, and available through them and other distributors.

25. Catherine Clark,"*CBC Evening News Report,*" March 12, 1990. The story took about three minutes airtime. In B.C. at the time, I watched the story twice and looked, over the next few days, for follow-up articles. There were none.

26. There are enough cautionary stories about official cover-ups of environmentally related deaths to urge reportorial caution in the coverage of almost any environmental damage or clean-up story. The issues of long-term health effects in the Love Canal toxic dump in the Niagara Falls region come immediately to mind. At a 1990 public forum, for example, Grand Island resident Luella Kenny, whose seven-year-old son died because of dioxin poisoning in that area, charged that "the state's whole investigation into my son's death was superficial, and it was meant to just placate me. In fact, I was told to stop flagellating myself and get on with my life." See Anthony Cardinale, "Mother Warns Not to Trust Officials on Dioxin," *Buffalo News*, April 26, 1990, A14.

27. *Health Database Plus* is a product of Information Access Company and available online through CompuServe Information Services.

28. Cost of the search, including full text retrieval, was $4.50 for database usage over ten minutes. The full research cost was thus $6.50, including ten minutes of line time paid to CompuServe for its service line.

29. Linda C. Higgins, "Worry over Power Lines Surges," *Medical World News* 30:17 (September 11, 1989), 22-24. *Medical World News* is also indexed electronically by *Biology Digest* and *Biology Abstracts*.

30. Higgins also notes in passing that the *New York Times* published   an article on these issues on June 11, 1989, following the first installment of the *New Yorker* series, which was published on June 9, 1989. Reference piles upon reference.

31. Higgins, "Worry," 24.

32. Junu Bryan Kim, "How Dangerous Is Electromagnetic Radiation?" *Bestways* 17:6 (June 1989), 13-15.

33. Paul Brodeur, "Annals of Radiation: The Hazards of Electromagnetic Fields," *New Yorker*, June 12, 1989, 51-87. This was the first of a three-part series later published in book form and reviewed extensively across North America. See Paul Brodeur, *Currents of Death: Power Lines, Computer Terminals and the Attempt to Cover Up Their Threat to Your Health* (New York: Simon and Schuster, 1989).

34. Brodeur, "Annals of Radiation," 57.

35. Ratings in the spring of 1990 showed BCTV to have the largest viewership in the province, followed by CBC-TV and then CKVU. I am indebted to BCTV reporter John Daly for bringing McCardell's story to my attention and for his information on the current standings of all three stations. John Daly, personal communication, March 15, 1990.

36. The use of the machine is discussed in the *New Yorker* article. Gaussmeters are simple to use and easy to obtain. At least one U.S. company rents them through the mails to computer terminal operators concerned about emissions from their cathode-ray tube display screens, the focus of the June 19, 1989 *New Yorker* article.

37. Paul Brodeur, "The Magnetic-Field Menace," *MacWorld* 7:7 (July 1990), 136-45. The whole July issue, which was composed of a group of articles on this topic, is, in fact, a model of clarity on a complex issue and an excellent summary for those interested in this subject. *MacWorld* is available online through *Computer Database* and *Magazine Index*, both products of Information Access Company.

38. Test results were included as a data summary with excellent graphics. See "Test Results," *MacWorld*, July 1990, 143.

39. Deborah Branscum, "Rating Radiation Screens," *MacWorld*, July 1990, 84.

40. Jerry Borrell, "Is Your Computer Killing You?" *MacWorld*, July 1990, 23-26.

41. Lora Grindlay, "Leukemia Study to Involve B.C. Kids," *Province*, June 26, 1990, 5. There was, of course, no mention in this story of the incidence of leukemia in Kamloops or of previous B.C. media treatment of that issue.

42. Grindlay, "Leukemia Study."

43. Reporters interviewed informally included Ann Reeves and Holly Horwood of the *Province*, personal communication, March 13, 1990, and John Daly of BCTV, personal communication, March 11, 1990. *Province* managing editor Don MacLachlan said in May of 1990 no database searches had been done on this subject by his newspaper. Donald MacLachlan, personal communication, May 6, 1990.

44. Allan Rachlin, *News as Hegemonic Reality* (New York: Praeger, 1988), 70-87.

45. Clarence A. Robinson, Jr., "U.S. Says Soviets Knew Korean Airlines 747 Was Commercial Flight," *Aviation Week and Space Technology*, September 19, 1983, 20. The quote is attributed to a ranking U.S. official and is one of dozens of similar quotes found in magazines, the *New York Times*, the *Washington Post, Time, Newsweek*, etc.

46. Taken as a whole, Pearson's reportage, alone and in conjunction with associates, is the finest piece of journalism of its kind that I know of. The brief analysis in this section is indebted entirely to his research. See: David Pearson, "KAL 007: What the U.S. Knew and When We Knew It," *The Nation*, August 18, 1989, 105-24. Also see David Pearson and John Keppel, "New Pieces in the Puzzle of Flight 007: Journey into Doubt," *The Nation* , August 17, 1985, 104-11; David Pearson, "007: Questions that Won't Go Away," *The Nation*, September 5, 1987, 181-87. For the alleged cover-up of these events by U.S. officials, also see David Corn, "Fear and Obstruction on the KAL Trail," *The Nation*, August 17, 1985, 110-12.

47. Pearson, "KAL 007," 107.

48. Some of this information first became available in the United States through release to Japanese news agencies of tracking information from Japanese radar installations, but much of it was already in the public record. *Aviation Week and Space Technology* carried a wealth of data on the flight paths of both the passenger airplane and the RC-135 in its September 12 and September 19, 1983 issues.

49. Corn, "Fear and Obstruction," 111.

50. Edward S. Herman and Noam Chomsky, *Manufacturing Consent: The Political Economy of the Mass Media* (New York: Pantheon, 1988), 29-30.

51. In 1990, on the other hand, a wide variety of international services are available to the writer or researcher including the Canadian Press, Tass, Kyodo News Service, and the *Manchester Guardian*.

52. Leonard Downie, Jr., managing editor of the *Washington Post*, insisted after the event that his newspaper, "like other major newspapers and TV networks investigated the flight of KAL 007 within an inch of its life." Quoted in Rachlin, *News as Hegemonic Reality*, 70-87.

53. Andrew Ippolito, "Databases in Newspaper Libraries," *Editor and Publisher* 118:19 (May 11, 1985), 61e.

54. These are government-created databases of information by and for members of Congress. They are also available online to the greater public through most major information services.

55. Bud Jorgensen, "A Company Should Be a Credit to its Rating," *Globe and Mail*, November 9, 1990, B9. Jorgensen was discribed in chapter 2 as assistant city editor at the *Province* in Vancouver. In the mid-1980s, he moved to Toronto and became a columnist.

56. Raymond L. Bancroft, "The Demographic Beat," *American Demographics* (November 1982), 30.

57. Tom Koch, "Cycle Wars," *Honolulu Magazine,* August 1990, 60-63.

58. *Nightly Business Report* sponsors include Kidder Peabody, Inc., Digital Computer, and Reuters, the leading European provider of electronic business information whose news service also contributes reportorial support to the show's coverage of current financial events.

4

Search Strategies:
Electronic and Traditional

So far, a perspective has been offered that allows for a progressively rigorous analysis of the role of actors—writers, editors, and sources—in the generation of news stories. For each participant in the process by which daily or weekly news stories are generated, specific goals have been identified, and the conflicts engendered among those goals (institutional, instrumental, functional) have been examined. The ability to examine the precise tensions through which news is synthesized has, in turn, been based on a distinction among story levels defined as ephemeral or trivial, contextual, and structural. The argument has been advanced that each is defined, in large, by the source of information used by the reporter or writer. This book's theme—that electronic libraries are a unique information source that empowers writers and changes their relations to the subject—requires that the nature of these databases and the means by which they are accessed be discussed in some detail.

This and the next chapter attempt to describe the effect computerized databases will have on the information potentially available at each of the three story levels: trivial, structural, and contextual. This description requires not simply a listing of those computer files currently available online but, in addition, a description of the general levels of information they represent and, simultaneously, the search strategies that are used to find specific data in the "electronic library." Just as the printing revolution not only made libraries possible but also made bibliographic search techniques necessary, so, too, have electronic databases resulted in specific types of data storage, organization, and retrieval procedures to allow for retrieval of specific and pertinent data. Indeed, it will be shown that the search strategies that these electronic resources necessitate are the single greatest impetus forcing a change from ephemeral toward structural or contextual story lines.

It is tempting to make of these technologies a panacea, and it is necessary to guard against the light cliché that states cheerfully that "the medium is the message." Since Marshall McLuhan's popular work of the 1960s,[1] it has been commonplace for academics and popular writers alike to argue that the medium by which information is transmitted determines, in great part, the content of the final transmission. Certainly, there is some truth in the formula. The printing revolution led to long-term structural changes in the way increasingly literate societies stored and processed information. It led to the creation of categories of public information impossible without both the libraries it made necessary or the profession of hack writer and journalist that it encouraged. But what McLuhan forgot, and other researchers have been at pains to point out,[2] is that the printing revolution created a radical change not only in the way information was transmitted but also in the sources people used when writing or speaking on any issue. While the marriage of television, McLuhan's "hot" medium, and satellite transmission technology does allow for the near simultaneous presentation of audiovisual information between two or more points on earth, if the message sent around the globe is defined traditionally (what an official said at a certain time), then little, really, has changed. The oral datum has not been transformed or changed. It has merely been speeded up.

The medium is not the message if by that one means that the means by which information is transmitted defines the resulting signal. A clear distinction must be made between the medium of transmission—the specific information system's mode of data production—and the technology by which the information that constitutes the message is collected. The medium itself—the technology of transmission—exists within a social context, political environment, and economic system that will influence data—the message—chosen for transmission, and determine the degree to which stories are accepted by "gatekeepers" as well as the extent of their final dissemination. It makes little difference if a news reporter with a notebook, a radio reporter with a tape recorder, or a television news crew with a video camera records a speech by President George Bush. All three will turn out stories whose messages are, at heart, identical: "Speaking from the Rose Room today, President George Bush announced he would ask Congress for billions of dollars to fund the nation's war on drugs." Whether a television announcer, radio broadcaster, or newspaper reporter crafts that introduction, the content is the same. It credits the president without analysis, affirms his insistence that the war on drugs is a necessary priority, and defines information essentially as what was said by that single official at a single time and place. The message is constant in each medium.

What is suggested here is that the medium—any specific medium—is only one element of the structure by which the context of information, its superstructure of both data accumulation and transmission, affects the data conveyed. McLuhan focused upon the structure of the medium, the nature of a signal's transmission, irrespective of other considerations. He thus largely ignored the content of information to be transmitted. But while the specific medium of transmission may influence the reception of a datum, it is not the message in its entirety. There is encoded in any public report—irrespective of its means of transmission or its mode of production—a series of assumptions and propositions that are the root data. They are the content, and it is in the arena of content—fact and context—that these new technologies affect the superstructure of information and achieve their greatest effect.

The printing revolution made possible, in McLuhan's words, the "Gutenberg reader," who compared texts and different editions of a single text, who made historicity a possible posture by allowing not only the dissemination but the storage in libraries of vast amounts of information. It affected both dissemination, the structure of the mode of production, and the cultural superstructure of information. In the same way, the electronic data storage revolution affects the superstructure of information organization (and ideology) as well as structural aspects of data dissemination. It creates, however, what might be called the "electronic reader," who is defined by specificity and plasticity rather than by the rigidity of fixed text.

Perhaps McLuhan's dictum needs to be reversed: the message is the medium. New technologies will create fundamentally different information only to the degree that they affect the content of the information signal, whatever the medium of transmission. The base information content of the news does not change because it is broadcast instead of printed but, rather, changes to the degree a specific news outlet defines its stories in terms of different sources of information. McLuhan argued that it "is the medium that shapes and controls the scale and form of human association and action. The content or uses of such media are as diverse as they are ineffectual in shaping the form of human association."[3] Here it has been argued that the scale of the medium is defined not simply by its range and speed of dissemination, but perhaps more importantly, by the context in which it places individual data of perceived social import. Its form is not simply a result of the medium chosen for broadcast but is a result of both the narrative form as a relay or transformation system and of any datum's source. Both of these elements are affected by technology in a way far more central than that described by McLuhan. It is not, as McLuhan suggested, that "the 'content' of any single medium blinds us to the character of the medium" but rather that concern with the medium of dissemination has blinded us to the relation between technology and the content of contemporary information.

Chapter 2's brief review of addiction issues suggested that reporters do not need electronic databases to pursue structural or contextual stories in which information from sources is placed in a broader context. After all, my story was written in the early 1980s without benefit of electronic libraries and many of the references cited in this text could have been (and, indeed, some were) culled from current magazines and newspapers readily available to any journalist or writer. But the article that finally ran in the *Province* was, at heart, a traditional story buttressed by some library research. It focused primarily on the work of two local psychologists and addiction researchers, Barry Beyerstein and Bruce Alexander of Simon Fraser University. Because of the skepticism of my editors, I asked the researchers for references to other articles in the field as well as reprints of their articles. I then used the local university library to obtain those references and incorporated their findings into my story. But throughout it all, I was guided by information provided by the interviewed source's perspective.

To have developed a story without reliance on that single point of view (and the research its subjects provided as substantiation) would have required hours in the library with *Index Medicus*'s yearly index of articles, searching for academic articles under the very general headings of addiction, heroin, morphine, marijuana, or cocaine. Locating articles in contemporary magazines on the efficacy of federal interdiction policies would have required further hours of research in the *Periodical Guide to Popular Literature* and, were newspaper stories to be a source, the *News Bank*. The former index lists articles published in general periodicals by subject while the latter catalogues, under general, bibliographic headings, citations based on headline information from stories in one hundred different U.S. newspapers. After these bibliographic searches, it then would have been necessary to procure the articles whose citations had been found through this research (and in areas lacking complete libraries, this work would mean writing or telephoning for copies of old news stories and applying for articles through an inter-library loan system).

This labor-intensive, time-consuming "term paper" approach is one that few reporters have the training, inclination, or resources to pursue. It requires one to be able to devote large blocks of time first to identifying the pertinent literature, then to procuring the articles or stories themselves. For this approach one needs a medical research library, a legal research library, and a decent university library if one is to complete the task without electronic assistance. Further, this approach is seen by many as "academic," an odious word in many newsrooms, and so time-consuming as to be prohibitive. Certainly, it is possible in theory to create contextual or structural articles without reference to electronic libraries, but, in practice, the constraints are generally prohibitive.

LIBRARIES AND SEARCHES

Fixed Text

There are important differences between electronic database "libraries" and their print antecedents that distinguish these information sources from their more traditional print counterparts. The most important is that print resources are fixed references stored in individual books, journals, or microfilm rolls, and electronic references are digitalized. Books and journals are closed systems, with each text a distinct entity whose information needs to be searched separately and located individually. While print made "literature objectively real and therefore subjectively conceivable as a universal fact,"[4] the immobility of the printed page and the isolation of a book or journal article on the library shelf meant that their information could be accessed only through the complex process of searching through indexes for a specific text among its millions of fellows, pursuing the whole article or book for data on a particular point, and then incorporating a recovered datum, it it was found worthy, into a new piece of lettered work.

This knowledge system created a whole series of roles based on the production of written materials (writer, journalist, editor, designer, typesetter, publisher, bookseller, reader, etc.) as well as necessitating a whole secondary class of researchers (bibliographer, librarian, cataloguer) whose job was to assist in, first, the storage and, second, the retrieval of information from those fixed information sources. It also created a two- or three-tiered system of information ranging from the general public (newspapers, mass market magazines) to the intellectual (specialty newsletters,[5] smaller circulation magazines[6]) to the technical (journals and newsletters written by and for members of a specific profession).

Until recently, journals and texts were mainly the exclusive intellectual property of closed, professional societies whose readers and contributors were members of specific trades or professions (physicians, lawyers, historians, economists, etc.). Writers for these journals were literary amateurs using a rarefied, professional language understood by their profession's members but not necessarily by the general public. Further, this literature was largely arcane and known only to those whose job category would argue for its perusal. Who, for example, but a pharmacologist or psychologist would know what journals to turn to for information on addiction and habituation? Few who are not members of the medical professions typically know of or use *Index Medicus,* which is usually catalogued solely in major university reference sections or specialized medical libraries. Only a lawyer or law librarian would know the journals and system of case references that make of the legal literature a potent research tool. In each of these cases and in others, the technical literature has remained isolated, like the newspaper clipping files, and accessible only to those whose job it was to know how to access it.

Fixed texts—the overwhelming mass of printed books and specialized literature—created a system, as Alexander Pope warned it might, in which there was "a lumberhouse of books in ev'ry head, forever reading, never to be read." Access to information has been constrained by the physical ability to search for the appropriate journal article, magazine article, newspaper story, or book that will pertain to a single topic. The general search model taught in schools to assist those in locating information on any specific topic is given in Illustration 4.1.[7] It moves from the broad, general background reference (general encyclopedias, specialized encyclopedias, and dictionaries) to books and then journal articles referenced in the topic's area. Books are organized by subject, author, or title, and a writer interested in a single topic must plow through library shelves of discretely stored data to find the appropriate material in which the specific information required is stored. To locate articles by topic or author in a specialized journal or magazine, one must use one of several series of references, each volume of the individual series covering only a year's worth of mate-

Illustration 4.1
Print Search Techniques

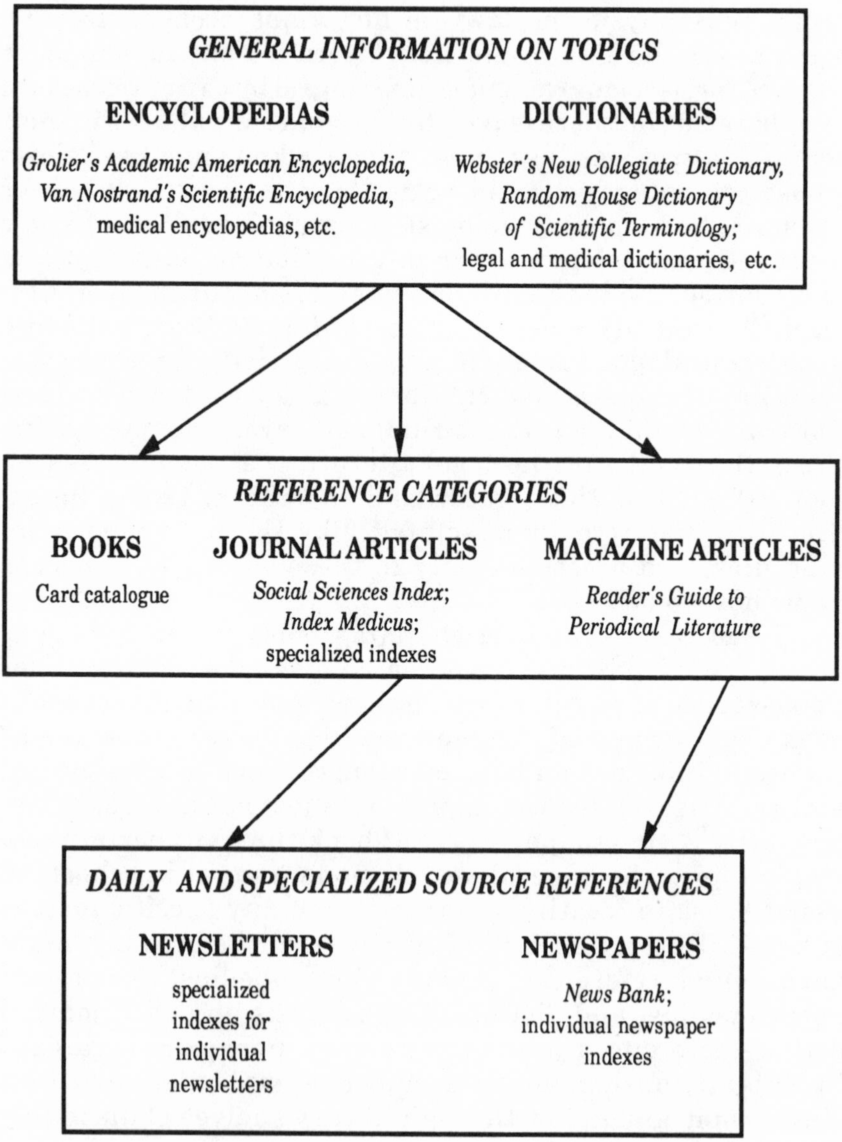

GENERAL INFORMATION ON TOPICS

ENCYCLOPEDIAS

Grolier's Academic American Encyclopedia,
Van Nostrand's Scientific Encyclopedia,
medical encyclopedias, etc.

DICTIONARIES

Webster's New Collegiate Dictionary,
Random House Dictionary
of Scientific Terminology;
legal and medical dictionaries, etc.

REFERENCE CATEGORIES

BOOKS

Card catalogue

JOURNAL ARTICLES

Social Sciences Index;
Index Medicus;
specialized indexes

MAGAZINE ARTICLES

Reader's Guide to
Periodical Literature

DAILY AND SPECIALIZED SOURCE REFERENCES

NEWSLETTERS

specialized
indexes for
individual
newsletters

NEWSPAPERS

News Bank;
individual newspaper
indexes

---

rial. These series would include the *Reader's Guide to Periodical Literature, Index Medicus, Social Sciences Index, Business Periodicals Index*, etc. These lead not to the article itself but instead to information that describes its location (for example: Linda C. Higgins, "Worry over Power Line Surges," *Medical World News* 30:17 (September 11, 1989), 22-34). It may or may not be physically available. Once found and read, it may or may not be relevant.

Thus for those interested in researching addiction to determine if the war on drugs makes any sense, one might go first to *Grolier's Encyclopedia,* whose general listing on addiction cites in its chapter notes several reference books. Even the encyclopedia's most recent edition will be several years out of date because by definition a new edition is a major undertaking requiring years of writing, editing, and production. Those books cited at the end of the article, if found in a local library, in turn cite journal articles or books by other authors and represent the thinking by experts at the time the article was written. To see if these individuals have written anything more recently, their names would be searched for in specialized indexes—*Index Medicus,* for example, and the popular literature's yearly edition of the *Reader's Guide to Periodical Literature* or perhaps another more scholarly index. Pertinent articles written since the last year's index was published or articles in a journal not indexed by the specific reference would not, of course, be found. For those using the most popular news sources, some individual newspapers (e.g., *New York Times, Los Angeles Times,Washington Post*) publish yearly indexes of their own stories, each entry catalogued with headline by general subject, and, for wider news coverage there is the newspaper story index, *News Bank.* Where articles or stories refer to other sources of information—congressional studies, presidential proclamations, etcetera—further use of other, equally specialized libraries would be required.

Traditional News Research Strategies

It is not surprising, given the economic constraints and general, oral perspective of the newspaper, that this classic "term paper" research method is used only infrequently by newspeople. If news is oral and concerned with "facts," then most of this method is not only time-consuming and expensive but, in addition, irrelevant. The general search paradigm espoused by newspaper research librarians has been geared to finding the isolated datum that can be used immediately and narrowly by the reporter or editor. As Jean Ward and Kathleen A. Hansen say in their article on news library research strategies: "Traditionally, librarians and journalists have focused on the 'fact.' A librarian usually helps [news] patrons find 'facts' much in the same way journalists seek facts on behalf of the public and for their news stories."[8]

"Facts" are specific bits of data that have been published in the newspaper, are easily available from cumulative statistical references (state data books,[9] for example), or are to be found in the most general reference texts. Thus in the event of a chemical spill, a librarian might use a scientific encyclopedia (e.g., *Van Nostrand's Scientific Encyclopedia*) to find pertinent "facts" on the toxicity and chemical make-up of the leaking substance. This focus on "facts" narrows the number of references to be searched, the potential information to be retrieved, and the time required for the whole research process. Thus one would not ask a news librarian for information on the general causes of deaths in hospital. That would require searches of a technical literature not available in traditional news libraries. Nor would one be likely to ask a news librarian if a single death that has occurred in a city fits a pattern of injury that had been observed in other circulation areas or broadcast regions. Even if a news librarian attempted to search *News Bank*, for example, for stories involving a similar pattern (e.g., anesthetic-related deaths caused by machine failure), the stories themselves would be difficult to obtain and the cumulative index's headings would be too general to target the search so specifically.

So the traditional news library has focused primarily on organizing and then retrieving information first presented in its own publication. If news is primarily oral in content, then clipping files preserving stories based on what officials have said will be the critical historical resource that reporters need. Thus, at the *Province*, requests for information on anesthetic deaths drew forth a series of thick clipping files, envelopes of stories published in that newspaper and its sister publication, the *Sun*. One file was labeled "coroners" and reported on public inquests that the local coroners service had ordered. Among these stories were some involving anesthetic-related hospital deaths. Another file was the more general series of clippings labeled "doctors" and included some "coroners" stories and general, physician-related wire stories from other regions. Even more general folders, bulging with stories on "medicine" or "hospitals" might also be culled from the stacks by the diligent librarian.

Not all reporters have access to this material, of course. Those who work in distant bureaus, for example, have very limited or no access to the print resources of their employer's news library. Reporters based in the city but away from the newsroom on an assignment cannot physically check the library's files from the courthouse, police station, or legislature news bureaus. They must call and ask a librarian to check the files for a "fact" or previous statement, a process that can take minutes or hours once that librarian is free to do nothing but address the specific reporter's research. Those who have both time and proximity may find the volume of clips to be so thick and the information cataloguing system so general as to be ultimately unusable as a viable resource. As Ted Weeger, an assistant managing editor at the *Los Angeles Times*, said: "We find that often when a reporter goes to the library and asks for clips on such-and-such a subject, he is likely to get five or six envelopes crammed full of stuff. There's no way he can read them all, unfolding every clip and then having to scan them."[10]

If one did read those files one might find apparently relevant, past news stories whose information is presumed to be true (as was that in the *Wall Street Journal* example). But each story's fact is usually based on prior, fundamentally oral information that is itself suspect. Each clip represents a reporter's previous summation of official or expert statements, usually delivered in one or another journalistic context (press conferences, inquests, court hearings, etc.). Thus the strength of a newspaper's library files—stories based on official, oral statements delivered in journalistic context—is that they typically present as "fact" verbal observations or opinions that have been relayed through two media (oral to print or oral to broadcast) without examination.

Thus traditional library research for newspeople is based on "facts" that can be easily searched, on isolated data or factoids originating in a specific geographic region, and on oral information, all of which, by definition, exclude broader contextual or structural issues. Ward and Hansen give the general newspaper library's "fact-oriented" search model (Illustration 4.2) as a five-step process in which the library's contribution occurs at stage three. It is the self-referential, closed nature of this data system that explains why "some reporters worry that the clips will prematurely establish a perspective and inhibit their independence and originality in developing the story."[11] If the reference basis is what the subject said at a previous point, if facts are defined as what an official has said at the level of the journalistic event, then the latitude of the reporter to judge current events is going to be severely limited. Any perspective on the official's statement in a current context will reflect at best "facts" enunciated by that official in previous statements to the press. Thus some reporters surveyed by Ward and Hansen did not follow their profession's established practice and ignored library files while doing research because they recognized that past stories indeed serve as a source of orthodoxies and stereotypes provided by officials, which limit a priori the newswriter's perspective.

Librarians working with clipping files and three dimensional texts have assumed that their general purpose is to support a narrowly defined search for an isolated datum usually contained in a previous newspaper or magazine story. The system supports a tautology that defines "fact" as what the official or expert said at a given place and time and bases future stories (fact checking) on what that official or expert said in the past at a journalistic event covered by a news reporter. In effect the unexamined, past statements of the source lawyer, doctor, politician, or university professor are the standard by which that individual's more recent statement is examined for accuracy. But as we have seen, officials' statements at any point are influenced by their own conflicting goals and perspectives. At best those statements are "weak facts," unsupported by other objective criteria. They cannot, by definition, be trusted as accurate outside the very limited frame of the moment. Data from

Illustration 4.2
Traditional News Librarian's Model

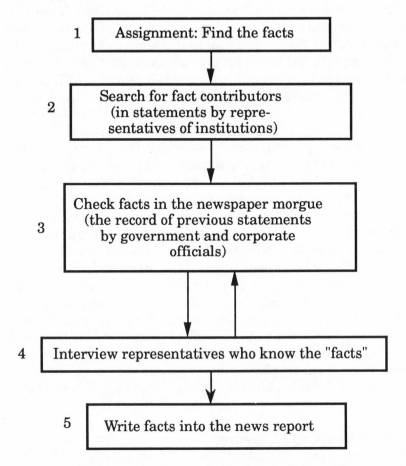

1 | Assignment: Find the facts

2 | Search for fact contributors (in statements by representatives of institutions)

3 | Check facts in the newspaper morgue (the record of previous statements by government and corporate officials)

4 | Interview representatives who know the "facts"

5 | Write facts into the news report

other information levels (academic journals, technical journals, news reports from other, diverse circulation or broadcast regions) that would place the individual's statement into a more objective context are not typically available in this "fact"-checking, bibliographic regime. This system works best when one wants to know the mayor's middle initial, the year a senator began his first term in Congress, or a jury's findings from an inquest whose victim's name (Loewen, Marvin) is known. The whole "fact"-oriented system provides data but not, necessarily, information.

What it does not do is facilitate or encourage a systematic program for uncovering potentially appropriate information from other sources. It offers no real search strategy for broader categories of information, no method by which systemic or contextual questions could be easily addressed. The whole process affirms and supports an oral definition of news as isolated "fact," offering little impetus to those wishing to integrate bibliographic sources with the reporter's more traditional sources of information. Ward and Hansen, attempting to enlarge the news librarian's function, defined these sources as informal and institutional.[12] The former is data gained in conversation from other journalists, official sources, and personal contacts—what the court reporter told the medical reporter, who then talked to his contact in the local branch of the AMA. As we have seen, this information is tainted by the personal perspective and interests of those sources and their own professional agendas. The latter would include information gained from public officials, public relations releases, and official documents (court records, government records, etc.) Institutional sources are beyond the storage capability of most media libraries or, for that matter, most public libraries. Official repositories are designated as destination sources for varying types of official documentation for each level of government. Informal sources—the reporter's stock-in-trade—are dependent on personal relations, typically oral and, as the story detailing Todd's and Habash's positions made clear, biased and therefore suspect.

The Electronic Library

Electronically stored information makes the discrete book, individual statement, or esoteric journal article a part of a larger, plastic whole whose sense and data can be accessed simultaneously by the generalist. Digitalized storage fundamentally alters traditional search methodologies by restructuring the lumberhouse of books, journals, and newspaper articles into an electronic code which can be searched for information on a narrowly defined topic at incredible speed and with previously impossible specificity. Once stored in a binary code, the text takes on whole new properties that allow not only for more efficient storage but for new means of retrieval. Tim Miller uses the following trivial example to make the difference clear:

> Take, for example, *Who's Who in America*. In
> the print version each word in the two-volume
> set is bound to one place only on a sheet of
> paper; the 75,000 biographies are arranged al-
> phabetically. Thus, we can find Caspar Wein-
> berger in the Ws.
>
> In the computerized version, by way of
> contrast, each word swims in a digital soup,
> ready to be dipped out in accordance with al-
> most any criterion the searcher wants to specifiy.
> Thus, last year, when librarians at the *San
> Francisco Chronicle* wanted to find members of
> the secretive, men-only Bohemian Club, they
> went to the on-line version of *Who's Who* offered
> by Dialog Information Services, a vendor of more
> than 300 data bases. Within seconds the com-
> puter located the word "Bohemian" each time it
> appeared in an entry. Among the club members
> found: Secretary of Defense Caspar Weinberger.
>
> A search of this kind in the print version
> of *Who's Who* would have taken a reporter ap-
> proximately eight years, not counting coffee
> breaks.[13]

This is the specificity of online databases. In the print
version of *Who's Who,* there is no way to find every mention
of the Bohemian Club except by methodically checking each
listing for a subject's possible membership in the organization.
But because the electronic version of the text is, in fact, a
"digital soup" in which the data's organization is unfixed,
one can draw from it a directory of the club or, should one
wish, determine membership in any other organization whose
constituency is sufficiently important to be noted in the
directory. One can, of course, be more specific. To discover
whether justices of the Supreme Court or their employees
belonged to the Bohemian Club, one could search the online
text for "Bohemian" and "Supreme Court" simultaneously, a
longer phrase that would return only those text entries
describing Bohemian Club members affiliated with the Supreme Court. If there was another organization that in-

cluded the word Bohemia (say, for example, "Children of
Bohemian Parents") or other members of the Supreme Court
staff also listed in *Who's Who* (say, the court's chief librarian) who belonged to either Bohemian group, those entries
would be included in the search's answer as well.

It is this very specificity, the ability to search volumes of
data with extremely narrow filters, that, interestingly, has
led many to believe, in Philip Meyer's phrase, that "it's the
same old journalism but with better tools."[14] After all, the
traditional news model is based on an assumption of discrete "facts" presented by individual experts or officials at a
specific journalistic event, so a research tool that allows the
writer to cull rapidly and precisely through masses of
newspaper clippings for that "fact" should be an aid to the
traditional research approach. In the late 1970s, when major newspapers first began to computerize their libraries,
this move was seen as an advantage. Rather than culling
through folders of news clippings catalogued in the publication's morgue, one could search with more specificity for
stories that might have previously appeared on a single
topic. What resulted was a chronology, a listing of pertinent
stories ordered by date and defined by search phrases that
cut across the boundaries of traditional newsroom divisions
(business, "living," sports, news).

If all that one could search was *Who's Who* or the files of
a single newspaper for a story one remembers reading six
months ago, then computerized information storage would
be, in fact, no revolution at all. Digitalized storage perhaps
would be justified by the economies achieved in storage
space and the added efficiencies that the Bohemian Club
search made evident. But what is searched is not simply a
single story but the whole of the digital soup. Rather than
five bulging files of clippings labeled "coroner," "medical,"
"doctors," and, perhaps, "medicine," the reporter searching
for stories on "anesthesia and death or injury" would receive
a chronology of stories in which those words occurred in
conjunction. Because what is being sifted through electronically is the whole story and not simply general file words
(coroner, hospital, doctor, etc.), the range of newspaper data
searched might retrieve stories not otherwise included in
the files. Thus if there has been a story on product recalls for

specific respirators or a news brief on problems elsewhere in their use, these would be retrieved by the electronic search as well. What the digitalized library yields, through search specificity, may indeed be more efficient, faster, and more complete than traditional search methods. But the computerization of, say, a single newspaper's proprietary files does not greatly expand the reporter's potential information base. "Information in clips is limited to what people at a particular paper already know about a subject. When a reporter is assigned a story unrelated to anything his or her paper has covered before, the clipping file is useless as a research source."[15] And, of course, the information contained in those files is limited by the system of oral transmission that at present defines contemporary newswriting.

Three things have happened, however, that make of this new technology a revolution. One has been that the expense of computerization has required the creation of new markets for whole classes of digitally stored materials. Just as the printing revolution made possible previously impossible economies of scale, enlarging the body of written materials readily available, so, too, has this computerization of information created its own economy of scale. The online library has become a commodity in its own right and its database is sold as a resource to any who wish to access it. Companies like Vu/Text, which computerizes newspapers, offer clients the opportunity to search the databases of all other newspapers that have chosen to participate in this system. These newspapers receive a royalty whenever their individual files are accessed, and editors have discovered they can partially recover the cost of computerization by making their digital libraries available online to the public at large and to other news organizations through a vendor like Vu/Text.[16]

As well, popular and specialty magazines, often owned by the same corporations that control daily newspapers, have also computerized their libraries, which are being made available in the same way by one or another digital information company. What began as an efficient means of storage for an individual newspaper or periodical has become a system of increasingly communal information retrieval for all participants. So reporters or writers can search not only the database of a single newspaper company, but instead—virtually simultaneously—can search more than sixty-five newspapers and hundreds of regional and national weekly magazines[17] as well. Reporters are thus not limited by their own library files but can access and work with the files of colleagues from around the country.

Second, computerization has made it economical and efficient to digitalize the work, research, and records of a variety of specialized publications and resources whose distribution previously was limited to individuals in specific fields. Law journal articles and court records from state and federal jurisdictions have been placed in electronic form, as has the work of academics and professionals writing in fields ranging from atomic physics to zoology. Just as the first printing revolution transformed writing from the leisure pastime of society's elites to a broadly based, print-oriented system of information, so, too, has computerization made academic writing a widely available resource. This material is also available to the reporter, writer, or news librarian interested in placing news "facts" in a context. Until this development occurred, professional, "objective" research was practically available only to a limited, professional audience that read journals such as *Pediatrics, Michigan Law Review, Professional Geographer,* or *Demographics.*

In the same vein, the federal government, whose bureaucracy generates an enormous amount of data, discovered it was both cost-effective and efficient to store their records—and to disseminate them—through digitalized systems. Thus in 1990, for example, public releases and information updates from various federal agencies were available to any citizen with access to a computer and modem.[18] In addition, the U.S. Supreme Court agreed to initiate Project Hermes, a system allowing the electronic distribution of the Court's opinions immediately upon completion through the Supreme Court Opinion Network to fifteen major legal and news publishing organizations that will, in turn, share those opinions with other organizations.[19] This system will make available immediately the court's complete brief, a process that, in the past, took at the least months to sift down through traditional legal reportage systems.

In addition, the U.S. government has begun to license outside vendors to digitalize government records and sell them in their electronic form to general users. Thus much of the information that is filed with the government but is a part of the public domain can be searched electronically. Each year, for example, more than one hundred thousand corporate reports are filed with the Securities and Exchange Commission, generating over six million pages of data. In 1985, the Disclosure Information Group contracted to store the data electronically and make it available, for a fee, to the public. Until recently, these SEC filings were submitted in print form—on paper—but now the majority are filed electronically and thus available to the online researcher almost immediately. As Alfred Glossbrenner has noted, today there is virtually no significant piece of information about the finances of a public company that Disclosure does not include.[20] Those filings can be searched with the same flexibility and specificity as *Who's Who*.

Finally, information storage occurs not as a separate part of the information process, following production of printed materials, but as an integral part of the production process itself. The newspaper Linotype operators who worked with lead type have been replaced by electronic equipment and "cold type," which makes a page plate from a computerized publishing system. Publications produced electronically code their stories or articles and information in a digital form, which can be organized bibliographically and stored electronically as soon as an editor sends the item to a page. Because searching is done by computer, stories need not be clipped and individually processed in the library but are "poured" into the digital soup. The result is that information is updated in all databases at an extremely rapid rate and that searchers need not use last year's index to find articles based on perhaps already dated work done two or more years before.

A comparison of "electronic" and traditional encyclopedia forms illustrates the difference in these two storage forms. Grolier's *Academic American Encyclopedia*, which costs $800 for a set of hardcover volumes, is updated annually. Its information is stored on computer-generated, magnetic tapes, and in the 1980s was offered as an online database to both

Dow Jones News Service and CompuServe customers. There is now also an electronic Grolier's, updated monthly, with two thousand more articles than its annual print cousin. The electronic version can offer those extra articles because it is freed of the space limitations its physical counterpart is constrained to accept and because articles can be easily added or subtracted to the digitalized version. Thus, during the 1988 U.S. presidential election campaign, the electronic Grolier's carried detailed articles and biographies on Democratic and Republican candidates, and then deleted the files when the election ended. In season, facts and figures on baseball's players and game statistics were also temporarily included in the encyclopedia, only to be replaced during the winter with data on hockey and basketball teams and players.[21]

The result of all these changes has been the radical transformation of the typical news organization's library where, until recently, the resource base was largely limited to dictionaries, encyclopedias, a few magazines, and traditionally stored clipping files. Now that library is linked to a mammoth electronic information resource in which the news organization's clippings have become a single component within the millions of specific and potentially pertinent electronic files generated by a geographically diverse selection of newspapers, journals, and magazines, which may have published stories on or about any single topic. Those news files are joined by a mass of digitally stored and electronically retrievable government documentation, legal case histories, and technical reports. To search only newspapers for stories on, say, addiction and habituation would, using traditional methods, require months. To absorb the technical literature on the causes of drug abuse might require weeks. The legal issues involved would demand weeks more for those unused to the very specific bibliographic system used in traditional law libraries. The mass of potential data is overwhelming. But the fears of some that computerized information would merely overwhelm the writer with extraneous information[22] have been balanced by the system's inherent capability to tailor information retrieval to very specific requests. It is the specificity of search technology in this digitalized information system that keeps

Illustration 4.3
Electronic Data Model

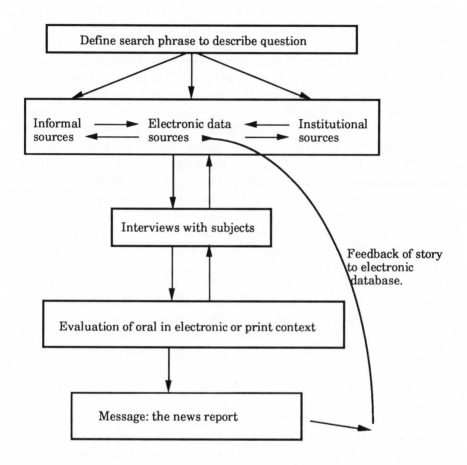

the mass of data retrieved on any subject from becoming overwhelming.

ELECTRONIC MODEL

The resulting bibliographic model that reflects these changes in the electronic news library can be seen in Illustration 4.3. It is based on a tentative model of Ward and Hansen's that attempted to describe the relation of electronic databases to more traditional news library models. Their description has been modified to better reflect the position of electronic searching. In this model, the request for a specific "fact" has been replaced by the need for a search phrase that will define the question or problem area. The question may be rooted in a specific event (coroner's court, an official proclamation, a legislative budget, etc.), but what is sought now of necessity is a general perspective that will winnow the mass of data in this digital soup down to an effective base of potentially relevant information. Reports stored in electronic databases inform the reporter or editor, as does information gained from informal (colleague's or source's tips) and institutional sources (press releases and official statements). They provide a base of data by which "weak facts" can be evaluated and, simultaneously, a context broader than that of a single, biased, official source. Interviews thus become part of the information process, not the whole. What a Dr. Todd is asked—and how his answers are treated—can be based on a whole range of stories, articles, and reports selected to deal with the issues of malpractice: cause, effect, and cost. The database (legal journals, medical journals, news stories detailing previous quotes) also offers a context in which the statement of the subject is mediated and evaluated prior to writing the news report, which is then added to the electronic library and becomes available for future use by other writers or editors.

Search Phrase

Search phrase is the term used for any specific word or combination of words entered into an electronic data system to access one or another file of computerized information. It provides the parameters that govern the degree of specifiity with which any search in a single database is carried out. The phrase replaces general, gross file names ("doctors," "coroners," "hospitals," etc.) with which traditional news libraries separated past clippings and allows for progressively specific examination of a wide field of electronically stored data. Phrases can be simple—a single name, title, or word—or complex, including a string of modifiers, depending on the degree of specificity needed to narrow the wealth of potential data to that which is usable for any given purpose. Search phrases are thus the operative filter through which the researcher sifts the mass of available information in any database to return the potentially crucial report, story, or journal article.

Practically, the search phrase is a strainer that allows the researcher to extract from the digital soup only those data that bear directly and specifically on the problem at hand. The trick is to assure the appropriate spaces in the strainer's mesh. If the grid is too narrow, then potentially pertinent articles will be excluded, and if it is too broad, the mass of information retrieved from a search will be too vast for careful review. As a general, operative principle, it is better to write a phrase so narrowly that a first search returns only two or three articles than to craft a phrase so broadly that one hundred citations are retrieved. It is always better, for example, to search first for recent articles, limiting the search by a six-month or one-year time frame, because this year's articles will, typically, include references to still-pertinent previous work. The narrow phrase also reflects a well-thought-out, testable hypothesis, a clear merger of events to be considered, and an aspect of that event that can be efficiently searched. What is called here the "simple search" exemplifies a narrowly defined search filter and is often a means to gather enough information to craft a full hypothesis.

Simple Search: EAF

The traditional news model presumes there is a single "fact" that will be required by the reporter—a name, a date, a judge's ruling—and that it is the librarian's task to find that discrete datum. Certainly, electronic data resources can provide this type of information, and this ability was emphasized in early articles on electronic resources and the news. Thus one can ask the computer to search for all references to Henry Kissinger ("Kissinger, Henry") in current news publications and report with assurance that the tally of references—10,187 in 1987—was the highest of any single reference for that year. In preparing this book, I searched an online medical database using "Bruce Beyerstein" as my search phrase because my notes did not have his middle initial (which is L.) and I wanted to include it in this book. Remembering that David Pearson had written an

article in *The Nation* about the downing of Korean Airlines
Flight 007 by Russian military personnel, I used his name,
"Pearson, David," as the operative search phrase in a database
of magazines to find the article's specific title and exact
date of publication. In some databases, the family name
precedes the Christian name while in others the order is
reversed.

"It's great for looking up the proverbial needle in the
haystack," says Dennis Rim, a librarian at the *Washington
Post*.[23] But the real value of the databases is in finding the
haystack itself. The nature of the digital database and the
language required to access it tend to lead the writer or
reporter from the fact to its context. A simple example will
demonstrate how this process works. In August 1989, Canadian television producer John Daly asked me to assist his
station in investigating a rumor about the dumping of U.S.
toxic wastes in Canada. An engineer passing through
Vancouver had told BCTV newspeople that a company called
Hawaiian Western Steel (HWS) was shipping something
called electric arc furnace dust (EAF) from Oahu to British
Columbia. EAF was supposed to be toxic, and Daly wanted
to know when and where the material was shipped, how it
got to British Columbia, what exactly EAF was, how dangerous
it was, and, finally, why a Hawaiian steel company would
send its waste products to Canada.

To find answers to these questions, I first called Hawaiian Western Steel on Oahu, but its officials refused my
request for information. I then called a local union representing Hawaiian Western members. But the union stew-
ard referred me to his supervisor, who turned out to be the
company official to whom I'd first talked. He again declined
comment. What was this stuff? Who would know? Why
wouldn't HWS officials discuss it? Online, I first searched
the *Wall Street Journal* and *New York Times*, using "electric
arc furnace dust" as my search phrase. I assumed that if
EAF was a major problem, one or the other newspaper
would have had at least one article about it. No information
was found. Then I repeated the search in a database of
metallurgical and chemical journals and newsletters, hoping
for something that would at least define the supposedly
toxic substance. Six articles were returned from the search,

each including source, publication date, and abstract. The following, from the September 10, 1988 issue of *American Metal Market*, gave me much of the information Daly and his reporters needed. The abstract is reprinted here in full:

> The EPA [Environmental Protection Agency] has listed electric arc furnace (EAF) dust generated during steel making as a hazardous material under the Resource Conservation & Recovery Act rules, according to J. F. Collins, National Steel Producers Association (Washington, D.C.). The US generates 0.5 mil tons of EAF dust. The dusts that have leachable lead, cadmium and chromium have been prohibited from disposal in untreated landfills since August 8, 1988. It costs up to $125/ton to dispose of EAF dust in a landfill having safeguards, but the cost could increase as the number of approved sites falls. Historically 73% of EAF dust has been deposited in landfills. Basic technologies meeting the EPA's requirement of "best demonstrated available technology" for EAF dust are high-temperature thermal treatment metals recovery and chemical fixation techniques.[24]

The most important fact in this report seemed to be that EPA regulations had changed and now defined EAF dust as a hazardous waste because of its heavy-metal content. That change meant shipping would be regulated and storage or treatment necessitated at the waste's destination. Knowing this, I knew a great deal. I had an idea of what EAF was and an assumption—that its transportation to Canada was a result of EPA regulation changes. A call to the EPA in Hawaii confirmed the assumption, placing the whole in a regulatory context, and provided the rest of the information BCTV had requested. On file in the EPA's electronic database was the name of the company carrying the material by sea from Hawaii, its destination before the EPA regulations went into effect (a Washington-state company), and its destination following the implementation of these new regulations: Cominco, Ltd., in British Columbia. The rumor that

sparked the search was both right and wrong. EAF was
being shipped to Canada, but it was not being dumped. EPA
regulations now required EAF to be handled as a hazardous
waste and that requirement meant it now paid Hawaiian
Steel to ship the material to a company large enough to treat
it and extract the residual metals from the dust. Cominco is
one of the world's largest mining companies and one of the
few West Coast facilities with sufficient "high-temperature
thermal" capacity (in short, a large and hot enough furnace)
safely to extract the residual heavy metals from the dust.
Daly then called Cominco, which confirmed it was handling
this type of steel production by-product as a sideline and
making money in the process.

The story, which began as a rumor of dumping toxic
materials, became an interesting business piece detailing
how a Canadian company has become a center for specialized treatment of waste products that U.S. firms can't or
won't handle. An article in *Chemical Marketing Reporter,*
also uncovered in the single search, listed EAF as one of
thirty-nine substances that had been reclassified as hazardous
and requiring either specialized landfill storage or specific
extraction before normal storage would be allowed.[25] In my
final report to BCTV, I suggested they might wish to find out
what other hazardous wastes were being sent to Canada for
treatment and to compare Canadian and U.S. EPA hazardous waste treatment standards. Were the BCTV report to
be integrated into a national story, it would have been easy
to check with eastern Canadian metal companies to see if
they were receiving EAF from eastern U.S. steel producers
for metal extraction as well. Since Cominco is a national
company with multiple plant sites, this possibility seemed
likely. But BCTV, a provincial outpost for the national
Canadian Television Network, was not interested in a story
at that scale.

Using a traditional reporter's model, a librarian who
took the time to look in a scientific or metallurgical dictionary could have discovered that electric arc furnace dust was
a by-product of the steel process containing heavy metals.
Such a search would not, however, have uncovered the
crucial fact that new Environmental Protection Agency
regulations had, in 1988, classified EAF as a hazardous

waste whose storage was now subject to specific regulations. The fact of its composition took on import only within the context of the EPA regulations. This type of synergy occurs frequently in electronic data searching. Using the electronic model, I entered a search phrase that was the simplest form possible—a single noun. The electronic data sources provided information that allowed me to identify the appropriate institutional sources of information (the Environmental Protection Agency's office in Hawaii) and to ask its subjects about EAF shipments from Hawaii under the new regulations.

It is important to stress that this electronic database search did not eliminate the need for traditional, reportorial interview techniques. Sources were still called, and requests for information were made. News files were searched. But in this process, information was not limited to the oral source (denials from Hawaiian Steel, from Hawaii-based unions). Information retrieved from specialized journals and newsletters identified the individuals whose information was crucial—local EPA inspectors—and allowed for an informed interview with them. That resulted in information no newspaper or single journal database was likely to hold: names of marine shippers, dates of EPA inspection of Hawaiian Steel, destination of the furnace dust. Had a full-scale story been done, these raw data would have been the information required to set up television filming schedules. Basic reportorial techniques were empowered by the electronic storage facilities, and the "haystack" of federal regulations was found, along with the "needle" of the EAF's destination.

In the end, this was a small story. Had heavy-metal waste products been, in fact, dumped in British Columbia, it would have been a far larger issue. In that case, interviews with officials at Hawaiian Steel, Cominco, and the company that transported the materials by sea between the two sites would have been based not simply on informal rumors but on the data drawn from these electronic sources. Had BCTV wished, and had it been necessary, further searches could have been run to investigate the financial stature and business nature of Hawaiian Steel, for example, which must file reports both with the EPA and with the federal Securities and Exchange Commission.[26]

But these things were not done. The rumor would have been great news. The actual story was pleasant news and a general business story, not what regional television stations necessarily do best. BCTV editors decided that the story of Cominco's treatment of these materials was not sufficiently newsworthy for them to invest more money in the story. The general system of priorities and perspectives that govern the news agenda was not changed. The information base which presents it with data was altered. The total cost of the database search of the metallurgical journals and newsletters, and of both the *New York Times* and *Wall Street Journal* databases was about $40.[27]

As a footnote to this specific case study, Raul Ramirez informed me in 1990 that the Center for Investigative Reporting (CIR) was working on a television documentary that would trace the shipment of U.S. waste products to Third World countries, where storage and containment regulations were lax. The documentary was attempting to determine the degree to which products like EAF, defined as toxic or dangerous by the EPA, were being shipped to countries where regulations were less strict. When informed of the EAF search and my recommendation to BCTV that they focus on the other thirty-eight substances added in 1988 to the EPA list, Ramirez said this was the CIR documentary's approach, albeit without a Canadian focus.[28]

Complex Search: A Medical Example

The EAF example was a simple search and used a simple search phrase. It employed a noun to locate references and information on a single and highly specific product. More typically, requests for information from electronic databases that say, in effect, "give me everything on 'X'" are too broad for efficient use of online resources. The accumulated resources of scores of newspapers and hundreds of journals provide a potential information base that requires narrower, contextual search parameters. In the early 1980s, for example, *Miami Herald* newspeople searched electronic databases for stories about football player Joe Montana, using just Montana's name as the search phrase. Their

undifferentiated request resulted in hundreds of citations—
most of them quite useless—and a bill of $140.[29]

Unless the subject is as esoteric, and therefore as specific,
as electric arc furnace dust, it is necessary in constructing a
search phrase to use modifiers that describe more precisely
both the exact subject and general context of reportorial
interest. A complex search phrase addresses a factor whose
examination is critical to the understanding of a boundary
event with modifiers capable of narrowing potential returns
to those that might bear on that event's general context. It
places statements of officials at the level of the journalistic
event within a context of prior research bearing on the
elements of the boundary event. Creating an appropriate
search phrase thus becomes the critical tool in the bibliographic search, defining not only general categories of
information but their relation to other potential information parameters as well. In a real sense, it defines, by
creating a hypothesis, what the final story will be.

Chapter 2's discussion of tort reform is a good example
of how this process works. To have asked *Vu/Text* for all
articles published in its online newspaper database on the
question of tort reform would have been prohibitively expensive, probably redundant, and largely uninformative.
Hundreds of newspaper stories and editorials have been
written on the issue. Many of them quote physicians in favor
of tort reform, legal representatives against it, and the
recapitulation of opinions by legislators supporting one or
another entrenched position. A search for all articles on
"tort reform" would not provide a context in which the issues
could be examined, merely the already established positions
of the very interested professional parties.

It was therefore necessary first to attempt to define
the context—for the reporter to decide what it was he or she
really wanted to know—and then to describe a search phrase
that would bring that information forward. Institutional
sources (in this case, Habash and Todd) seemed at odds over
who was to blame: incompetent physicians or avaricious
lawyers. Testing the venality of lawyers would be difficult
(and comparing that to the avarice manifested by members
of other professional groups, impossible), so the question
chosen was: Why are people injured or killed in surgery?

Todd's point has a certain logic—if people were not injured or killed in surgery, there would be no malpractice cases. So who is to blame in cases of surgically related misadventure? But medicine is so broad (neurology, obstetrics, orthopedics, etc.) and surgery so large a category (dental, thoracic, abdominal, etc.) within medicine that a common element in all surgical specialties, like anesthetic administration, was needed to define a context for the literature search.

To search the general newspaper, popular magazine, and specialized medical literatures for information on the relation between anesthetic administration and cases of injury or death in surgery requires a search phrase that would narrow the broad subject (anesthetic administration) to specific problems (death or injury). Anesthetic administration involves, for example, use of and problems with specific drugs (like halothane), mechanical problems with respirators and other equipment, the complex of physician interaction with both mechanical and pharmacological components, and issues of standard operating-room procedure. A search could be defined to highlight any one of these areas individually, but the first search needed to be more general. Thus, the first phrase used in this search was written: "anesth/ and (death or injury)."

The phrase includes a series of logical operations designed to limit information to be returned and define its priorities. These Boolean search operatives include conjunctions, parentheses, and a slash (/) to target the search more effectively. Illustration 4.4 attempts to show graphically the general function of these specific search operatives. The slash is commonly called a "wild card" or, more technically, a "truncator." It instructs the computer to search for any word that begins with "anesth," whatever the word's suffix might be. Thus stories including, as a partial listing, anesthesia, anesthesiology, anesthesiologist, and anesthetic will all be recovered. Stories using the British spelling "anaesth/", will not, however, be brought forward, and those searching technical journals, newspapers, or newsletters that use British spelling would need to write their phrase: "(anaesth/ or anesth/) and (death or injury)."

The conjunction *and* instructs the computer to search for the first phrase (anesth/) only where it appears in a story

Illustration 4.4
Boolean Search Connectors

OR: Retrieves all the elements of the search term. Includes articles in which either or both phrases are included.

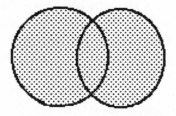

*anesth/ **or** (death or injury)*

AND: Retrieves only citations or articles that include the selected search phrases.

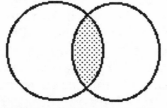

*anesth/ **and** (death or injury)*

NOT: Excludes one search term or group of terms from the primary phrase or phrases. This retrieves all articles including the word anesthesia, except where the words *death* or *injury* appear.

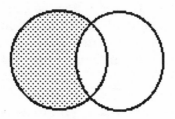

*anesth/ **not** (death or injury)*

in conjunction with the single word *death* or *injury*. Thus all stories involving anesthetics and anesthesia will not be brought up, only those in which the search includes accidents leading to death or injury. The parentheses further instruct the computer to join either "anaesth/" or "anesth/" with either death or injury. Were the phrase written "anesth/ and death or injury," the computer would retrieve all articles that contained either "anesth/" or "death," as well as all articles containing the word "injury," irrespective of its subject. In this case and without parentheses, "or" says get "anesth/ and death," as well as all stories with the word "injury." That instruction would result in the return of thousands of unwanted stories.

My first search used the phrase "anesth/ and court," in an attempt to find news stories about juried cases (from civil, criminal, and coroner's courts) involving anesthetic-related matters. Unfortunately, what was found instead was scores of basketball-related stories in which players were judged, by sports writers, to be anesthetized on the playing court. Even the search phrase "anesth/ and (death or injury)" brought forward a score of sports stories in which anesthetized players were dead on the court or in which those who played as if they were anesthetized were judged to have injured their team's chances in a game. These stories could be removed by including another line to the phrase directing the search to exclude either basketball or, more generally, sport or sports stories: "(anesth/ or anaesth) and (death or injury) not (/ball or sport)." Here "/ball" would remove all stories in which football, basketball, or baseball were included in the text.

There is, at present, no single, uniform search language recognized by all database services, a fact that complicates the life of any researcher who uses several different services. While at present all must use Boolean search indicators, each service has defined the truncators in a slightly different fashion. The truncation mark, for example, may be written as "/", "?", "!" or "*" (anesth/, anesth?, anesth!, or anesth*), depending on the service used. Some services, *Vu/Text*, for example, allow search phrases to include instructions defining the conjunction between search words. Thus one can limit a search on *Vu/Text* by including in the search phrase a symbol limiting retrieval to only those stories in which the phrase's first element ("anesth!") appears within either the same sentence ("/s") or the same paragraph ("/p") as the second phrase ("death or injury"): "anesth! /p (death or injury)."

Dow Jones New Retrieval Service provides a similar service but in a slightly different way. It allows for the search to insist that both elements of the phrase appear either adjacent to each other (but in any order, i.e., "anesth/ and death" or "death and anesth/") or separated by any specific number of words. Thus a search for "Data adj General" would retrieve any story in which either "data general" or "general data" appeared. "Data adj7 general," on the other hand, would retrieve those stories in which the two separate words appear in any order within seven words of each other, for example: "*Data* is often found to be a *general* topic of reporters" or "In *general*, police find the issue of legally admissible *data* to be an issue."

To make this procedure even more confusing, different data services allow the user to search different categories of information. Some data sources are only bibliographic, searching and retrieving no more than author, title, source, key word, and data of publication for the materials they have stored in digital form. This form is the electronic equivalent of bibliographic index cards traditional to most libraries in which one searches by author, title, or subject. Others may search only this information and an abstract filed with its journal article. Thus one searches both the headline or title, key words, and a one-paragraph abstract that is filed electronically. But if one wants to read the whole article, one must then go to the library and look it up by conventional means. Finally, some databases—*Vu/Text* is one—include the whole text of articles online and allow the writer to search the entire database for the search phrase's conjunction.

This diversity of search languages and retrieval methods is a result of the newness of these services. At the beginning of the printing revolution, as increasingly large numbers of printed materials needed to be effectively catalogued, techniques for indexing and shelving books varied library by library and, sometimes, librarian by librarian.

Each worked according to general principles but sometimes different rules which were, in the United States, finally standardized by the Dewey decimal system. Digital information storage has evolved to the degree that, even where different symbols are used, the search characteristics are similar. Boolean truncations, use of the conjunctions *and*, *or*, and *not* in phrases, and general organizational principles are rapidly being standardized. Further, current explorations of new data techniques may, in the coming generation of online data facilities, allow for common language searches in which Boolean phrasing is no longer necessary.[30] Just as, on the science fiction television show *Star Trek*, the science officer, Mr. Spock, cavalierly asks the computer "for information on sentient, humanoid life forms in Star System Beta Seven," data researchers will be able to ask their computer "for stories on financial mismanagement and medical problems in the Veterans' Administration hospital system." As Chapter 5 attempts to demonstrate, there are already a variety of data vendors with increasingly simple databases whose programs emphasize ease of use for the amateur researcher.

SOURCES

The traditional librarian's "fact"-oriented model assumes that a single datum is required by the reporter and further assumes that, in the majority of cases, it will be found in a very narrow range of sources. These include specific compendiums of data (the encyclopedia, almanac, state data books) and the files of past stories published by the newspaper or magazine. To the extent that the data are isolated and discrete, they provide no necessary links to larger structural or contextual issues, and they are trivial or ephemeral. "Facts," as we have seen, take on meaning only in a broader context, and their validity can be determined only when the information's source and quality have some impartial judge. Defining that broader perspective is made difficult, it has been argued, because of the very nature of print data storage techniques (news library files, library shelves, the broad categories of card catalogues), as well as because of the reliance by news clips on oral information that is typically presented at the level of the formalized, journalistic event. At best these are "weak facts," at best true within their own context but, without external context, anything but objective or unbiased. I do not suggest that those traces of past journalistic events are useless but, rather, that the limits of the news morgue must be recognized and placed in perspective.

The searching of the files of any single newspaper, journal, magazine, or newsletter to the exclusion of other sources will yield specific data that, if essentially a compendium of ephemeral reports, may suggest patterns and issues. In theory, journalists have always checked "the clips" in their search for information. What is suggested here is that examination of a newspaper's past stories, typically the traditional journalist's primary research method, is only a first step in which general patterns may be revealed and from which a hypothesis can then be fashioned. Consider the following example. In 1987 an Abbotsford, B.C., adolescent, Marvin Loewen, died during dental surgery in a local clinic.[31] Following this death, the local coroner announced an inquest into Loewen's death would be held. A search of the shared library of the two local newspapers, the *Province* and the *Sun*, recovered a series of stories describing prior inquests into deaths resulting from both general and dental surgery. In many of them, an anesthestic was described as a critical element leading to the death, and most inquest juries criticized the failure of the dentist or operating physician to be prepared for emergencies. This material was suggestive but not conclusive. In eight years there had been at least ten inquests resulting from surgical misadventure, and in all of them anesthetic was a contributing or primary factor. To see if this pattern of B.C. deaths was exceptional, a reporter could then search regional newspapers in other jurisdictions (Toronto, Los Angeles, Boston, etc.). As case piled upon case, patterns in all of these stories would emerge. Time after time, death was attributed to anesthetic overdoses, failure to monitor equipment that delivered anesthesia, and equipment failure.

Because most U.S. newspapers report on court and not simply inquest cases, news copy often includes assignment of blame and an assessment of monetary damages against the physicians and dentists. These stories thus reflect a social definition of precisely who is responsible in medical misadventure and the degree of that responsibility, calculated in dollars. Coroner inquests in B.C., on the other hand, are public forums and prohibited by statute from assigning blame or assessing damages. So a search for court stories in newspapers—"anesth/ and (death and injury) and (jury or court) not /ball" would be useful. Because U.S. court cases are themselves stored electronically, those with access to an electronic database of U.S. court records (like *WestLaw*) could search there as well.

One could, of course, first do a general search of all court jurisdictions, but the newspaper search would generate case names, which can themselves more precisely and economically be accessed in the electronic court record system. Thus in the 1980s the *Los Angeles Times* reported on a number of anesthetic-related cases, including those in which a dentist was convicted of murder after injuring over thirteen patients in separate anesthetic-related incidents. His conviction was appealed and upheld at several levels, and, at each step in the legal proceeding, the court (jury and judges) made clear that legal and professional standards required physicians to adhere to specific standards of drug administration and patient monitoring, which were not followed by this doctor.

Both legal and news searches focus all deaths on physician actions: proper monitoring, properly maintained equipment, administration of appropriate levels of anesthetic drug. A judicious search of the medical and biomedical literature on a specialized national database (*Medline*) returns, then, a series of articles on anesthetic mishap in which physicians themselves acknowledge that a large percentage of surgical deaths or injuries result from failure by members of their profession to follow approved standards of patient monitoring and use of appropriate monitoring equipment in the operating theater (hospital or dental clinic).

Thematic Sources

The progression is clear. One moved in this case from the local newspaper to regional or national newspapers as

indicators of recurring events. The vehicle for this explora-
tion was a search phrase whose crafting created a context
(death and injury) through which a specific action (administration of anesthetic) could best be understood. Court records
and the technical literature laid bare the broad context of
social and scientific judgment against which individual
statements (conflicted at the institutional, instrumental,
and functional levels) by boundary-event actors could be
evaluated. The result was an ability to weigh the denials of
boundary-event participants ("I didn't screw up") against
the combined voice of the published medical professor and
amateur writer. The reporter can write with authority on
the basis of this type of information that, in effect, "If Dr. N
didn't do x, y, and z, then everyone—judges, juries, medical
researchers, and his professional colleagues—agrees he was
at fault."

All this wealth of information from a variety of sources
can be brought to bear on a subject as narrow as an individual inquest in which the physician says blandly, "It was
just a one-in-a-million freak death" or on a subject as broad
and complex as tort reform and the social cost of contemporary medicine. The whole story begins with and ends with
the narrowly defined newspaper report but extends the
concept of its information base from the unexamined oral
statement to the written resources of legal, medical, and
official authorities across North America and around the
world.

Interview and Evaluation

This material in itself can be used as research for a story
but, more frequently, it arms reporters or editors with data
that allows them to challenge directly, on the basis of comparable information, the official, the expert, or the academic. This possibility was made clear in the EAF search in
which reports retrieved from the electronic database on
new Environmental Protection Agency regulations directed
the research to branch officials in Hawaii. Freed from an
absolute reliance on a response from Hawaii Steel officials
(who refused comment), I could intelligently phrase issues
of toxicity of the hazardous waste, and the relation between

the new regulations and the Hawaiian company's change to a Canadian reclaiming site. Later questions by BCTV to Cominco, Ltd., were similarly informed. In these cases, interviews become the forum by which general information is focused on the specific case, and evaluation is a matter of placing the local or regional event within the broader context of professional standards or environmental concerns.

In the Loewen case, in which both dentist and anesthesiologist insisted they lacked any responsibility in a teenager's death, a reporter armed with electronic research could have questioned the status of the respirator prior to surgery (there were, in fact, holes in its bellows), preparedness for emergencies (the defibrillator was broken), and degree of patient monitoring during surgery (minimal, by standards described in the literature). As testimony on these points was given, the newswriter would know its significance and be able to relate it to other cases, trends, and patterns. Further, when specific issues were raised in the court, the reporter would know precisely where and how to obtain information on the issue and test, in the literature, its relation to the boundary events. At the Loewen inquest, for example, the anesthesiologist suggested under oath that the teenager's death might have resulted from "carotid sinusitis syndrome," a complication so rare that a search of medical databases found no examples whatsoever resulting from procedures like the one performed on Loewen. Thus at each step the data returned provides a context in which to weigh the evidence, a means by which the oral fact is weighed against past incidence and research traditionally stored in written form but, until now, inaccessible to the public information writer.

Who Controls the Search?

In the late 1980s, the presence of electronic information retrieval systems has grown at U.S. newspapers and magazines, although its use is usually restricted to news librarians or, less frequently, editors who accept questions from reporters, phrase the search appropriately, and access databases on the writer's behalf.[32] The issues seem to be education and cost. Librarians are trained in general and specific means of research, are familiar with Boolean search languages, and, as traditional custodians of resource materials, are believed to be the logical members of a publication staff to access these new resources. And if, as some believe, electronic retrieval resources are simply more efficient incarnations of traditional resources, then it is appropriate that traditional overseers of information should be in charge. On other newspapers, specific editors are charged with supervision of database use. The rationale seems to be the presumed ability of editors to assure that these potentially expensive resources are not abused (e.g., should a staffer wish to find information to assist a child in a school project) and of the perceived difficulty of using online resources. Ward and Hansen noted the importance of the territorial issues raised by these technologies when they wrote that: "Budgeting for database services, controlling costs for online searching and assigning either librarians or reporters the chief responsibility for such searches are among the practical issues now arising."[33]

Complaints by librarians charged with the guardianship of electronic resources focused, in their study, on the failure of reporters to appropriately frame search parameters and on their desire to use the database resources in new and complex ways. Librarians both resent, in general, this incursion upon their research role and worry that the costs, usually assigned to their budget, will be excessive and without sufficient results to justify the expense. As Fredric Endres noted in 1985: "They [news librarians in charge of databases] complained that reporters were not specific enough in their request for information or that some reporters had become so reliant on the databases that they would not begin to write a story without asking for a thorough database check. Again, the librarians thought this was a waste of time, effort and money."[34]

It is necessary to recognize that the role of the news librarian has traditionally been ill-defined. Although trained in a broad range of information storage and retrieval skills, the primary tasks of news librarians have been menial ones. Their job has been limited, in the main, to clipping and filing stories that appeared in a specific periodical or journal, and then assisting the newswriter in retrieving information and answering questions based on file information. But Hansen and Ward found that 63 percent of the reporters interviewed prefer to search and evaluate traditional files themselves rather than ask for a librarian's assistance. And yet, at many newspapers today, reporters are not allowed into the physical library but must request all files (and, if there is an electronic database facility, all searches) from the librarians.

Librarians, in turn, expect the reporter to know what electronic resource is to be searched just as, previously, they expected reporters to be able to define the "fact" they were concerned with ("I want the Loewen file." as opposed to "I'm looking for a pattern of deaths related to administration of various anesthetics."). But without online experience and without sufficient training to understand the database or databases that a specific publication's library may have, reporters are unlikely to be able to frame their requests with sufficient specificity or know where that information is located in the electronic world. Finally, the focus of database searches is not on the isolated "fact" but on the context of a prior event. It is a hypothesis, with which neither public information librarians nor newswriters in general have a great deal of experience.

It is the very nature of these electronic libraries that reporters must formulate their own search phrases. This skill will become as much a part of the newswriter's repertoire as typing is today and shorthand was a generation or two ago.[35] To the degree that these are new resources whose effect on the news is only beginning to be felt, one must have sympathy for librarians used to "factual" queries who are now faced with reporters whose vague questions and inclination to use electronic resources extensively might, indeed, seem like a waste of time. Because the story is no longer necessarily tied to the level of the journalistic event, questions addressed to library resources may indeed be far broader than the traditional search for a single datum— statistic, fact, or prior story. To the extent that stories are defined by the content they carry, data defined by the information newspeople bring to an event or interview, reporters or researchers will, increasingly, have to gain control of their electronic resources.

Growing acceptance and use of these electronic libraries will, of necessity, change relations between public information writers and the librarians who serve them. The librarian's primary, traditional function—to catalogue, store, and direct the user to potentially important files—will remain. The emphasis, however, increasingly will be on the last function, that of information directors and consultants, and not on the menial chores demanded by the maintenance of physical files. In addition, to the extent that librarians are gatekeepers of the electronic libraries, they will need to be more directly involved in the creation of a story, more aware of the relation among general information, a specific boundary event, and the means through which theories are generated and tested in the literature.

The position of librarian—the very idea of the job—was an outgrowth of the printing revolution, a result of the need for specialists who could catalogue and direct the storage of volumes of information. That role will change as electronic storage takes precedence over physical collection and data are stored not in discrete volumes but as individual bits of information connected to others in the digital soup. As this happens, the position of the news librarian will become a supervisory, editorial role and the job of story research will become a part of the whole training process for public information writers. Just as young lawyers and law clerks do research for senior partners and judges, so may young reporters eventually have, as a first assignment, the research chores of their professional seniors. But just as law clerks cannot necessarily judge the importance of a specific case, and a medical librarian cannot be sure when a seemingly ephemeral article on retro-viruses holds the crucial bit of information for a researcher, so, too, the secondary researcher or librarian cannot necessarily judge, in this context, the reporter's exact information needs on any specific story. In news as in other fields, research will become an increasingly critical part of the reporter's technique, and news librarians ever more necessary and sophisticated partners in the story process.

Current confusions and tensions between news librarians, writers, and editors are transition problems, part of the tug and pull that typically occurs when a new technology begins to replace an older, more traditional and socially entrenched system. Costs of system use are decreasing, in large part as a result of new technologies (like CD-ROM storage disks) and in part through sheer economies of scale. Large, frequently accessed systems are cheaper to use. If the thesis that pervades this book is correct and the technology is to become the primary means of accessing public information, then not only will the role of the public information writer change in the process, but the task of librarian in general will be simultaneously transformed.

A LEGAL PARADIGM

What a well-crafted search phrase does, at least in theory, is inform reporters about the characteristics of a boundary occurrence and provide them with information at least comparable to that of the speaker at a press conference or other journalistic event. The search phrase places those prior occurrences in a context of previously published academic, judicial, and periodical statements that, together, allow the newsperson to evaluate the statements of official actors on the basis of prior, printed research and previously recorded statements.

The idea that a specific current affair must be consciously and perhaps self-consciously considered as a member of some broader class of recurring event is not new, although it may be relatively new to newswriters and editors. The U.S. legal system, for example, is based on a series of past judgments—legal precedents, officially promulgated regulations, legislation, the Constitution—that are the a priori context in which any current issue or event must be considered. The legal model presents an example of a system in which contemporary and often newsworthy events are framed through historical context and their relation to established social principles. Whether they search electronically or manually, first-year law students are taught in research courses "to appraise the relevant issues factually, recognize and weigh the following factors":

T-Thing or subject matter
A-Cause of Action or ground of defense
R-Relief sought
P-Persons or parties involved[36]

"Thing" refers, simply, to place or property as a significant element in the problem or issue being considered. In the ELF example, this was the electric arc furnace dust. Defining the "thing," as the anesthetic examples suggested, is the task of the search phrase and a crucial element in defining the context of the event.

"Cause of action" focuses the issues of a problem. In law, the cause may be a breach of contract, negligence, or some other claim. For newspeople, it is the structure or context that frames the whole. EPA regulations in the ELF story and medical standards for anesthetic administration in the case of tort reform were the contextual "cause" within which the "thing" or "event" was framed.

"Relief" sought in law refers to what the plaintiff may be asking for: damages, an injunction, compensation for loss of consortium, and so on. In the context of the news, it describes what the individual actors want out of the story, the frame that defines the prejudices of the subjects being interviewed. Todd, for example, wanted lower malpractice insurance rates for his organization's members. Habash wanted, for his constituency, the ability to seek high awards for their clients (which results, in contingency cases, in larger fees for the lawyer). The concept of relief allows reporters, in their evaluation of the data, to see the subject not as an unbiased information source but rather as a biased participant in the events on which the subject is speaking. Tort reform is the result of cases of alleged medical malpractice. Lawyers and physicians have vested interests in the outcome of the legislative debate. Physicians testifying in trials or coroner inquests do not want to be labeled as incompetent or ineffectual, and the relief they seek is from adverse publicity. Ideally, the database's information allows the reporter to put the subject's needs and prejudices within the wider context of impartial information and thus to judge the subject's statements accurately.

"Persons or parties involved" is not always immediately clear. In the ELF story the active and crucial role played by the EPA, which drafted new regulations in 1988, was hidden until the database turned up the changes. And yet the whole story hung on the EPA, its regulations and those who enforce them. Problems in identifying the crucial parties involved in a story—or the bias of known participants—are common in news writing wherever actors involved in an event may, for one or another reason, choose to hide their role. But there is almost always a paper trail—a document, statement, or illuminating article that is accessible to the researcher. Habash made good use of this when he quoted Todd's statements, made in an earlier context, in which the doctor blamed fellow physicians for acts of malpractice. As a lawyer, Habash understood very well that officials will take positions that may be at variance with their private views and that a good lawyer looks for the trace of that real position in previous quotes and articles. For Habash, Todd's involvement became twofold—as a physician and as a representative of his association—and Todd's views in both roles, separated by time as well as title, were not identical. The search phrase uncovers not only hidden agendas and broad context but defines the actors in terms not only of their immediate statements and postures but of their previous statements as well.

The legal research paradigm thus places any single event into a complex context with potentially broad social and historical boundaries while making over, within that context, the positions and personal interests of actors in the event. Someone is seeking "relief " or demanding "restitution" because of injuries suffered in the past. That desire is based on the argument of improper performance, failure to adhere to established guidelines, or violation of accepted statutes that define the society's notion of responsibility and establish a system in which blame can be assessed, violators identified, and damage calculated. Enforcement of a regulation, legal restriction, or prior court decision is sought in a current context. If a building collapses, what is important is not simply the testimony of its owners or

Illustration 4.5
Law Model: Sources

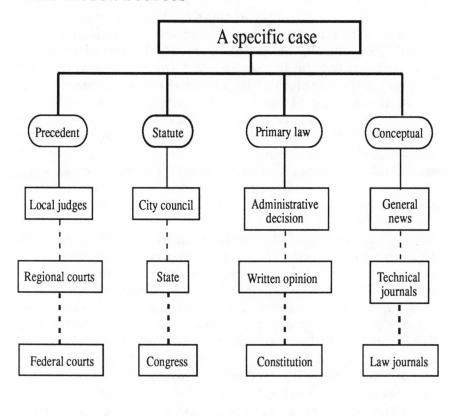

scale: Local to federal jurisdictions

builders (who may well deny all responsibility), not just what happened, but what happened within the context of the antecedent causes of that collapse and the responsibility for the structure's failure. The legal paradigm is thus a matter of matching what happened recently with what has happened before in a context in which responsibility was clearly assigned and assessed. It interprets present events in the light of past occurrences and official statements in the context of precedent, regulation, and published analysis.

Illustration 4.5 describes in graphic form the range of sources traditionally used by lawyers and legal researchers in placing a single case within the broader history of prior events and legal precedent. Like the earlier news-based Illustration 3.1, this diagram incorporates levels of geographic scale and general information. Whether one searches for precedents at the circuit, district, or supreme court levels, for example, or pursues information at the level of city, state, or federal legislation, the appropriate source will depend on the problem at hand and the precedents needed. These three general levels—local, regional, and federal— roughly correspond with the story levels defined in an earlier chapter: the ephemeral, isolated story; the structural story based on multiple cases from a wider geographic region; and the contextual story itself. The contextual story incorporates national, regional, and local information in an attempt to define the broader social context of regionally replicated events.

This issue of scale is emphasized in the U.S. legal paradigm in which primary law, those principles empowered by the Constitution, takes precedence over administrative decision (EPA regulations), legal opinion, and local court decisions. Federal law supersedes state laws which, in turn, are the context in which city and county laws are written. Using the range of available databases provides the public information writer with a similar scale of experts, authorities, and officials from all jurisdictional levels whose intelligence and weight can be brought to bear on a specific local event.

Thus reporters made aware of these levels through their use of regional and national databases can focus their queries not simply on a boundary event's participants (Dr. X, Police Chief Y) but on those who, at other information levels, are quoted as authorities on a topic or as having general responsibility in a broad legislative or legal or professional area. The degree to which information from a greater geographic scale illuminates events at the regional scale was made clear in the discussion of the CBC story on the incidence of childhood leukemia in Kamloops. There, a huge body of evidence bearing on what local officials had to say existed internationally. Its employment placed in question the official assurances, published and broadcast in the news, that no systemic or structural problem existed. "Relief," here, is defined by the broader context and not by the local statement.

The "conceptual" category describes the appropriate use, in law, of "expert opinion" by legal or other professionals concerned with and knowledgeable of the issues under dispute. Thus Todd might be called (or Habash) to give expert testimony to a legislature on the issue of tort reform or his articles may be read into the record by legislators supporting his organization's position. Those "conceptual" articles (the *Smithsonian*'s review of building collapse is one example) provide for the public information writer not only background information (the names of authorities, general chronologies of past events, generalized information) but an umbrella of theory and the general thesis of responsibility and cause, which must then be localized and applied.

Thus online electronic resources provide the public information writer with an enormous range of information at various geographic levels of occurrence. The writer has recourse to information in legal, legislative, and technical fields written at the local, regional, national, and now international levels. Court decisions, newspaper stories, magazine articles, and the work of amateur experts writing in everything from *Aviation Week* and *Space Technology* to the *Zoological Record* can be obtained with incredible specificity through the properly defined search phrase. This wealth of information brought to bear on a single boundary event creates, for almost any story, a context in which the individual occurrence is revealed as one of a recurring class, events, of legal and social decisions, for which exist impartial and expert opinion. This context makes of the statements of experts or officials in court, press conference, or press release—whatever their title and power—no more than a single voice whose own agenda and personal or professional interests can be questioned as critically as the information they present.

Other areas like law and science have functioned in this way for years, and it is no great surprise that they have been quicker to adapt to the potential of online libraries and information storage systems. News will function increasingly in this way, as electronic information sources gain greater and greater acceptance. In the 1920s, Walter Lippmann said that the books and papers were on the desks not of his fellow journalists but of the officials. That statement is no longer necessarily true, and it is this change that is revolutionary.

In the first chapter's review of coverage of the Stuart murder case, *Newsweek*'s criticism of the *Boston Globe*'s failure to report on the murder case with a sense of skepticism was mentioned in passing. There was a holier-than-thou sense about the weekly magazine's evaluation of the daily newspaper's coverage of an event that both had written about so extensively, especially since *Newsweek*'s coverage in late 1989 had not evidenced the "skepticism" it insisted the daily needed to apply. In general, one can say with authority that skepticism, like the instrumental goal of objectivity, cannot be realized until or unless the single boundary event (and its actors) is examined within a broader context of prior occurrence. It cannot happen when the primary function of daily or weekly news is the promulgation of oral information. There is no doubt that in Boston most information in the Stuart case was oral—including that of *Newsweek*'s coverage. Examples of electronically generated news presented in Chapters 2 and 3 attempted to demonstrate the degree to which operational skepticism and journalistic objectivity develop out of both contextual research to news events and the perspective that comes from using bibliographic materials to write daily or weekly news.

At least in theory, it is the function of the law to redress injustices and to place the immediate boundary event within a social context of legal precedent and social knowledge. Since these functions are similar to the institutional goals of the public information writer, it is not surprising that a paradigm of use to one profession may, with modification, be of use to the other. But lawyers have clients and, instrumentally, it is those individuals they are hired to serve. Representatives of the Fourth Estate have, in theory, no single client but rather serve a more general function in which full disclosure is seen as a social good in and of itself. Newswriters and editors do have agendas, however—both as individuals and as members of large, information-based corporations. The potential for progressive freedom from absolute dependence on the official press conference and statement will place in sharper relief the economic and social filters that also influence the news. Historical evidence suggests that the new technology will affect these filters, but the degree to which this effect will allow newswriters to approximate their institutional goals is, at present, uncertain. No writer of Samuel Johnson's day could have accurately predicted the degree to which changes in printing technology would affect society's information base, in great part because those changes occurred within a much broader social and economic transformation. No writer in the late twentieth century can fail to acknowledge, in the description of modern technologies, that the result of their acceptance will likewise be dependent on broader sociopolitical changes in the society about which he or she writes.

Access to electronic information sources is based on a logic whose result is the search phrase. But even the best-crafted search language will be of little use (and its generating hypothesis of little value) without a field of data on which to impose it. The utilization of these new resources is ultimately dependent on the organization and availability of information in a digitalized form. Since information from all these sources is now digitalized, reporters are free to draw from identical areas of data in their work. Local newspaper clips are not the only source. Regional and national newspapers are equally accessible. Decisions by courts—from the U.S. Supreme Court to the Ninth District Circuit Court—are equally accessible, as is a range of general interest and specialized journals. Where this information is stored and how it can be most effectively accessed are the next issues that must be considered in this analysis of the potential effect of electronic databases on public information in general and the news in particular.

NOTES

1. A distinction should be made between McLuhan's clearly academic treatment of the printing revolution and his more messianic work promising the imminent arrival of a "global village" because of improved technologies of au-

diovisual transmission. Thus *The Gutenberg Galaxy* (Toronto: University of Toronto Press, 1962) stands as a substantial, if perhaps dated, contribution to our understanding of the printing revolution. Later work, based on the distinction between "hot" and "cold" characteristics of specific media seems, in retrospect, to be of little substance. The complexity of any single medium and its relation to modes of production, information source, socioeconomic conditions, and historical imperatives were largely ignored in, for example, *Understanding Media: The Extensions of Man* (New York: McGraw Hill, 1964). For a review of the attention and interest his theories generated in the 1960s, see Harry H. Crosby and George R. Bond, *The McLuhan Explosion: A Casebook on Marshall McLuhan and Understanding Media* (New York: American Book Co., 1968).

2. Again, I rely on the work of Alvin Kernan, *Printing Technology, Letters and Samuel Johnson* (Princeton: Princeton University Press, 1987), 153. Kernan is used here not only as a writer on Johnson or on technology but as a historian who concentrated a wide body of previous research into a single, tightly focused study.

3. McLuhan, *Understanding Media*, 7. Quoted in J. Herbert Altschull, *From Milton to McLuhan: The Ideas Behind American Journalism* (White Plains, N.Y.: Longman, 1990), 334.

4. Kernan, *Printing Technology,* 153.

5. *I.F. Stone's Weekly* would be an example of this type of limited circulation, but extremely important newsletter. *Defense Weekly*, published in Washington, D.C., which reports on the Pentagon and military efforts in general, might be another example. The *Wall Street Journal*, a legacy of the nineteenth-century commercial newspaper tradition, is attempting to become a general public newspaper but, until recently, could have been considered a part of this news class.

6. In this category I would include as examples *The Nation, Commentary, Harper's*, and the *New Yorker*.

7. This model is based on a "Search Strategy for Library Use," Columbus: Ohio State University [OSU] Libraries, Office of Library User Education, 1988. The flow chart has

been modified to reflect a more general search methodology. OSU's model emphasizes the central place of the university's electronic card catalogue system. The location of references in a card catalogue—electronic or print—to journals or books in any single library is, for our purposes, irrelevant.

8. Jean Ward and Kathleen A. Hansen, "Commentary: Information Age Methods in a New Reporting Model," *Newspaper Research Journal* 7:3 (Spring 1986), 54. Interestingly, the literature on specialized search methodologies relating to computerized information systems in general and news use of such libraries in particular is relatively meager.

9. In Hawaii, for example, this would include the official *State of Hawaii Data Book* (Honolulu: Department of Business and Economic Development, 1988).

10. Cathleen Hunt Baird, "Computerized Libraries Aid Newsrooms," *Presstime* 11:12 (December 1989), 28.

11. Ward and Hansen "Commentary," 719.

12. The distinction between informal and institutional information sources is taken from Ward and Hansen, "Commentary," 56.

13. Tim Miller, "The Data-Base Revolution," *Columbia Journalism Review* 26:3 (September/October 1988), 36.

14. Miller, "Data-Base Revolution."

15. Andrew Ippolito, "Databases in Newspaper Libraries," *Editor and Publisher* 118:19 (May 11, 1985), 60e.

16. Tom McNichol, "Databases, Reeling in Scoops with High Tech," *Washington Journalism Review* 9:6 (July 1987), 29. At this early stage of development, the result is that online resources tend to be larger, richer, more established newspapers and not alternative or radical periodicals. Vu/Text is a division of Knight Ridder, a publishing company whose newspapers, not surprisingly, are well represented on the system.

17. There is in this category, for example, *Data Times,* a computer library of regional business publications, and *Magazine ASAP*, which provides the full text of several hundred contemporary publications. The organization and use of these resources are discussed in the next chapter.

18. Mark S. Leff, "Phoning for Facts Doesn't Have to Mean Dialing for Dollars,"*Quill* 78:2 (March 1990), 38. The story includes a list of electronic bulletin boards accessible by members of the press.

19. Steve Nevas, "Coming Soon to a Screen Near You: The U.S. Supreme Court," *Quill* 78:2 (March 1990), 24.

20. Alfred Glossbrenner, *How to Look It Up Online* (New York: St. Martin's Press, 1987). An excellent, almost encyclopedic book on online resources and what each vendor offers.

21. Cathryn Conroy, "This Is Not Your Father's Encyclopedia," *CompuServe Magazine* 9:1 (January 1990), 56.

22. See, for example, the editor who suggested database technologies would be a bothersome luxury because "We get more information now than we know what to do with." Fredric F. Endres, "Daily Newspaper Utilization of Computer Data Bases," *Newspaper Research Journal* 9:1 (Fall 1985), 29.

23. Tim Miller, "Information, Please and *Fast*: Reporting's Revolution: Data Bases," *Washington Journalism Review* 5:7 (September 1983), 53.

24. "Electric Furnace Dust Is Still a Problem," *American Metal Market,* September 19, 1988, 15a.

25. "US Turns Screw on Hazmat," *Chemical Marketing Reporter,* August 15, 1988, 749.

26. See discussion of these filings in the next chapter.

27. The *New York Times* and the *Wall Street Journal* were searched on *Dow Jones News Retrieval* at a connect time of $24 an hour. The searches took approximately five minutes. Metallurgical databases took place through CompuServe's *IQuest*, which charges a connect time of $12.50 an hour and a flat search fee of $9 per search. That search took approximately twelve minutes with one $9 charge.

28. Raul Ramirez is currently metro editor at the *San Francisco Examiner*, formerly headed up an investigative team for the newspaper, teaches journalism at Berkeley, and has been for a number of years a member of the Center for Investigative Reporting. We met while Gannett Fellows at the University of Hawaii in 1981-82. Raul Ramirez, telephone conversation, May 6, 1990.

29. Tim Miller, "Information, Please," 53.

30. In 1989, Dow Jones News Retrieval introduced *Dow-Quest*, a computer information system that searches, through "plain English search commands," 175 publications stored online. Thus a search for information on "impact of health consciousness on fast-food menus" can be written exactly like that, rather than as "health /s conscious/ and (fast food)." See Donald B. Trivette, "What's Different about DowQuest?," *Dowline* (Summer, 1989), 20-26.

31. This case is exhaustively examined, its electronic search described, and the results for news and public information detailed in Tom Koch, *The News as Myth: Fact and Context in Journalism* (Westport, Conn.: Greenwood Press, 1990) 123-43.

32. Endres, "Daily Newpaper," 33.

33. Ward and Hansen, "Commentary," 51.

34. Ward and Hansen, "Commentary," 51.

35. I am informed by British colleagues that reporters trained in Great Britain have traditionally been required to demonstrate an expertise in both typing and shorthand before working on Fleet Street. Shorthand has been, lamentably, a less ubiquitous skill among North American newspeople.

36. Myron J. Jacobstein, *Legal Research Illustrated* (Mineola, N.Y.: Foundation Press, 1987), 9.

5

Electronic Libraries:
Files, Vendors, and Databases

To understand fully the practical potential of online information, one must consider the organization and retrieval system of these electronic libraries. It is not enough simply to urge the use of appropriate search phrases because each phrase must be applied to one or another storage archive. Just as it is of little use to know that a book or article is germane if it cannot be retrieved from a traditional library, so, too, must each search phrase be applied to a specific section of the electronic library, from which it can be "downloaded" and later read. Here, unfortunately, is a problem because there is at present little consistency among the multitude of databases currently available online. The enormous volume of data now stored in digital form and the unique problems this system of organization and retrieval presents have given rise to a whole range of somewhat different solutions to the bibliographic problems that this new technology has created. In 1990, for example, there were over four thousand different databases available online and more were being added, virtually month by month, to the digitalized reference system.

Most of those databases are not accessed directly but, rather, through distributors—Dialog, Lexis, Dow Jones, and CompuServe are the best known—that package and offer a series of electronic information services to their clients.

None offers the complete range of stored online information (the most any one service may carry is perhaps one-third of the total number of databases stored digitally at any one time), and each uses a slightly different search language and system of user retrieval in its operation. Some databases offer the full text of articles while others supply only the bibliographic information (called the "bibcite") required to locate an article or book in conventional libraries; some of the former allow the user to search the whole, digitally stored article while other databases or vendor systems can be searched only through key words stored online with the article; in the case of newspapers, some systems will apply search phrases to the whole of a digitally stored article, which can then be retrieved in full, while others search and can retrieve only a story's headline, date, and page location. Further, there is an astounding redundancy within this disarray. A few critical databases are offered online by all major vendors, while some specialized vendors simultaneously offer the same information in several different databases. Thus *Medline*,[1] a major medical database published by the U.S. National Library of Medicine, catalogues and permits retrieval of references to individual articles published in 3,070 different journals. But the database *Medline* is itself composed of three separate databases—*Index Medicus, International Nursing [Literature] Index*, and the *Index to Dental Literature*. Each of these is, in turn, carried individually by some, but not all, data vendors that offer *Medline* as an online resource. To complicate matters further, some of the individual journals that appear in these databases, and thus in *Medline*, are themselves indexed on large data services. Thus one can search for information on *Medline* as a whole, its component databases like *Index Medicus*, or the electronic files of digitally stored, individual journals like the *New England Journal of Medicine* or Britain's *Lancet*.[2] Further, much of the information that can be retrieved from *Medline* is duplicated in the electronic files of *Excerpta Medica*, catalogued in Amsterdam, Holland, which abstracts 3,500 separate journals dealing with medicine and biological sciences.

To increase the confusion (and the specificity), this biomedical material is also catalogued and retrievable by general topic through specialized, subject-oriented databases like *Biosis, Ageline*, or *CancerLit*,[3] which individually pull from the general medical, pharmacological, and medical engineering literature information on, respectively, bioengineering, gerontology, and cancer. Finally, specialized vendors have cropped up to facilitate access to all this literature, wherever it is stored, through simplified access language systems that dedicated users can subscribe to alone. Thus physicians may choose to access the available medical literature neither through *Excerpta Medica* nor directly from *Medline* but, rather, through PaperChase,[4] a service designed to facilitate online research by medical personnel unfamiliar with the use of other, more general data suppliers.

At the beginning of the printing revolution, when cataloguing was a new science and the idea of the right of public information was a new concept, similar inconsistencies existed. The very idea of the consistent, logically ordered array of knowledge that the encyclopedia presented was a radical attempt during the Enlightenment, not only to catalogue information as it poured in, but to organize that information in a systematic and uniform fashion. Ordering of texts concerned with biological science, for example, occurred only as that science grew and the varying categories that librarians may recognize today (pharmacology, zoology, internal medicine, genetics, etc.) were needed to systematize and store what was once a single, simple grouping of materials on "natural science."

Electronic databases, which began as a more cost-effective means to store certain types of static data—court records, government records, scientific records, and business company data—have matured to cover interactively a range of technical, scientific, and governmental literatures. The technology for digitalized mass storage is barely a generation old, and today's means of access—the personal computer coupled with a modem—has been readily accessible to most users for at most only a decade. That the consistency and efficiency that typically result from maturity in an industry have not occurred in so short a time is not, perhaps, surprising.

There are at present some indications that even newer technologies may eliminate some of the worst problems of redundancy and facilitate a universal search language across varying storage systems. CD-ROM storage technology, for example, makes it possible for individuals to access enormous bodies of information (like a year's records from *Index Medicus*) at home and at their leisure. Advances in fiber optics technology are creating systems that will increase both the amount of information that can be carried by any one data line and the speed of its transmission between host and home computers. The linking of serial computers to simultaneously search large databases with simpler search phrases is a technical advance so new at the time of this writing that its potential effect cannot yet be evaluated.[5] The history of technological innovation suggests that, as the industry matures, redundancies will decrease and ease of use will increase. But in an industry barely a decade old, what is needed today is an understanding of the data storage system's general organization and its viability for general researchers at present.

The contemporary anarchy of storage retrieval systems and search languages is, strangely, a boon to the writer or researcher seeking inexpensive access to complex electronic databases. A general understanding of both the storage systems currently in use and of the very redundancy which seems so inefficient allows one to find the least expensive but most comprehensive source for any single information bit. It is the purpose of this chapter to describe current storage systems of digitalized information and to suggest ways in which search phrases can be applied to varying, easily available systems in an inexpensive and yet cost-effective manner.

VOCABULARY

To make sense of this situation, one needs to adopt a specific vocabulary. Because there is as yet no single accepted lexicon describing the interlocking hierarchy composed of specific files, at one level, and large digital service companies at the other, the following descriptors will be used in this book:

- *File:* A single article, bibliographic citation, or abstract retrieved from an electronic search.

- *Database:* A single collection of articles or citations stored by one company, which may or may not be the vendor. Thus newspaper articles are stored on the *Vu/Text* database, medical files may be stored on *Medline* or *CancerLit*, etcetera.

- *Supplier:* Companies that make one or more databases available by providing the combination of telephone lines and electronic technology necessary for the accessing of digitally stored databases. PaperChase supplies the database *Medline*, for example. Vu/Text is both creator and supplier of the *Vu/Text* database, which may also be accessed through other vendors.

- *Packager:* Some suppliers, Vu/Text, for example, package and sell their own database product. These are the equivalent of specialty retailers in the general commercial world. Other companies, like Dialog or BRS, package and sell a number of databases created by individual suppliers. Most users access the electronic library at the level of the packager.

- *Gateway distributors:* Vendors that make available the services of one or more packagers on a one-time, fee-for-use basis.

- *Wholesale Distributors:* General service distributors that offer a variety of services, including "gateways," in a general service system. CompuServe is perhaps the best example.

To see how this works, consider the results of the online search that obtained citations and information on articles by David Pearson which appeared in *The Nation* about the destruction of Korean Airlines Flight 007 by a Russian military fighter in 1983.

> *Heading #1*
> TI: K.A.L. *007;* questions that won't go away. (Korean Air Lines jet shot down in Soviet air space).
> AU: *Pearson-David.*
> SO: The *Nation* (NATNB), volume 245, Sept 5, 1987, p. 181(6)
> PD: 870905.
>
> *Heading #2*
> TI: New pieces in the puzzle of Flight *007:* journey into doubt.
> AU: *Pearson-David.* Keppel-John.
> SO: The *Nation* (NATNB), volume 241, Aug 17, 1985, p. 104(7)
> PD: 850817.
>
> *Heading #3*
> TI: K.A.L. *007:* what the U.S. knew and when we knew it.
> AU: *Pearson-David.*
> SO: The *Nation* (NATNB), volume 239, Aug 18, 1984, p. 105 (19)
> PD: 840818.

These three "files" were retrieved with the search phrase: "Pearson and Nation and 007" from *Magazine Index,* a database that contains references ("bibcites") to several hundred magazines published since 1959. It contains neither abstracts nor an article's full text, and thus all searches of this database must focus on article titles, authors, and specific journal names. The asterisks around Pearson's name, that of the magazine, and 007 indicate that these words or phrases were elements of the search phrase that has been retrieved. The search returned three story citations with the information necessary to locate the article electronically or in a traditional library. The subheads of each "file" are clear: TI indicates the full title of the piece as it appeared in the magazine. AU is short for author or writer. SO is the original source of the article, including publication date, volume number, the page the story started on, and the total number of pages in the article itself. Finally, the PD number is an electronic locator in the digital soup through which the article or citation can be retrieved.

Had I wished, I could have applied the same search phrase to *Magazine ASAP*, another database whose files contain and will return the full text of approximately one-quarter of the articles referenced in *Magazine Index*. Both magazine databases are products of a single supplier, Information Access Company, a subsidiary of Ziff-Davis Publishing, whose business since 1978 has been both to store magazines in a digital form and to make them accessible (as citations or in full text) to electronic searchers. Dialog Information Services is a primary packager of Information Access Company's product. To access these databases, I also could have linked electronically with Dialog to find these citations on *Magazine Index* or, through *Magazine ASAP*, to locate the stories in full.

But I subscribe neither to Dialog or Information Access Company. To access this information, I dialed a gateway distributor whose purpose is to make available online the services of a number of packagers, including Dialog, for those who need occasional access to a number of different services but have neither the training in their use nor the sufficient need of service to justify a personal subscription. This gateway, a product of Telebase Systems, Inc., is called EasyNet, and it is available either as an independent service or, under the name IQuest, on the CompuServe system. CompuServe is a wholesale distributor of the products of other distributors, packagers, and suppliers. CompuServe provides a gateway to Telebase Systems computers, which in turn rent time from Dialog's computer system. Dialog stores and sells a series of specific databases, like *Magazine Index*, whose specific files (individual stories or articles) are what one wishes to find. This electronic wholesaler is the world's largest, a huge electronic information system with, in 1990,

more than half a million subscribers. It offers access to an
incredible array of digitally stored information through an
interlocking system of gateways and direct services.

Thus the series of system levels accessed to retrieve
these three citations were, as follows:

1. **CompuServe**
   (Wholesale Distributor)
2. **EasyNet**
   (Gateway Distributor)
3. **Dialog**
   (Packager)
4. **Information Access Company**
   (Producer)
5. *Magazine Index*
   (Database)
6. **Pearson David and 007 and Nation**
   (Specific Files)

In my search for references to the articles by Pearson, I
could have entered this system at any level. For example,
were I interested in accessing only these files—and had I
known where they were—I could have gone directly to Information Access Company for permission to use their system. For a price, one can sign up with almost any distributor
or producer, and, in return for a monthly or yearly fee (in
addition to charges for each minute of online use), subscription to the service provides access to the data that producer
or distributor supplies. If all a researcher is going to use is
files from popular magazines catalogued in these databases,
then signing up directly with Information Access would be a
cost-effective way to go.

If, however, I frequently needed to search for a wide
range of information—from articles on medical affairs to
business reports and, perhaps, some federal documents as
well—Information Access would not answer more than perhaps one-third of my research needs. Packagers like Dialog
(BRS, Lexis, etc.) make available hundreds of different databases covering a number of subject areas, and, for frequent
users of a wide range of digitalized information, they are a
better alternative. On Dialog, access to the *Magazine Index*

is billed at $75 an hour, but for those familiar with the system's search language and organization, finding the appropriate file holding Pearson's articles from *The Nation* would take less than five minutes and be more cost-effective than the gateway route.

Direct subscription to a specific packager is also the most efficient way to use electronic databases when the supplier has specialized in an area of highly technical data with an eccentric system of organization. For example, WestLaw, the digitalized compiler of court records, is perhaps the best example of a producer individuals almost always sign up with directly. Legal researchers and law librarians seeking information from the volumes of previous legal judgment use such a system on a daily, sometimes hourly, basis. In addition, those needing WestLaw's services with enough frequency to justify its cost will almost certainly be familiar with the specialized techniques of legal research. These techniques have been required because of the eccentric system of information storage traditionally used by the U.S. legal system and the specialized needs of the legal profession.

Cases are stored and retrieved—electronically or manually—not simply by subject and case name but, as importantly, by jurisdiction and court location. Those seeking precedents from New York State courts, for example, must use a specific Court Reporter—case compilations for a single jurisdiction—to review the pattern of judicial decisions on any topic. But because the U.S. legal system is national, researchers must simultaneously seek for judgments or decisions rendered in all other jurisdictions. Finally, because federal judgments supersede state-level decisions or local precedents, lawyers must also look for pertinent case law at the federal level when researching a legal problem.

In addition, there are highly specific tasks unique to the legal field but critical to legal research. It is, for example, often necessary to take a legal citation and "shepherdize" it, to look through all court records occurring after but based on a single decision (like *Roe* v. *Wade*) to determine if that decision has been challenged, modified, affirmed, or overturned by any U.S. court (at any level). This type of specific search is facilitated and simplified by electronic searching but is so unusual that even the general reference librarian may be ignorant of its need or use. Thus WestLaw represents a producer whose services and search system are designed to fulfill the specific needs of a highly specialized type of research. Because of the individualized search needs of legalists and the volume of data this database holds—two hundred years of court records generated at federal and district levels, as well as state and federal statutes—West-Law's customers typically sign up directly with the provider for its service. Thus those who seek legal databases will find few gateways leading into such a service, although WestLaw customers are offered more general access, through different links, to general information services.

To search for files from a magazine like *The Nation*, on the other hand, presents no unique problems of storage or retrieval. Magazines in general provide thousands of stories which can be catalogued in a consistent and simple fashion by publication name, subject, and author. Thus the file for any one magazine story is part of a broad class of publicly presented information compiled by a single packager or producer and simultaneously made available through a distributor like Dialog Information Services. If I subscribed to Dialog, I could have entered the system at that level and, using its printed and online directories, found the file for *Magazine Index* and retrieved these citations in that way. The advantage of using EasyNet is that, had Dialog not contained the necessary databases to successfully conclude this search, EasyNet's gateway would have accessed the products of other major packagers and producers that might contain the necessary information. For more specialized subjects or periodicals less frequently accessed, the possibility to simultaneously search the products of two or more packagers can be an enormous help. Further, as a general, introductory service geared to the occasional user and neophyte, EasyNet offers free online assistance to clients having trouble locating the appropriate database and crafting a satisfactory search phrase.[6]

CompuServe is the supraorganization, offering access to EasyNet (and through it to Dialog) under the name of IQuest, much as Sears used to sell major brands of appliances manufactured for the wholesaler under its own house name.

I used it because I do not need either EasyNet's or Dialog's proprietary databases with sufficient frequency to justify the expense of a full subscription to either company. Since I use the services of any one producer (Vu/Text, BRS, PRS, etc.) only occasionally, it is cheaper and more efficient for me to be able to rent time on all of their services through a gateway like CompuServe's. Another benefit is that by using either EasyNet alone or CompuServe's IQuest, I do not have to worry about the fact that each of the major producers uses a slightly different search language. The EasyNet/IQuest gateway provides a translation filter that allows the subscriber to employ a single search language, whatever the packager or producer may use as a stand-alone service.

Certainly, CompuServe charges for this convenience. I spent $12.60 an hour for "connect" telephone-line charges and $9 for the successful search of the EasyNet gateway to Dialog, Information Access's primary vendor. The basic pricing system for access through the gateway is a unit price of $9 for the first ten citations received. If one wants more information, one has to pay an additional $9 for the next ten "hits" and then pay again for the next series, and so on. Since my online search took only five minutes and I received fewer than ten "hits" in this search, the whole cost was only $1.05 connect time plus $9 for the references, which were available at the library down the street from my office. Through Dialog, on the other hand, one is charged a flat fee per hour, which varies depending on the database accessed through its lines. *Magazine Index*, for example, costs $75 an hour on Dialog, while *Medline* costs only $30. But because a good researcher is online only briefly, it may still be cheaper for a skilled librarian to use a service like Dialog rather than a gateway service. The search for references to Pearson's articles, for example, took about three minutes, and thus would cost only $3.75 on Dialog (presuming familiarity with the location of the files and the system's search language and retrieval mechanism) while, through IQuest, the charge was $9.

Those doing frequent, long searches through a gateway system like CompuServe's IQuest may find the unit charging system prohibitively expensive. To retrieve one hundred citations from a variety of sources, with a price of $9 for every ten units of retrieved citation, becomes costly. The number of citations returned can be limited by appropriate search phrases (limiting articles by date, by seeking only "review" articles, etc.), but those who need frequent access to a wide range of subject categories find that direct subscription to individual database producers (Vu/Text, WestLaw, Information Access, etc.) or packagers (Dialog, BRS, Lexis, etcetera) is more cost-effective. For those with only a sporadic need of access, however, gateways provide a relatively simple, convenient, and inexpensive data access system. In addition, for the purposes of this book, focusing on access through the gateways (and wholesale distributors) makes the general digital system's organization clearer and allows the examination of several packagers and suppliers.

COMPUSERVE

Few people, excepting perhaps those professional data brokers whose business is to carry out online searches for clients, use even a portion of the total range of databases available from any producer. Users quickly find there is a small core of databases that they access repeatedly and a smaller number that may be needed only on occasion. Physicians and medical personnel typically focus on one of a score of biomedical, medical, or medical-economic databases, while ignoring files like *Magazine Index*, where Pearson's story citations were found. News reporters will use medical files infrequently but may make constant use of newspaper records, including their own publication's, made available by the producer Vu/Text. Business writers and investment brokers have frequent recourse to specific files describing the financial health of regional industries, important markets, exchanges, and specific businesses but may rarely, if ever, use medical files.

For the generalist or the individual who uses electronic resources infrequently, a gateway distributor like EasyNet or a wholesaler like CompuServe provides perhaps the best opportunity to access a variety of digital information services and categories. For the novice, this type of general information service also offers perhaps the best and most cost-effective introduction to online services. Not only is the range of potential services unusually broad, but the amount of online assistance provided is far greater than what is offered by more specialized electronic data storage systems. Experienced librarians and researchers may sneer at this "hand-holding," but ease of access and online help in everything from honing a search phrase to information on where one can look for appropriate materials allow the neophyte to learn easily what it may have taken the professional researcher years to master.

In addition, focusing on CompuServe's information storage and retrieval system reveals much about the world of electronic information and its accessibility to public information writers.[7] As it is the largest and most diverse online system currently available, a description of its components provides the opportunity to examine the full range of online library and data service resources. In addition, because CompuServe does provide gateway access to a number of producers and packagers like Dialog, BRS, PaperChase and EasyNet, it is an excellent vehicle through which to examine the range and type of files currently stored electronically. It is not the purpose of this chapter to advocate one service over another because those choices will depend, ultimately, on the individual user's ability, specific data needs, and financial resources. Nor is it the intention of this text to duplicate the work of those who have written tutorials for specific gateway services,[8] for producers, or for the use of online resources in general.[9] Rather, the intent is to make clear the general organization of online "libraries" so that the effect of these resources on public information can be better evaluated and discussed.

Informal Sources

Illustration 5.1 presents in graphic form the general facilities available to CompuServe members. The news librarian's model of the news search presented in Chapter 4 (Illustration 4.2) included both informal sources—the statements of friends, colleagues, and topical advisers in any subject area—and formal news sources—previous story clips, articles, official statements made at the information level of the journalistic event, and attributed quotes—as sources of news information. Most electronic information vendors and distributors focus only on the formal sources, but CompuServe, through its "Special Interest Groups (SIGs)," commonly called "forums," provides a whole range of informal information sources that allow the newswriter to communicate directly with specialists in most major fields.

SIGs are systems of data storage and communication in which individuals sharing interest in or concern about a specific subject area can exchange information or question others with expertise in that area, hold "online conferences," and store files of stories, programs, or graphics for use by the forum's membership. They began in the early 1980s as technically oriented groups who largely traded computer programs, programming tips, and general information on the use of the then newly available personal computer and its software.[10] While computer- and software-oriented programs remain popular,[11] they are now matched by interest groups representing aviators, physicians, lawyers, investors, newspeople, educators, travelers, public relations professionals, and space technology enthusiasts. Each interest group has a specific electronic area on the service and a specific area within the CompuServe computers that includes a "library" for longer files a member may wish to have stored in digital form for future communal use. There is also a "message board" on which members post comments or statements for others to read and comment on at some future time and a Citizens' Band radio-like electronic area available for real-time discussion should two or more members wish to use their computer terminals to communicate directly with other members of the group. Finally, any SIG may host a "conference" in which a guest (usually an authority in the field) will be available to answer questions as forum members plug into the system on their computer keyboards.

These services can provide informal but potentially critical background information to the public information writer. Membership in any professional forum is dominated by, but not limited to, members of a specific profession—all CompuServe subscribers are welcomed in any interest group or forum. Thus a reporter interested in tort or tort reform could

Illustration 5.1
CompuServe Organization: General

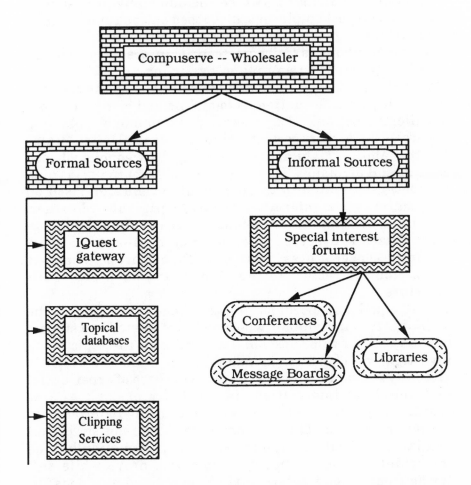

leave a message with both the physicians' forum and the
lawyers' forum asking for information on how members of
each group view the issue. In addition, when a news event
breaks, forums whose members are involved or interested in
that occurrence will typically carry a large amount of information on the specific event itself. Thus, when Pacific South-
west Airlines Flight 1771 crashed in California in December
1987, reporter Tony Russomano of KGO-TV, San Francisco,
accessed the Aviation Forum (AVSIG) to see if its members

had information not otherwise available from police, airport, and crash-investigation officials.[12]

AVSIG participants, which include many professional pilots and airport employees, discussed online rumors that a man had smuggled a gun on board the plane at takeoff and complained about lax airport security procedures that allowed easy access to any plane by airline and airport employees in general. Russomano thus arrived at the scene of the crash with information from airline and airport personnel alleging not only the presence of a gunman but blaming generally lax airport security throughout the United States for the ability of hijackers to smuggle weapons aboard commercial airplanes. He therefore had from the beginning a hypothesis related to the immediate event and based on information given informally by airline personnel. Further, that information provided a context greater than the immediate disaster, a perspective based on airline and airport employee concerns over lax security for airport personnel as a contributing factor to the immediate *and* previous air disasters.

Of equal and perhaps greater long-term value is the availability of individuals who may be interested in a subject but may not have professional expertise in the topic being investigated. The huge membership of CompuServe SIGs virtually guarantees newswriters a wide base of experiential and anecdotal information. In 1990, for example, I was researching a story on motor-vehicle licensing requirements in North America. The assignment included not simply all available medical, legal, and academic information but, as importantly, case studies of people who drove while suffering from vision impairments.[13] I explained my needs online to two SIGs, one composed of those interested in journalism (JForum) and the other for police, firefighters, ambulance technicians, and other emergency service professions (SafetyNet). From the former I received a number of messages suggesting stories that had been published or produced on different national TV shows, most of them focusing exclusively on elderly drivers. SafetyNet subscribers responded with detailed information on legal statutes in various states and general perspectives on the problem. But in both forums, individuals responded who were either themselves young, sight-impaired drivers or who were worried about relatives with debilitating visual conditions who continued legally to drive automobiles despite those infirmities. Several agreed to discuss their concerns and personal problems on camera.

It is difficult to assess the value of this type of resource precisely because it is "informal." These two anecdotal examples suggest a utility that remains, at present, largely untapped and certainly unstudied in any meaningful way. But then, the impact of traditional, informal sources on news reports—the unattributed information and tips provided by colleagues, editors, and sources—is similarly difficult to evaluate. What seems to be clear is that news reporters and editors have traditionally relied on a variety of sources—professionally based and community-generated—to gain background information on topics of potential interest.[14] Both broad information categories are represented online and can be focused on both breaking news and more general, longer-term, "investigative" and public affairs stories.

Formal Sources

If the efficacy of these informal sources is difficult to evaluate, the value of more formal electronic resources is not. The previous chapters' analysis of published articles and public issues (e.g., the shooting down of KAL 007, tort reform, deaths resulting from the improper administration of anesthetic) has been largely dependent on information gained from these formal resources. Most of the research for this book was carried out in the electronic equivalent of traditional, print libraries, in the files of specific journals, magazines, and newsletters organized for use by professional researchers or specialists in specific fields. But in the late 1980s a series of specialty databases were introduced which attempted to assure that the layperson would have access to the broad base of information through simplified search procedures. Illustration 5.2 shows in greater detail than Illustration 5.1 could the range of formal resources currently available online and the interrelation of the system's three major formal components: specialty databases, clipping services, and the IQuest gateways.

Specialty Databases

Increasingly, CompuServe offers not only a gateway service to major vendors like Dialog but, simultaneously, a series of specialized databases that provide journal and newsletter information on specific topics. These databases typically consist of fewer total files than those accessible through specialized vendors, provide a search system with "menus" that guide the novice through their use, and, finally, are less expensive to use than their more detailed and encyclopedic counterparts.

These databases are sometimes called "unbundled" because they provide a core of information from a smaller base of journals and newsletters than the "bundled" databases offered by full-scale packagers or specialty producers like PaperChase. They thus promise a simpler search procedure and language of file materials on a specific topic. The trade-off for this simplicity is that the search is carried out on a small, less technical database. By 1990, one or more of them on CompuServe covered these major fields: health, law, marketing and management, media news (through newsletter coverage), data processing, and a general business database drawn from the financial sections of a selection of North American newspapers.

An example of both the utility and the limits of this type of database can be seen in the following example. In February 1990, *Health Database Plus*, consisting of electronically stored articles from a select number of specialty journals and popular magazines on medicine, was searched for information on the relation of anesthetic or anesthesia and death or injury occurring from anesthetic use. The following text records that search, with minor editing to remove redundancy and increase legibility. It utilized the search phrase "anesth/ and (injury or death)," which is, in the course of the search, narrowed only to those articles dealing with dental injury or death in an anesthetic setting. Figures or words in bold were entered by the author. Information in italics explains, where necessary, the progression of stages in the search. The series of prompts and responses is that of the interactive system:

Illustration 5.2
CompuServe: Formal Sources

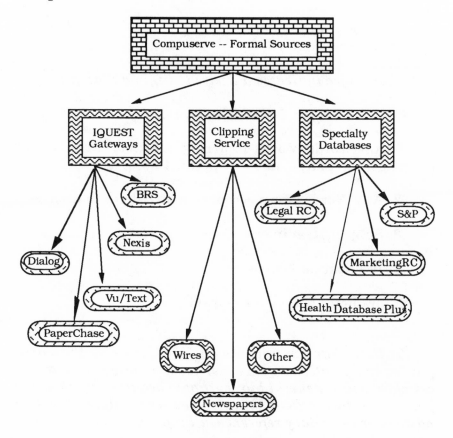

HEALTH DATABASE PLUS
Health Database Plus
    Copyright 1990 Information Access Company
    Copyright 1990 Ziff Communications Company

(Health Database Plus's producer is Information Access Company, which is owned by Ziff Communications Company.)

Enter choice (<CR> for more) !

  1 Search Health Database Plus

2 Quick Reference
3 Exit

Last page, enter choice !
->1

(This choice indicates a desire to begin a search.)

START a Search for Articles by Specifying:

1 Key Words (words occurring in article titles, subject headings, company names, or product names)

2 Any Words (words occurring anywhere in articles)

3 Subject Headings

4 Publication Names

Enter choice (<CR> for more) !
->1

(To limit the potential data retrieved, one asks the search phrase (here called key words) to be applied only to the article's title or general bibliographic heading. By choosing option 2, a larger field in which the issue might be only a passing or secondary reference, all references would be chosen.)

Enter key word or phrase
(? for help):

(Keying in a "?" brings assistance to the neophyte uncertain of how to phrase the search.)

(anesthetic or anesthesia) and (death or injury)

Words Anywhere: [anesthetic I anesthesia] & [death I injury] 254
(Only) Full-text articles matching ALL search methods: 250

(The total response to this search is a large and unmanageable 254 articles or citations. Even when those citations that are only abstracts or bibliographic references are eliminated, the number returned is still large.)

(Further) CHOICES:

1 Display a Menu of Matching Articles
2 Match Full-text or Abstracted Articles
3 Narrow the Search
4 Replace (Erase) an Existing Search Method
5 Widen the Search Using an Existing Search Method

Enter choice (<CR> for more) !
->**3**

NARROW the Search for Articles by Specifying:

1 Key Words (words occurring in article titles, subject headings, company names, or product names)

2 Any Words (words occurring anywhere in articles)

3 Subject Headings

4 Publication Names

Enter choice (<CR> for more) !
->**2**

Narrowing the Search. Enter word or phrase
(<CR> no change, ? for help):
->**dental**

(Only cases involving injury or death resulting from application of anesthesia during dental procedures will now be returned. One could also have added the word "review" to the 250 citations first returned, to narrow the whole to review articles, or similarly narrowed the search by asking for only those citations published in the last one or two or three years.)

Words Anywhere: [anesthetic or anesthesia] & [death or injury] & dental

Full-text articles matching ALL search methods: 23

Having narrowed the file to twenty-three articles, I was again offered the choice of displaying the retrieved articles in either full text or only as an abstract, further narrowing the search, or creating a new search. By choosing to review only abstracts, the cost of the system's use is reduced and a general idea of both the information that can be retrieved and its journal location is gained. Since each full-text article downloaded carries a surcharge of $1.25 in addition to the database's $15 an hour user fee (and CompuServe's $12.50 an hour access charges), those on research budgets will use the full-text service sparingly. Even with faster baud (transmission) rates currently available on modern modems, the cost of downloading even twelve articles can become prohibitive. I find it is cost-effective only when there are fewer than five review articles whose references can then be checked at a local library.

Further, if abstracts are available, they sometimes provide enough information for the public information writer seeking general background on a specific topic. Consider the following example returned by *Index Medicus*, logged through PaperChase for information on review articles in the medical literature on the relation between anesthesia and injury or death:

TI: Anesthetic Mishaps and the Cost of Monitoring:
  A Proposed Standard for Monitoring Equipment.
AU: Whitcher C., Ream, A.K., Parsons, D. et al.
SO: J. Clin. Monit. 1988; 4: 5-15
ABSTRACT: Review of insurance data indicates that approximately 1.5 claims are paid per 10,000 anesthetic procedures, a conservative estimate of the incidence of preventable serious injury associated with anesthesia. Insurance data permit estimation of the premium cost for the anesthesiologist and hospital, per operating room per year, of $69,429.00.

We propose the use of an enhanced monitoring standard requiring a pulse oximeter, capnograph, spirometer, halometer, automatic sphygmomanometer, breathing circuit oxygen analyzer, stethoscope, electrocardiographic monitor and temperature monitor. We suggest that this premium cost, together with the estimate that 50% of incidents would be avoided, predicts a resultant saving of over $27,000/operating room/year, a saving equal to the entire cost of the enhanced monitoring system in approximately 8 months, or a yearly saving of over five times the annualized expense of the monitoring system. Thus, in addition to the moral imperative to monitor a patient during anesthesia to avoid injury and death, there is an economic incentive to monitor efficiently.[15]

KEY WORDS: Monitoring: standards, Injury. Risk. Anesthetic mishaps.

The value of both returning abstracts in a search and including "review" in the search phrase is evident here. The article as a whole reviews a specific data collection or literature and thus, if retrieved in full, provides a wealth of sources that can be manually searched in the library. For the public information writer interested in the issue of anesthetic administration (or tort reform or medical performance), the abstract itself is a gold mine. Here is hard clinical evidence, presented by physicians and phrased in economic terms, that failure to use widely available, cost-effective monitoring equipment contributes to 50 percent of the operating room, anesthetic-related incidents. It equates monitoring (a moral imperative) with prevention of death or injury and, further, argues that the cost of appropriate monitoring equipment would pay for itself in less than a year.

The full text of the article, later retrieved from the library, is even more complete, but, were one checking for information the day before a court hearing or inquest, even the abstract alone would empower the reporter (or lawyer) intent on finding out precisely why a healthy person died during anesthestic administration. In cases in which anesthetic death has occurred and an attending physician who did not appropriately monitor the patient disclaims all responsibility, Whitcher et al. give the lie to the physician's assurances that "everything that should have been done was done." The article lists equipment that could and, according to the authors, should be in an operating room, while eliminating the possible rejoinder by doctor or hospital administrator that monitoring equipment is prohibitively expensive. It suggests that half of the incidents of anesthetic mishap would not occur if a full complement of monitoring equipment was in place (and in use), while suggesting there is a "moral imperative to monitor a patient during anesthesia to avoid injury and death."

For a story on tort and tort reform, this article also is an important piece of information. If the deaths that lead to litigation are preventable and if by not using appropriate equipment, physicians violate a "moral imperative," then perhaps the issue is not the size of awards made by juries. After all, one-half of all "incidents" would not occur if proper monitoring techniques and equipment were used. The articles insist that the real cause of these accidents is the failure of hospitals and their anesthesiologists to assure proper monitoring equipment is available. To decrease malpractice claims, the article states, increase monitoring of patients.[16]

The use of serial menus that, at each step, direct the user to specific options is a key attraction of both unbundled services and those, like EasyNet/IQuest, designed to facilitate electronic research for the generalist or occasional electronic researcher. At each step the options offered—of narrowing a search phrase (by year, date, subject, or key word), defining the amount of information to be returned (full text or abstract), previewing the number of articles returned, accessing online "help" functions where the user can seek assistance—assure that the best possible search is conducted while keeping costs at a minimum. By charging only for stories or abstracts retrieved and keeping to a relatively low hourly charge, both unbundled and gateway-accessed services provide a cost-effective alternative to the more expensive and more complex, if more complete, full-scale bibliographic products available through dedicated packagers like Dialog, which charges $30 an hour for access to *Index Medicus*.

In addition to the $12.50 hourly charge for CompuServe, the unbundled *Health DataBase Plus* charges users an additional $15 an hour and $1.50 per article retrieved. PaperChase charges a flat $15 an hour connect time (in addition to CompuServe's charges), and *Index Medicus* on Dialog costs $30 an hour. Retrieving 250 articles (which, downloaded, would probably take more than an hour) would be expensive on all systems. The menu system of unbundled and gateway services is designed to assist the inexperienced researcher in narrowing potentially large data fields to as few critical references as possible. For a reporter covering a medical inquest into the death of an individual during dental surgery, a bill of over $400 (230 reprints at $1.50 per reprint, additional charges for use of *Health DataBase Plus* and $12.50 an hour for access to CompuServe) would be, at most newspapers and broadcast stations where I have worked, considered prohibitively expensive. By limiting the retrieval costs to the abstracts of 23 articles (or less), the bill is kept under $50 for current references in the field.

For reporters and other public information writers who often need only general background in a field like medicine, unbundled systems may provide sufficient information to allow for intelligent questioning of a coroner, physcan, or other medical official. Further, the magazines indexed here, unlike those in *Index Medicus* and PaperChase, include popular publications like *Hippocrates*, as well as more technical publications like the *Harvard Medical School Health Letter*. Unbundled services thus provide a bridge between the popular magazine field, catalogued in *Magazine Index* or *Magazine ASAP*, and the technical literature of a database like *Index Medicus*. If the results are not sufficient or if the topic requires a more detailed examination of the biomedical, pharmacological, or another specialized literature, then the occasional researcher might wish to use a gateway service like IQuest (or the CompuServe gateway to PaperChase), where more complete databases can be accessed.

This simple example underlines, again, both the importance of the search phrase and its absolute relation to the ability to access materials from the digitalized library. Like the traditional library card catalogue, understanding the digitalized storage system is the key to finding the appropriate information and receiving it in the desired form (full text, abstract, or citation). It is also the means by which these libraries can be used cost-effectively. One could retrieve all 250 full-text articles, but it is doubtful that most would be of interest or of use to the layperson. Typically, scientific articles on any subject are narrowly focused and often redundant, replicating and commenting on the work of previous researchers. Appropriate search phrases that progressively narrow potential files to the clearly pertinent, topical story (with references to past works) allow for highly specific and cost-effective research. When applied to specialty databases, which include popular summaries of academic research, the advantages for the layperson or generalist are clear.

IQuest: Screens

Sometimes information offered by the unbundled services is not enough. They did not, for example, contain information on electric arc furnace dust, or law journal references to tort reform, and may not cover the critical technical articles like Whitcher's. For this type of information one may need the resources of a full-scale packager like Dialog, in which the sheer volume of available sources can be daunting. If one were to search all the medically related databases on Dialog, which includes not only medical journals but those related to chemical, biomedical, and bioengineering fields, the results of a search for relevant articles on anesthesia and death or injury would be unmanageably large. A skilled medical researcher could probably pare the thousands of potential articles to a manageable size, but those unfamiliar with medical issues, uncertain which databases would be critical, and perhaps less than expert in the system's use might simply resign the search in despair.

In its gateway service, IQuest provides a service called "screens," which allows the user to see both the number of citations that will be retrieved for any single search phrase employed and the specific databases in which those articles or citations can be found. The importance of the latter cannot be overstated because full-service packagers require searchers to direct their queries not to the system at large but, rather, to a specific database in particular. One cannot simply say, "Find me review articles on anesthesia and death or injury" and expect the computer to do the work. The search phrase, at this point in the development of these technologies, first must be directed at a single database (*Biosis, Embase, Index Medicus,* and so on). Thus honing the search phrase to define the context of a problem is only half the task. The second and no less critical part of full-service online research is to apply the phrase to the appropriate database.

Much the same thing happens in contemporary print libraries. In a typical city library, one can search in vain for references to specific problems in biomedical engineering, anesthesiology, or any other specialized area of knowledge. For those, one must go to a specialized or university library where medical texts (or law journals, engineering newsletters, or marketing guides—whatever the specialty sought) are stored. The same division of storage is replicated in the electronic world, although access is facilitated by the computer network itself. But one still must know where the information is and go to it, electronically, before it can be retrieved.

These screens, in effect, apply the remedial assistance of the unbundled service's menus to the power of full-service packagers, whose very wealth of bibliographic resources is often an impediment to their use. Since these screens cost only $5 per search, they provide an enormously cost-effective arena in which a search phrase can be tested against the full complex of available databases. Simply, they allow a person to test a hypothesis, framed as a search phrase, against the multiplicity of available online resources. To see how this system works, consider the following examples. The first uses IQuest's menu and screen system to locate information on injuries or death occurring from anesthetic application in general. The second is specific to anesthesia in dental surgery.

PRESS TO SELECT   * Main Menu *
  1 IQuest-I   System helps select the database
  2 IQuest-II   Search a database of your choice
  3 SmartSCAN   Search multiple databases
  4 Instructions
  H for Help,   C for Commands
-> 3

(This is the command to begin a scan and narrows the parameter of searches through a series of questions and screens.)

PRESS TO SELECT
  1 Business
  2 Science & Technology
  3 Medicine & Allied Health
  4 Law, Patents, Trade names
  5 Social Sciences & Education
  6 Arts, Literature, Religion
  7 People
  8 News
  9 General Reference
  H for Help,   C for Commands
-> 3

(Clearly, the general subject area is databases storing information on Medicine and Allied Health. The other categories would be important were a different search to be instituted.)

PRESS TO SELECT
  1 Medical Research
  2 Pharmacology
  3 Nursing and Allied Services
  4 Consumer Health
  H for Help,   C for Commands
-> 1

(Medicine has been subdivided as a general topic into the subspecialties. If one were interested in a case involving a nurse anesthetist, number 3 might be preferable.)

Enter your medical topic
Type H for Search Guidelines.
-> **(anesth/ or anaes/) and (death or injury)**

*(Since many journals do use the British spelling, anaes/
is included as an alternate to the U.S. spelling.)*

Is: (ANESTH/ OR ANAESTH/) AND (DEATH OR IN-
JURY)
Correct ? (Yes/No) -> **y**

*(If the answer is no, one is prompted to write a new search
phrase.)*

Scanning, please wait...

Scan completed.
Medical Research scan results for: (ANESTHETIC OR
ANESTHESIA) AND (DEATH OR...

PRESS TO SEARCH

Title		*Format*	*Source / Type*
Ageline	2	abstract	journals
AIDS Database	0	reference	journals
AIDS Knowledge Base	0	full text	journals
Books in Print	1	reference	books
Cancerlit	168	reference	journals
Combined Health Information	5	abstract	multiple sources
Embase	2486	reference	journals
Health Instruments File	0	abstract	multiple sources
*Medline (1982 to date)	1271	reference	journals
Rehabdata	2	reference	journals
Sport Database	23	reference	journals

* Good choice for professional literature.

A ADDITIONAL CHOICES
(Choices listed include beginning a new search, narrow-ing these results by adding additional qualifiers to the cur-rent phrase, etc.)

H Database descriptions
(Retrieves a description of all databases named in the search.)

SOS Online assistance
(This brings research assistants online at no charge to assist those having trouble in the search.)

Total charges thus far: $5.00

What has happened is that a second, selective process similar to that employed in the search phrase has been used to identify specific databases to which that search can be applied. The total number of potentially relevant articles returned is far larger than that of the unbundled service, and the journal categories in which they occur indicate the type of information that will result. By entering "H," a description of the individual databases is provided. *Embase*, for example, where 2,486 references answer the query's parameters, is described by the command "Database De-scriptions" as: *"Embase—*From January 1974; updated weekly. Includes extensive abstracts of articles related to biomedicine from medical journals worldwide. About 60% of the records contain abstracts." *Embase*'s packager is BRS and was surveyed, here, through the Telebase Systems gate-way, called IQuest by wholesaler CompuServe. Its research base begins with articles published in 1974 and new articles are added to the database each week.

Medline, on the other hand, where the next largest number of returns is found, is carried by Dialog, is updated every month, and its oldest online files are from the year 1982. The description included from the screen is as follows: *"Medline* (1982 to date)—Updated monthly. Indexes articles from medical journals published worldwide. Corresponds to *Index Medicus, International."* Thus the database *Medline* is an electronic version of the traditional print reference,

Index Medicus, International. Clearly, these two databases (*Embase* and *Medline*), which cover the issues of medical equipment and procedure, are where the required information will be, but, equally clearly, the search phrase needs to be honed further. This information is just too much even to begin to sift through it. One could add "Review" to the search phrase, which would limit results solely to review articles or, if any of the phrases can be more narrowly defined, that step will also limit the returns to a manageable size. Using the word "dental" in the search phrase to modify "anesth/" is one example of a modifier limiting a search's returns. The following screen represents a second search using the phrase "(anesthetic or anesthesia) and (death or injury)":

Title		*Format*	*Source/Type*
Ageline	0	abstract	journals
AIDS Database	0	reference	journals
AIDS Knowledge Base	0	full text	journals
Books in Print	0	reference	books
Cancerlit	0	reference	journals
Combined Health Information	0	abstract	multiple sources
Embase	30	reference	journals
Health Instruments File	0	abstract	multiple sources
*Medline (1982 to date)	19	reference	journals
Rehabdata	0	reference	journals
Sport Database	0	reference	journals

While the use of two such screens, each costing five dollars, may seem somewhat extravagant, the advantage of this system for one unfamiliar with the databases covering any one field is evident. Accessing *Medline*, one of the least expensive databases available on Dialog, costs $30 an hour. *Embase* is more expensive on an hourly basis. To download over one thousand (or even one hundred) references on a fishing expedition for information would quickly run up a data search bill of several hundred dollars and require days of reading before one could find the truly pertinent articles. The screens, by identifying individual databases and their general subject boundaries (and there is, in fact, some overlap between *Embase* and *Medline*, which, for example, both catalogue the *Journal of the American Medical Association*) and allowing one to preview a search before it is run, show the writer or researcher how to narrow the parameters of a search. Further, because these screens list the format of materials in each database, those who wish not only the bibcite but also a formal abstract (or the full text) can choose their databases accordingly. Finally, the whole allows one to avoid duplication by showing overlap of the subject areas of major databases (*Embase* and *Medline*, for example). It has been my experience that, when the search can be narrowed (especially through the use of the search qualifier "review") to under fifteen citations, retrieval of abstracts along with standard locational information provides sufficient direction and, sometimes, enough general information to warrant the time and expense.

IQuest: Simple Searches

Gateways also provide menu-driven services that choose the appropriate databases from the array of packager services they carry and automatically retrieve pertinent citations. The advantage of this system is that, if one has no clue at all about where to address a highly specific search phrase, the system goes into "automatic" and does the work itself. Unlike the screens, which identify databases where appropriate information may reside, this menu-driven system retrieves targeted articles themselves. When BCTV asked for information on electric arc furnace dust, for example, I had no idea what database would have information on so esoteric a subject. It was a topic quite beyond my experience. Rather than search through a catalogue of databases to find one that dealt with environmental issues or metals or metallurgy, I used the gateway distributor's screens, which assist in defining a subject and automatically find the appropriate supplier, database, and file. After logging onto the Telebase Systems network via CompuServe, I recorded the following session. Again, numbers or phrases in bold were entered by me, and information in italics is a commentary on choices made through this system:

1 IQuest-I   System helps select the database
2 IQuest-II   You name the database
3 SmartSCAN   Scan a group of databases
4 Instructions
-> 1

(Had I known where to look, I could have named the database and gone directly to the subject. Were this a contextual search, like that in the anesthetic example, I might have chosen a screen. As it was, I needed to know, first, what electric arc furnace dust was. So I allowed the system to find the most appropriate database for me.)

PRESS TO SELECT

1 Business
2 Science & Technology
3 Medicine & Allied Health
4 Law, Patents, Trade Names
5 Social Sciences & Education
6 Arts, Literature, Religion
7 Entertainment & Travel
8 Persons
9 News
H for Help,   C for Commands
-> 1

PRESS TO SELECT

1 Accounting
2 Banking & Finance
3 Companies
4 Economics
5 Industries
6 Insurance
7 Management
8 Marketing

   9 Real Estate
  10 Taxation
   H for Help, C for Commands
-> 5

(Because I was interested in the steel industry's relation to EAF)

PRESS TO SELECT

   1 Agriculture & Food Science
   2 Construction
   3 Energy
   4 Finance, Insurance, Real Estate
   5 Government & Defense (U.S.)
   6 Manufacturing
   7 Retail Trade
   8 Services
   9 Transportation, Utilities, Communication
  10 Wholesale Trade
   H for Help, C for Commands
-> 6

Enter Search Phrase:
-> Electric Arc Furnace Dust

Is: ELECTRIC ARC FURNACE DUST
Correct ? (Yes/No) -> **y**

Ten citations with pertinent abstracts were returned in this search. All came from a database whose files were composed of articles from the following magazines or trade newsletters, none of which I previously had heard of: *Chemical Marketing Reporter, Journal of Metals,* and *American Metal Market.* The stories and abstracts included reports on the announcement and later implementation of Environmental Protection Agency regulations concerning EAF, defined its metal content, and announced creation of a special high-temperature furnace in France designed to reconvert European EAF to usable metals. These files were drawn from *Trade and*

Industry ASAP, a database covering approximately four hundred publications. Its supplier was Information Access Company, and the distributor was Dialog. Had I examined a dictionary of databases for an appropriate place to address this query, I would probably not have thought to access *Trade and Industry*, and, although technical information on EAF would certainly have been available elsewhere (perhaps in a database of federal regulations), this means was sufficient to find all the data I needed. The abstracts provided the technical information I lacked (on both the heavy-metal content in EAF and requirements for removing those metals) and placed it in the social context (new EPA regulations) that the story required.

The whole cost $9 for the IQuest search (a flat rate for the first ten responses) and $12.50 per hour for CompuServe online charges. Since the search took at most ten minutes, final cost was $9 + $2.08, or $11.08.

Gateway versus Packager-based Services

Experienced reference librarians and trained data researchers may dismiss gateway services and their menus as time-consuming and unnecessary. Those users familiar with Dialog, BRS, or other full-service specialty packaged services like Dow Jones News Service, PaperChase, or Vu/Text, can and do bypass the steps of screen and menu search. Familiarity and practice have given them the experience to know either what databases will be most useful in any search or how to find quickly, on any system, the appropriate database to address when searching for information on a new topic. A trained researcher interested in EAF but uncertain where to look for information could have logged onto Dialog's electronic *Database of Databases*[17] or, on BRS, the *Database Directory*.[18] On IQuest, the electronic database directory is the *Directory of Online Databases*,[19] although it seems to me the menu or screen systems do the same on this service and costs less to use. Each of these electronic directories provides general card-catalogue-style information on the databases carried and could be best searched by asking the computer to match "metals" or "steel processing" with the appropriate database. Experienced researchers would more likely have used the general *Trade and Industry ASAP* database in the past, and experience might therefore have told them to try there first. But most news professionals are not trained researchers. They are not familiar with the thousands of online sources (or traditional library resources) through which arcane information can be both located and accessed.

For the free-lance writer, periodical reporter with limited resources, or advocate on a budget, screens and menu-driven searches are a cost-effective way to define a search phrase and limit a search before hundreds of dollars are spent browsing through the electronic library. Screens are basic tools that allow writers new to electronic researching to limit and define the areas they wish to examine. If the search phrase is so narrow that no "hits" are returned, there is no charge. If the phrasing is too broad and thousands of possible matches are returned, the search language can be tightened at minimal cost. Gateway services assure the widest possible mix of providers at the least potential cost, and these search aids assure that lack of familiarity with those services will not prevent their broadest possible use.

Librarians versus Writers

For neophytes with the means to both hone their search phrase and identify potential sources for that information, these unbundled resources, screens, and directed search systems offer one possible resolution to the practical conflict between writers and librarians over control of electronic databases. As the previous chapter noted, librarians are often exasperated by the failure of reporters to phrase their searches appropriately or to know precisely where the data sought may be located. They dislike badly framed questions, and demands for general, unfocused searches can, indeed, be expensive, time-consuming, and wasteful. Furthermore, many reporters want to conduct their own searches. They do not want librarians to decide for them what information is most pertinent to a specific topic.[20] These unbundled resources—screens and menus—provide an economical means by which both reporters and librarians can share the work of focusing not only on traditional "fact" at the level of journalistic event—what was said by an individual to a fellow reporter at a previous time—but rather, as in this case, on the context of the boundary event itself.

Reporters need to know the general parameters of available information and, while creating a theory to fit the general facts of boundary event and official statement, need some access to the electronic resources currently available in the newsroom. Librarians who are charged by their employers with supervision of all resource materials and placed under budgetary restraints need to be able to exercise some authority over the use of these potentially costly electronic resources. A logical compromise might be to delegate screen searches to the reporter while reserving control of the full and still expensive databases to the librarian. Reporters then can hone their phrase, develop a knowledge of potential databases, and, in this "pre-search," define the parameters of information sought. Full searches of whatever service is subscribed to by the publication would be the librarian's job, and decisions on limiting those searches would remain the resource specialist's prerogative.

When, on occasion, I've had the opportunity to access directly a large packager like Dialog or needed the services of a specialty supplier like Vu/Text or PaperChase, I've first done an IQuest-style screen search to learn exactly which databases had the largest number of files pertinent to my subject area. A similar system may be equally effective if institutionalized in a periodical news office where budget restraints imposed by corporate home offices continue to create shortages in specific editorial departments. Even though most news organizations subscribe to one or more major services (Dialog, BRS, Lexis, etc.), this type of gateway or wholesaler's screen may still be efficient and economical. Because of the duplication among services, it is often the case that sources identified by the screen search as available on one service will also be available through another. For those times when that duplication is not the case, a tightly written, menu-driven search through the gateway wholesaler would allow the public information reporter to access the truly critical datum on a one-time and cost-effective basis.

Specialty Services

It is necessary at this point to enter a caution concerning the use of databases and to correct the impression that all sources are equally and easily available through distributors and wholesalers. At least at present, availability is a more complex issue. While there is considerable overlap among the information bases of major packagers like BRS, Dow Jones News Service, and Dialog, each will maintain databases to which the other does not have access. Further, some sources can be accessed in only a limited fashion through gateway services when compared to the full range of services offered by the supplier to individual subscribers. Thus Vu/Text's files of more than 65 regional newspapers are available to users of EasyNet (IQuest), but no global search system is offered to these gateway fee-for-service clients. Through these secondary distributors, one can search only individual newspapers, not the accumulated information of all files simultaneously. Corporations or individuals who subscribe directly to the Vu/Text service, however, can use a global search system that applies any single search phrase to the combined databases of all its member newspapers. WestLaw, the supplier that stores U.S. court cases, offers its subscribers access to other data storage systems, but users of most other packagers and distributors cannot access the court files on an occasional basis.

Thus, choice of vendor is in reality the first step in an electronic search because it determines the type and form of the data that will be retrieved. I subscribe to CompuServe as a general wholesaler whose greater access to a number of systems promises the widest possible range of occasionally used information. In addition, I have at various times subscribed to one or more packagers or suppliers—like WestLaw or Vu/Text, whose more specialized databases were critical to a specific project or job.

One can predict with some confidence that the disparity between producers' and distributors' systems is a temporary phenomenon. Links between individual suppliers will increase as the technology matures, and the ability to access disparate files stored by a variety of producers and distributors will become increasingly common. The gateway linkages are only one example of the growing interconnection among all these services. The increasing purchase of electronically stored services by university libraries[21] also suggests that, in the future, online information services may be generally available as an adjunct to the traditional print storage system.

Clipping Services and Business News

One final category of CompuServe's news system needs at least brief description. Both Illustrations 5.1 and 5.2 included the clipping service as a subset of the general information resources offered online.[22] The clipping service is a system that will automatically identify and electronically store articles or stories from the electronic versions of various news services. The service matches a user's search phrase—stored online—with the electronic version of specific newswires, updated daily or hourly. Any stories that match the search phrase are retrieved and stored electronically for the reader or researcher. At present, the services monitored and to which search phrases can be applied on CompuServe include: the Associated Press (AP) national newswires (i.e., *AP US & World*, *AP Sports*, *AP Financial*), United Press International (UPI) news wires, *Reuters Financial Report*, *McGraw-Hill News*[23] (another business newswire), *Over the Counter NewsAlert*, and the electronic edition of the *Washington Post*.

If one subscribes to this service, whose use carries a surcharge, one places a search phrase online and directs that it be applied to one or more of the newswires the service covers. After the search phrase has been logged in, any story carried on a monitored news system will be identified and automatically stored online until the user calls up that personal file for review. Thus if the search phrase logged for clipping were "anesth/ and (death or injury)," stories about anesthetic-related deaths carried on the AP or UPI wires or in the *Washington Post* would be captured auotomatically, as would stories relating to manufacturers of anesthetic-related equipment if an individual was reported killed or injured by that product. Unfortunately, the service is at present heavily weighted to business-related information.

Regional wires and general newspaper coverage are not yet as available on this service, although it is likely that, as the technology advances,[24] what can be continually searched automatically and the number of sources that any individual can thus access, will increase.

Dow Jones News Service

CompuServe's clipping service competes with that of Dow Jones News Service (DJNS), which offers another business-oriented news tracking system keyed to stock and industry symbols of potential interest to the investor or business writer.[25] That system is called *Track* and is designed to allow investors to follow both the prices and general news concerning the fortunes of specific companies. Each *Track* folder—called a "profile" by DJNS—can contain up to twenty-five stock symbols (i.e., IBM, CNS, S, TL, etc.) or codes for a specific area of production (computers, news, automobile manufacturing, retail, etc.). After filing the symbols online, the user can automatically log onto the system and call up the "profile," and the value of each stock so listed will be returned immediately. In addition, those symbols function as individual search phrases for stories appearing in publications monitored by the Dow Jones News Service. In retrieving the folder, one also simultaneously receives notice of any articles in which the company name or industry at large was mentioned. Citations so stored are displayed by title and date and can be read in full through Dow Jones News Service's full-text news database package, *Text*.

Those not using the clipping service can, of course, search the digitally stored business library independently. Its holdings are a good example of how the broad spectrum of any one field—in this case newspapers, wire services, and periodicials—is tailored by an individual packager to provide a focused electronic service. *Text*'s databases include the full text files of the weekly *Barrons* (1987 to present), *Business Week* (1985 to present), the *Wall Street Journal* (1984 to present), Dow Jones News Service (1979 to present), the *Washington Post* (1984 to present), McGraw Hill's online database of twenty-five business publications, and *DataTimes*, a database of 150 regional and specialized business magazines.[26] Also on this service is a press release newswire that digitalizes and makes available corporate statements by company public relations departments.[27]

In addition, DJNS offers an almost overwhelming array of databases from a variety of suppliers concerned with almost every aspect of business and industry. These range from *Disclosure*, an online library of mandatory Securities and Exchange Commission filings (10-K and 10-Q) submitted to the government by companies operating in the United States, through corporate reports by Dunn and Bradstreet or Standard & Poor's, to a database listing mandated filings for ownership of 5 percent of any company.

The service's business orientation and corporate affiliation have earned the computerized library a large following among corporate research divisions, although for the general reporter, writer, or researcher its deficits, at present, may outweigh its advantages. The prestige of the Dow Jones cachet and the size of the system's database offerings made Dow Jones News Service the premier distributor of computerized corporate information in the early to mid-1980s. By 1990, however, many of its databases were simultaneously offered by other wholesale or gateway distributors (like CompuServe) and packagers (like Dialog). Its higher yearly membership charges and connect fees, coupled with an unusually complex online search and command language,[28] make it a frustrating resource for all but those specialty researchers concerned primarily with financial and business news who took the time to become familiar with its eccentricities.

Just as medicine was used, earlier, as a topical example to describe the means by which pertinent information on a specific scientific area could be accessed, Dow Jones News serves as an example of an online research tool that focuses a number of computerized resources to provide information services for those interested in financial issues. Where PaperChase was conceived as a specialized tool for the medical professional, so DJNS was conceived as a broad array of finance-related, computerized suppliers that would be of interest to the corporate official or business writer. The increasing availability of its various component services elsewhere diminishes the researchers' necessary reliance on the individual service itself, however. A number of alternate, more general information services now offer similar databases and the products of the same packagers, making it possible to report on business affairs by using the services of independent distributors.

Subscribers accessing daily stock prices on DJNS, for example, were until recently unique in their ability then to immediately access published news reports on the company whose stock price per share had just been electronically searched. This ability to key news stories to changes in the price of an individual stock was one of the great advantages of the *Track* program. Now CompuServe offers a similar service. Subscribers accessing a specific stock price are informed when a news story has been run by one of the news services included in the clipping service. Those wishing to read these stories can then immediately access the news stories. Thus, after typing "AAPL," the exchange symbol for Apple computer, and the command "Go Stocks," the online service provided me this morning with the price of the company's stock. A bulletin simultaneously informed me there were news stories about the company and, by typing the command "CoNews" (surcharged at $15 an hour), I was given a menu of current stories about Apple computer from both Reuters and AP newswires.

A Business Example

Whichever the wholesaler or distributor chosen, the effects of this technology on business reportage are evident in the following example. In 1987, the Akron, Ohio, *Beacon Journal* won a Pulitzer prize for its 1986 coverage of the takeover of Akron-based Goodyear Tire and Rubber Company. When, in October 1986, general wire stories stated that Goodyear was among the New York Stock Exchange's most actively traded stocks, it was perceived by both the media and financial traders as a possible takeover target. To track the rumors, analyze potential buyers, and follow the attempt, *Journal* reporters used several computerized resources. These included specialized databases like *Disclosure*, composed of information submitted by U.S. businesses to the government, whose detailed financial information on possible buyers allowed news reporters to determine with some degree of certainty whether those companies would be able to command sufficient capital to take over so large a corporate target. *Disclosure* is available on DJNS, Dialog, and, among other gateways, Information Access Company's EasyNet.

In addition, *Journal* reporters made good use of stories filed by colleagues for other hometown newspapers in the cities where Goodyear's potential suitors were located. "If a rumor came up on deadline, in a matter of a few minutes, several of us could access a lot of information on Vu/Text."[29] It is likely that, had the *Journal* used only DJNS, which does not provide a gateway to *Vu/Text* files, it could have accessed similar information from the regional business services of DataTimes's database. Whether it used *Disclosure*-based information through DJNS's or CompuServe's gateway is irrelevant. It is probable that other databases, like those tracking insider trading,[30] were also used, and the information recovered from these regional news services and the Securities and Exchange filings was sufficient.

The critical point is that an array of databases covering federal filings by private corporations and general news files from around the country allowed local reporters to analyze actively and monitor the possible sale of a major hometown employer. Rather than accepting the word of involved corporate parties, *Journal* reporters were able to determine, step-by-step, the actions taken by Goodyear's suitors and also to make informed guesses at the potential effects for their city of those possible changes in the corporate structure of their principal employer. Newspapers in those cities where bidders for Goodyear had home or branch offices could be searched for indications of corporate health (and therefore if there was sufficient capital to justify the bid) and for the bidder's degree of participation in community affairs. Where suitors had taken over other corporations in the past, newspapers in the target cities (as well as corporate reports) provided information on the effects of those previous mergers or acquisitions. Was the target company broken up to pay for the takeover? Were wholesale layoffs at the target company instigated? Was the original management left in place? Did the suitor keep, after the fact, promises made during the period of bid, counterbid, and negotiations?

Here again we see the degree to which conflicts among the institutional, instrumental, and functional goals of the subjects must be judged within a broader context than statements delivered at a press conference. Corporate officials are charged, institutionally, with protection of the shareholder's investment, the care of their company, and (hopefully) its improvement. Instrumentally, these goals become a pledge to produce a product or provide a service so unique, valuable, and necessary that the public will not only accept it but choose that product or service over others. Functionally, those officials earn their living through employment in the company and their ability to advance in the corporate world is defined by the success of the parent corporation under their stewardship.

Those pursuing the successful purchase or merger of one company by another must insist on the long-term benefits of that action for both companys' products or services as well. CEOs must state that this change will benefit all shareholders. They must assure the public at large and investors in particular that a board's decision to make or accept a merger is in everyone's interest. But these assertions are uniformly suspect because the corporate executive's primary obligation is to the firm's financial condition, not the greater community's benefit. The company officials' careers, incomes, egos, and reputations are bound up in the takeover or merger move. Successful financial marriages, like the 1989 merger of Warner Communications and Time-Life, made multimillionaires of corporation executives who, before the deal, may have been only wealthy millionaires. Those who spoke most forcefully and publicly for the merger were often individuals who stood to gain the most and whose views on the deal should have been most suspect.

Thus to weigh the future effect of any deal whose value is trumpeted by participants (the sale of a local newspaper to an information conglomerate, the choice of a public transit system for a city, or the courting of a specific industry for a depressed region), one must examine the uniformly rosy statements of corporate leaders through an analysis of the past actions of their companies and, perhaps, a good look at the potential benefits any successful negotiation will bring to them as individuals. By using these databases and receiving an accurate and complete picture of a company's financial structure (from federal filings), one can predict the possibility that a successful merger will overextend the purchaser, with disastrous results for employees and stockholders. Where a company has, in the past, swallowed and dismembered smaller rivals, firing longtime workers and decimating the symbiotic relations between company town and local residents, it is likely that local newspapers have written about those actions.

If skepticism is an important component of objective journalism, as *Newsweek* suggested in its analysis of the Stuart murder case in Boston, it is critical when the future of a town's primary employer is at stake. To wait passively for the public announcement by suitor or target board members is to accept without either thought or skepticism the statements of individuals whose objectivity (as participants and financially interested parties[31]) is clearly open to question. By using federal documents and the reports of colleagues in a dozen different cities, however, one can put together an actual picture of the financial effects for both suitor and target.

CRITICAL DATABASES

In the mid-1980s, those interested in buying a first computer but bewildered by the array of products then on the market were sometimes advised to choose their hardware only after deciding what software would be used. Whether one bought an Apple Macintosh, whose graphics system was superior, or an IBM-compatible computer with extremely limited graphics capability, depended, in large part, on the type of work for which one needed the computer. Drawing and painting programs were, at one time, available for the former but not the latter system. If, on the other hand, one needed to analyze large amounts of almost any type of data, the clear choice was an IBM-compatible system. At that time, Apple vendors offered nothing as powerful as the sophisticated database, mathematic, and computational software marketed for the IBM-compatible computer. By 1990, however, the software bases of the two systems were similar and the potential of both had become, for the average

user, virtually identical.[32] Both computer systems now offered software and hardware to facilitate graphics, data
analysis, telecommunications, and page-layout functions.
Both provided large storage systems and a variety of acces-
sories (i.e.,scanners, modems, laser printers, plotters, and
so on) that made it possible to customize, through software
and hardware choice, the system chosen.

In the early 1990s, the choice of digital information
supplier depends not on the power of any one vendor's
computers but on the availability of databases that can be
accessed through any single online distributor. It makes no
sense to subscribe, for example, to Dow Jones News Service
if the files that will be most constantly accessed are from
past issues of popular magazines, scientific reports, or non-
business sections of regional newspapers. Dialog, on the
other hand, would be a needless expense for those whose
primary information requirement was to gain informal information from members of a professional community like
the forums that are CompuServe's stock-in-trade. To use
CompuServe primarily for its IQuest gateway when the
writer needs daily access to highly technical or academic
databases would be similarly inefficient. The choice of distributor depends, then, first on the availability of databases
from primary suppliers and, second, the cost-effectiveness of
the system for any user.

While a complete listing of databases used or discussed
in this book can be found in Appendix 1, it may be useful at
this point to describe briefly a small series of databases that
provide general or category-specific information of likely use
to the generalist and newsperson.

BUSINESS AND FINANCIAL

Disclosure
Files from: Eighteen months
Supplier: Bechtel Corporation
Provides: Detailed financial information contained
in federally mandated filings to the Securities and
Exchange Commission by public and private corpo-
rations (10-K and 10Q filings). On Dialog it is *Dis-*

closure / Spectrum Ownership, a database updated quarterly with summaries from all SEC filings. On BRS it is updated weekly under the name *Disclosure* and contains slightly different information. Both are available through EasyNet gateway.

ABI/Inform
Files from: January 1971
Supplier: Data Courier, Inc.
Provides: Lengthy abstracts from business and management magazines, stressing general business management and, secondarily, product information.

Business Periodicals Index
Files from: June 1982
Supplier: H.W. Wilson Company
Provides: An electronic version of the standard Business Periodicals Index with references from most major English-language business magazines concerned with marketing, economics, industry, and finance.

Dun's Market Identifiers
Files from: Yearly reports
Supplier: Dun's Marketing Services
Provides: Basic information from public records on virtually every U.S. business with more than ten employees. A variety of services, including *Standard & Poor's*, provides a wealth of information in varying degrees of detail on U.S. companies, private and public.

PTS databases
Files from: 1972
Supplier: Predicasts
Provides: A family of databases whose individual files index information on worldwide business literature. Individual databases include: *PTS U.S. Forecast*; *PTS New Product Announcements*; *PTS Mars* (advertising and marketing); *PTS International Forecasts*; *PTS F&S Indexes* (company, prod-

uct, and industry information including information on mergers and acquisitions worldwide).

GENERAL INFORMATION

Magazine Index
Files from: 1976
Supplier: Information Access Company
Provides: Files covering 370 magazines with a wide range of subject matter. Also see *Magazine ASAP*, a holding file for recent articles that are then stored in *Magazine Index*.

National Newspaper Index
Files from: 1979
Supplier: Information Access Company
Provides: Full coverage of the *New York Times*, the *Wall Street Journal*, and the *Christian Science Monitor*.

NewsSearch
Files from: Updated monthly
Supplier: Information Access Company
Provides: A short-term index of stories, articles, and reviews from more than fifteen hundred magazines, journals, and newspapers. Files are placed, at the end of a month, in databases like *Magazine ASAP*. Holds on a temporary basis files that will be transferred at the end of each month to the *Legal Resource Index, Management Contents*, and *Trade and Industry Index* databases.

GOVERNMENT

CENDATA
Available from: 1980 Census
Supplier: U.S. Census Bureau
Provides: Demographic and economic information from both the 1980 census and more recent, intercensus surveys. Also included is the text of Census Bureau press releases.

Congressional Record Abstracts
Available from: 1976
Supplier: Capital Services International
Provides: Abstracts of the proceedings of the *Congressional Record*, which is the record of debates and actions by the U.S. Congress. Includes coverage of committee and subcommittee reports, laws, executive communications, speeches, floor debates (including inserted material), data on bills, roll-call votes.

Federal Register Abstracts
Available from: 1977
Supplier: Capital Services International
Provides: Coverage of federal regulatory agency action published in the *Federal Register*. Includes presidential proclamations, executive orders, text of proposed regulations, and compliance requirements and legal notices issued by federal agencies.

MEDICINE AND SCIENCE

Enviroline
Available from: 1971
Supplier: Environmental Information Center
Provides: Digital version of printed indexes: *Environmental Abstracts* and *Environmental Issues*. Provides abstracts of articles on environmental issues published in government documents, industry reports, conference reports, newspapers, and magazines.

Medline
Available from: 1966
Supplier: U.S. National Library of Medicine
Provides: Indexes articles in medical and biomedical sciences from three sources: *Index Medicus, Index to Dental Literature,* and *International Nursing Index.* Also offered in a simplified search version with some full-text services through PaperChase (Beth Israel Hospital).

SciSearch
Available from: 1970
Supplier: Institute for Scientific Information
Provides: A multidisciplinary database whose references are expanded from those printed in *Science Citation Index*. It covers virtually every journal of both pure and applied sciences.

PRIVATE VERSUS PUBLIC ACCESS

The writer, reporter, or researcher needs to be able to describe not only the context of information pertinent to a specific event but also its likely location by database. Then the question arises whether that database's supplier is available either through a gateway subscription or a full-service distributor to which the writer or reporter—individually or as a corporate employee—has access. This search is not dissimilar to the print researcher's search through various library systems for a book, journal, or document whose temporary acquisition requires a trek through the hierarchies of library storage.

Contemporary print libraries exist within a hierarchy that provides a rough parallel to the computerized complex of files, databases, suppliers, and distributors. There is the neighborhood library, for example, which carries very general reference materials and popular fiction. It is linked to and can draw on the resources of a city's major library, whose holdings include a far greater number of technical and popular resources. In some systems, the city facility is a subset of the state library system, which links its urban members through a program of interlibrary loans to facilitate the efficient sharing of resources among all members. In addition, state (and sometimes city) libraries may be repositories for official state or federal documents. Use of the system is time-consuming, as all who have waited weeks for an interlibrary loan to be dispatched must know, but addresses the essential issue of allocating information resources through a huge network.

Parallel to this general public system may be one or more specialized library networks, of which the state or provincial university library is the most important. In both Canada and the United States, university libraries house extensive collections that, in many areas, far exceed the state system's resources. These include specialized collections in law, medicine, engineering, and the sciences, whose holdings may be part of individual colleges or schools within the greater university system. In the United States, private libraries serving specialized needs also exist, often duplicating the holdings of state or university libraries. Thus, in Columbus, Ohio, the federal court's law library largely duplicates, in its holdings, those of Ohio State University's law library. The latter is reserved for the exclusive use of members of the OSU faculty and community while the former is available to the public. In Honolulu, a special medical library is available for the exclusive use of state physicians while the University of Hawaii's library holdings on medical topics (textbook and journal) are available to all state residents.

Today most people take for granted the rather hard-won notion of general access through this interlocking library system to a range of public information. Both the right to and the necessity for citizen access to these print storage resources are assumed, in terms of both public documents and general research tools. Private libraries are no longer a critical part of the printed information storage system, although in Sam Johnson's day they were the critical repository, especially when the private library belonged to the royal family. In contrast, in this early phase of development, electronically stored information is at present squarely in private hands. The history of the printing revolution suggests that this may be a transient phase in the development of digitalized information resources. Just as books stored in public libraries became part of the communal knowledge system at no direct cost to the user, so, too, electronic databases will eventually enter the public domain. The increasing availability through university libraries of computer data stored on disk, the subsidization of interactive databases by specialty libraries,[33] and, finally, the increasing use of computerized storage as a primary means of information access in academia,[34] are all indications of this trend. Experiments in the late 1970s and early 1980s by the French government, which has made computer terminals available at no charge to citizens interested in accessing official information stored digitally, also suggest one way in which this revolution will progress.

Private versus Public Information: United States

In the early 1980s a number of barriers existed that denied the majority of citizens access to computerized information. Chief among these was a lack of the physical equipment (computer and modem) required to go online and an inability to use the equipment appropriately where it was available.[35] Of perhaps equal importance and greater long-term importance were the trend to privatization of information by the U.S. government and its insistence that all computerized information, even public records, should be sold—preferably through private corporations. In the 1980s the U.S. government under President Ronald Reagan acted to assure that federal information stored in a digital fashion would be "privatized" and that citizens seeking to access this data could do so only through private vendors. This action, in effect, created the specter of private corporations controlling the dissemination of public information. In addition, federal officials in the 1980s attempted to draw a distinction between the right of public access to printed information and its right to digitalized information. Where citizens had a right under law to the former, the latter, according to officials supervising compliance with the Freedom of Information Act of 1966, was not to be covered by similar guarantees. Public records stored in digitalized form were thus officially removed, despite previous accessibility to their printed form, from the public domain.[36]

The debate over these decisions, which first became public in late 1989, centered around the more than four hundred computerized databases then maintained by the federal government,[37] many of them covering research and general information that, traditionally, had been considered in the public domain. Federal databases cost, at present, between $15 and $30 an hour to use, while privately controlled databases, often based on that same public information, cost between $50 and $100 an hour to access. Examples of the former include the Environmental Protection Agency's *Toxic Release Inventory* (TRI), mandated by the 1986 Superfund law; the Department of Education's *ERIC* educational resources database; and the National Library of Medicine's *Medlars*, costing, at present, $20 an hour. Examples of private databases of federal information include *Disclosure*'s summaries of SEC 10-K filings, which retail for at least $70 an hour from private suppliers, packagers, and distributors, and the proposed *Edgar* database of other SEC documents, whose projected cost to the public is between $50 and $125 an hour.[38]

The debate on access and the rationale behind this privatization are complicated by the role played by large information and news-oriented corporations—Knight-Ridder is perhaps the most prominent example—that have entered the increasingly lucrative digital information field.[39] As news corporations, they are institutionally committed to the best and most economical systems of information dispersal possible. Their institutional goal (and the basis of their First Amendment protection) is based on public access to information. The news professional's institutional role as guardian of the public's right to information would be meaningless were the professionals and their employers also dedicated to the limited access of data in any form.

But as providers of those privatized records through their digitalized information services, companies like Knight-Ridder (which owns both Dialog and Vu/Text) have a vested interested in maintaining and increasing private corporate control of digitalized information—whatever the source. Their agents—the reporters and editors who supposedly prepare the news while free of restraints—are thus in an unenviable position of having to question the corporate position and uphold their institutional goals (and perhaps thus jeopardizing their functional goals) or refrain from entering the debate. While the debate is, at this writing, focused on the storage and retrieval of public documents, the issue will

probably become one of general public access to all digitalized records and the degree of accessibility that will be
guaranteed to the public.

As governments and private corporations both move to
computerized filing and storage of documents, public records
and documents in general will be increasingly accessible
only to those with the ability to access required data by
computer. Experiments have already begun at various levels
in North America to assure public access to official records
and information. Thus, in the province of British Columbia,
officials in 1989 were making available on an experimental
basis many computerized, digitalized records to news organizations and concerned citizens with computer and modem.[40] In 1990 citizens of Hawaii with access to computers
were being urged to use a local number to access the state
legislature's daily calendar to check on the status of bills
coming to the floor or committee. In addition, the U.S.
Supreme Court's Project Hermes[41] and electronic bulletin
boards run by various federal departments provide another
indication of the degree to which access to information—
either at cost or at a premium—will increasingly be defined
by the individual's access to computer technologies.

Just as public libraries were born to assure general public access to books, journals, and magazines printed and sold
for profit by private companies, one suspects that the resolution of issues concerning access to digitalized information
will require an equal assertion of the right of the public to
both its own records and to official files in general. Public
libraries grew out of a need not only to address the storage
needs of a progressively massive volume of printed information,
but to guarantee that access to information was not limited
by privilege or class. It has been noted that some university
libraries have begun to allocate some of their resources to
assure that faculty and students have access to computerized data in a variety of fields. In this way, the library
retains its role as purveyor of information irrespective of the
mode of storage, and the concept of public access is asserted.
One may assume that, although currently unusual, this
policy will become generally accepted and that with public
access, attempts will be made to lower the cost of electronic
services through reassertion of the public nature of federal

records (and thus the necessity of their dissemination at cost) and through market forces that assure that individual databases may be offered by a variety of distributors. In the short term, issues of control may create a conflict among corporate officials serving information companies that simultaneously act as suppliers of a variety of information types and as public representatives of the Fourth Estate, which, at least in theory, is a guardian of public information. In the long run, such a system (as production increases and the market becomes saturated) would retrace the steps that have brought about the print-oriented public information system many now take for granted.

CONCLUSION

Digital information storage systems provide an interlocking and to some degree hierarchical resource whose data can be used by popular writers (whatever the medium) to consider critically the statements of traditional news sources. The organization of this data matches, in some ways, the search phrases used to address the data in toto. Just as the online researcher must define a problem or topic in such a way that appropriate references will be retrieved, so, too, must that search phrase be addressed to an appropriate information packager or producer.

Within the current division of newsroom labor among librarian, reporter, and editor, there is disagreement about what information is pertinent and about control of available online libraries. An issue of "how much" should be searched, "where" information should be sought, and "what" is appropriate is a function of both appropriate phrasing of any particular problem and knowing the general resources available through online subscription services. At present there are three levels of data vendors offering a wide array of information, much of which may also be accessed in printed form. Individual suppliers, like WestLaw, offer specific services directly to the subscriber; packagers make available the products of a number of suppliers for the researcher whose information product needs are both consistent and broad. Finally, gateway distributors make available on a fee-for-use basis the services of more specific packagers as well as informal information sources.

These categories are not hard and fast. A supplier may offer subscribers a link to the resources of one or more packagers, and it is possible that a packager may have links to specific services also provided by the gateway distributor. By describing menu and screen systems on a gateway distributor, available systems accessing the widest array of packagers have been discussed. These "user friendly" mechanisms allow even neophytes to gain control of their own data search and offer one way in which the control of information can be shared between the electronic resource's librarian gatekeeper and the client writer or researcher.

The overlap and repetition of service of current vendors are a result of the youth of the industry and disjunctions created by the rapidly changing nature of a new, swiftly advancing technology controlled by private corporations in an evolving market. Because of the rapid changes in this industry and the almost certain assumption that new vendors will emerge as older ones disappear, change, or merge, the emphasis in this chapter has been on the broadest possible classifications and not on the currently available services of any single company. While it is clear that the digital storage of information will become increasingly common during the 1990s, the structure of corporate access is not yet defined. Indeed, the public's right to information stored in digital form will be as critical an issue in the coming years as the potential these resources may provide to writers or researchers in any specific segment of society.

Because digitally stored information is not yet free to the public through a system of government-supported libraries, issues of cost are as critical today as those of technical ability to access electronically stored information. Understanding the potential of an online database to provide critical information is of no value if the writer or researcher cannot afford to access the data. Thus the argument returns full circle to the relation between economic priorities in society and the institutional goal of news and public information corporations to provide appropriate information to its clients and society at large.

NOTES

1. *Medline* is carried by Dialog Information Services.

2. Both the *New England Journal of Medicine* and *Lancet* are independently carried as files by BRS Technologies, which simultaneously offers *Index Medicus*.

3. *Biosis* is a database containing articles on biology and bioengineering, and *CancerLit* is an electronic index of articles abstracted from various sources pertaining to cancer research. Both are available as individual files through Dialog Information Services while *Ageline*, a database of gerontological and geriatric information, is available through BRS Technologies. These few examples do not begin to exhaust the potential for specialized electronic files. A similar wealth of information is available in other fields, including law and business.

4. PaperChase was developed by Beth Israel Hospital, a teaching hospital for Harvard University Medical School. See, *Your Guide to PaperChase, the Service That Helps You Search the Biomedical Literature to Get the Information You Need* (Boston: PaperChase, 1989).

5. In 1989, Thinking Machines Corporation introduced commercial applications of a system of thirty-two thousand linked processors, each relatively weak in itself and yet each with its own memory. The resulting "connection machine" is used by Dow Jones News Retrieval to search a database of business magazine articles with relatively simple, non-Boolean phrasing. Thus rather than typing "health same /s conscious/," one could simply ask the system for articles on "the impact of health consciousness on fast-food." See Donald E. Trivette, "What's Different about DowQuest? Ease, Content and Text-retrieval," *Dowline*, Summer 1989, 20-26.

6. My early experiences with online searching were all carried out in this manner. The ability to query online librarians familiar with the products of various producers, able to suggest appropriate databases, and willing to criticize and explain search phrases made it possible for me to learn not only the gateway system but those of specific producers and suppliers as well.

7. Predictably, there have been a number of books written describing the most efficient ways to use CompuServe's

services. Those interested in its resources or applicability to their particular needs are referred to Alfred Glossbrenner, *Alfred Glossbrenner's Master Guide to CompuServe* (New York: Brady, 1987). In addition, the company publishes a variety of user manuals for those interested in accessing specialized data libraries. See, for example, *CompuServe Financial Services Users Guide*, and *CompuServe IQuest Database Directory*.

8. Tutorials are written constantly both by the distributors and vendors themselves and by specialty writers. All major services (Dialog, BRS, Dow Jones News Service, CompuServe, PaperChase, etc.) provide volumes of material for the user. These user guides, often provided free to the user, list in exhaustive detail varying files available and the means by which they are accessed. Free-lance writers have attempted to take this basic information and make it accessible in a more folksy, relaxed, narrative style. See, for example, Glossbrenner, *Master Guide to CompuServe*.

9. A number of books are now on the market providing general introductions to online data searching in general, while others focus on how to use electronic resources for financial, academic, scientific, and business research. An example of the general introduction to online resources is Alfred Glossbrenner, *How to Look It Up Online* (New York: St. Martin's Press, 1987). This is, perhaps, the best introduction to accessing database packagers and suppliers on the market. The 1989 edition of *Books in Print* listed over thirty-five titles beginning with "online" for texts describing the use of online resources in various fields.

10. For a short history of the development of CompuServe's forums, see Charles Bowen, "Forum Growth Creates Information Mecca," *Online Today* 8:7 (July 1989), 20.

11. At this writing there are, for example, forums dedicated to the use of software manufactured by, among others, Borland and Microsoft; forums dedicated exclusively to the use of Apple, Toshiba, and IBM computers, a forum for disabled computer users; etcetera. Increasingly, manufacturers of computers and software, which organize and supervise the forums, use them for product testing and as customer service outlets.

12. "Aviation Writer Scores Scoop by Using On-Line Data Base," *National Association of Science Writers*, Summer 1988. A short story on Russomano's use of this database is included in a series of readings used by J.T. Johnson in a course on the use of computers by journalists at San Francisco State College. I am indebted to Johnson for making it available to me. J.T. Johnson, personal communication, February 1990.

13. The assignment was from the CTV television network's public affairs program W5, perhaps the premier public information program on television in Canada at that time. The supervising producer, Gary Dweyer-Joyce informed me they had earlier considered doing a similar story but it had been shelved because researchers in 1989 had been unable to find individuals with visual problems willing to discuss their problems on air. A show segment based on this research was scheduled to air in 1991, about the time this book went to press.

14. In this interest they are no different from any member of society who may be professionally or personally concerned with specific issues. A bicyclist concerned about his city's road network may talk, for example, to a city planner who is a fellow church member, the councilperson who belongs to the same bicycle club, or the engineer who is a client. These SIGs provide a similar context, albeit one with vastly enlarged geographic range in which common interest may generate shared information.

15. C. Whitcher et al., "Anesthetic Mishaps and the Cost of Monitoring: A Proposed Standard for Monitoring Equipment," *Journal of Clinical Monitoring* 4 (January 1988), 5-15.

16. One could then use the *Social Sciences Index* (online or in the library) to find a list of articles in which Whitcher et al. are cited. It is always difficult to base an argument on a single review article, but, in most cases, articles like this are repeatedly cited and the position thus strengthened. On PaperChase one can also look for later articles in which the article's author is used as a subject reference, thus finding similar citations.

17. The *Database of Databases*, Dialog file number 230, is an electronic version of the American Library Association's two-volume *A Directory and Data Sourcebook*.

18. The *Database Directory* is published by Knowledge Industry Publications, and the American Society for Information Sciences. It can also be purchased in print form at a cost, in the late 1980s, of $215 a year. For that amount one receives two editions, published in the spring and fall,, and twelve monthly issues of the magazine *Database Alert*.

19. This directory, published annually in print form by Cuadra/Elsevier of New York, is also available on WestLaw. Since IQuest is the CompuServe gateway name for EasyNet, this directory is, of course, also available to the Telebase System subscriber. There are in addition specialized directories for individual research fields. Thus Cuadra Publications issued in 1987, for example, a specialized directory called *Online Databases in the Medical and Life Sciences*.

20. Kathleen A. Hansen, Jean Ward, and Douglas M. McLeod, "Role of the Newspaper Library in the Production of News," *Journalism Quarterly* 64:4 (1987), 717. "While 32 percent who request assistance ask [newspaper] library staff to help identify the 'best' material, 66 percent say they decide on quality of material by themselves."

21. At Ohio State University, for example, each school of the university has one electronic service at its disposal. Thus the School of Journalism's library is in charge of Dialog, the School of Veterinary Medicine is in charge of the CD-ROM disks for *Medline* files, the Law Library subscribes to WestLaw, the Main Library has, among others, responsibility for the census files, etc.

22. For a general description of this service on CompuServe, see Cathryn Conroy, "News You Can Choose: Nonstop Global Coverage Delivered Online," *Online Today* 8:1 (January 1989), 16-21.

23. In early 1990 this service was slated for removal from the CompuServe electronic information system. It is included here as an example of a type of specialized "news service," like the sports wire or *OTC NewsAlert*, which has gained popularity on electronic information systems.

24. It is sometimes difficult to remember how new this technology is and how rapidly it is changing. CompuServe

was founded in 1979 and has grown, in eleven years, to include more than 600,000 subscribers. Its success was dependent on a number of technological innovations of the 1980s, especially the inexpensive personal computer and the modem. Advances in chip technology, fiber optics, and CD-ROM storage systems all suggest strongly that in the coming decade the speed and capability of these information systems will increase dramatically.

25. For a discussion of *Track*, see *Dow Jones News Retrieval User's Guide*, (Princeton, N.J.: Dow Jones & Co., 1989), 87-88.

26. DataTimes, like Vu/Text, provides a computerized library of daily publications. The service offered on DJNS focuses on regional business publications and is also accessed by the "plain language" search system, DowQuest, introduced by DJNS in 1989.

27. *PR Newswire*, a product of PR Newswire Association, Inc., is also available at this writing on Dialog, Vu/Text, and Nexus information services.

28. Like almost all distributors, DJNS offers training sessions for new users, provides specialized software to make accessing information easier, and publishes an enormous array of user-oriented guides, including a monthly magazine.

29. Donna S. Willmann, "Vu/Text's Online Databases Aid in Pulitzer Prize-Winning Coverage," Vu/Text Information Services Press Release, June 3, 1987. This public relations blurb is used in part to demonstrate the type of background information available on the *PR Newswire* as well as the limits of such information. Vu/Text is interested less in the analysis of the journal's prize than in its own contribution to that effort. But within the parameters of that self-interest, one can credit its assertion that the use of electronic services was critical to the newspaper's award-winning coverage. From that starting point, interested parties can check the newspaper's files, other articles on the Pulitzer prize, stories linking "online" and "Goodyear or Akron," etc.

30. Because it is necessary for those seeking ownership of more than 5 percent of a company to file their intentions with the SEC, there are several databases that track this information. The government publication is *Official Sum-*

mary of Insider Transactions, whose database is supplied by FCI/Invest-Net; on Dow Jones the database is called *Insider Trading Monitor*; on Dialog it is file 540 and called *DIS-CLOSURE / Spectrum Ownership*. For a review of these and other business-related databases, see Glossbrenner, *How to Look it Up Online*, chapter 16.

31. It is not uncommon in takeovers for management to receive lucrative bonuses which, some believe, may bias their decisions and serve no long-term purpose in the re-structuring of a company. The merger of Time-Life and Warner Communications in 1989 included just such "golden parachutes," whose extravagance angered some shareholders.

32. The introduction of Microsoft's Windows software, which provided a Macintosh-like screen system for IBM-compatible, MS-DOS operating systems, was one factor bringing these two systems together. Another was the decision by Apple to use drives that would accept 3.5inch disks formatted either on an Apple or an IBM-compatible system. These factors meant that a story written using Microsoft Word software on an IBM-compatible machine could be opened and used by an Apple Macintosh owner running Microsoft's Word program written for the Apple Macintosh.

33. In 1989, the Ohio State University made available Dialog's network to faculty members through the Journalism Department, and a department of the main library had census information online and on CD-ROM disk for those who needed those resources.

34. The educational database *ERIC*, a repository for academic papers presented at conferences on a wide range of subjects, is an example. Articles catalogued in this reposi-tory are frequently cited with their computerized location number (like the ISBN number allotted to books) to assure prompt retrieval. *ERIC* database is available through dis-tributors like Dialog and Nexis, through packagers like EasyNet, and, therefore, from wholesalers like CompuServe.

35. In 1989 approximately one-third of all personal com-puters, about 18 million, were equipped with modems, and it was estimated by one columnist that "only about a quarter of those who own modems know how to use them." John Markoff, "Fast Modems: All Dressed Up, With Only a Slow Way to Go," *New York Times*, February 25, 1990, F10.

36. The issue has received considerable attention in both news and computer-oriented publications. An example of the latter, which provides a good summary of the issues, is David L. Margulius, "Your Right to What Uncle Sam Knows," *PC/Computing*, October 1989, 79-85. Another article that focuses on access to SEC documents is: Paul McMasters, "Government Information, at a Price," *Quill* 77:9 (October 1989), 17.

37. For a listing of these databases, see the *Federal Database Finder* (Chevy Chase, Md.: Information USA, 1989). It costs, at present, $125.

38. *Federal Databases,* 83.

39. For a brief review of Knight-Ridder's focus in this area, see Jeff Shear, "Knight Ridder's Data Base Blitz," *Insight*, October 31, 1988, 44-45. For another view of the degree to which information conglomerates have lobbied for privatization, see Margulius, "Your Right to What Uncle Sam Knows."

40. John Daly, BCTV, personal communication, December 1989.

41. Steve Nevas, "Coming Soon to a Screen Near You: The Supreme Court, *Quill* 78:3 (April 1990), 24. Project Hermes is the code name for a system that will simultaneously disseminate full court decisions in an electronic form to major news agencies and bibliographic legal systems.

6

Conclusions

It is possible to argue that the diffusion of electronic database technologies is a certainty simply on the basis of the history of the diffusion of previous information-related innovations. Comparisons with the earlier history of the printing revolution have created the impression that increasing utilization of this technology is inevitable. That thesis is strengthened by the rapidity with which general computer technologies have, since the 1970s, become commonplace adjuncts to the mode of production in both print and television news facilities. Stories from the wires are now read by news professionals, irrespective of their specific medium, not on paper printed by the old, slow Teletype terminals but in a continuous electronic stream that passes online through the newsperson's computer and from which, should one choose, a paper copy can be printed. Linotype has been replaced by cold typesetting and by computerized setups; the traditional typewriter with the computer terminal; and—again irrespective of the medium—stories that in 1975 were written and then edited on paper are now composed on screen, transmitted electronically, and first edited and then laid out on a succession of office terminals. Electronic databases are, in one sense, simply an extension of other computer-based technologies that have already revolutionized the North American newsroom. The technology of computer terminal, screen, modem, and fax is now in place. News libraries have been and are being computerized rapidly, both because it is more efficient to retrieve electronically written news in a digital form and because electronic storage requires fewer full-time staff members and less office space.

The inevitability of the use of databases also can be argued on the basis of their near ubiquity in other areas of public information. If lawyers, public relations writers, academics, government officials, physicians, engineers, and so on all use electronic library services, then newspeople must inevitably follow. To the extent that reporters cover active and computer-equipped segments of the society, they will either ape or adopt—depending on one's view of the news— the tools and language of their subjects. Increasingly, documents are filed directly onto databases, so reporters who seek, for example, federally filed information must search for it online. The facts of this argument—its constituent parts—are demonstrably true, but none of it speaks clearly to the way these resources will be integrated or the degree to which control of electronic databases will be ceded to journalists who may or may not use them in the ways suggested in this book.

The position of those who insist that the mode of production of public information is defined by corporate and official agendas must be considered. The diffusion of any innovation can be retarded or facilitated, channeled into different modes or encouraged in specific directions, all depending on the economic and social climate in which it takes root. The history of the newspaper and newsmagazine, whose mode of production was defined by the printing revolution, makes this clear. Noam Chomsky is correct when he insists that the economic and social agenda of publication owners and political leaders affected and, in some cases, determined both the development of news as a mode of production and the limits of expression that grew up around that public system of information diffusion.[1] It may be useful, then, to review the economies that electronic libraries bring to the news before summarizing the other effects these technologies will have on the form of the news.

COST BENEFITS

Efficiencies

It is possible to argue solely on the basis of cost efficiency that online technologies represent, when used intelligently, substantial economies in labor and plant resource use. Corporate managers unconvinced by the empowerment of writers in relation to their subjects and unconcerned about the potential improvement in the quality of the news "product" will likely approve increasing use of these technologies because of the potential savings they create in the newsroom. The adoption of electronic databases for news storage at any medium outlet offers marked efficiencies in space and employee staffing, as well as a separate and potentially profitable product on its own.

For example, Andrew Ippolito, a librarian at *Newsday*, pointed out in 1985 that "before going online at *Newsday* in February of 1979, two librarians using conventional sources and search routines were able to handle 50 to 60 queries a month. Now they handle 50 to 60 queries a week."[2] Not only are news librarians handling larger volumes of queries, but their specialized bibliographic training can be used, despite the increased volume, in a more intelligent and efficient way. Freed of the labor-intensive chore of physically clipping stories on a daily basis, making multiple copies of those clippings, and then cataloguing them manually in one or more files, they have more time to be reference librarians and to search through varying databases and information sources that may more precisely address the context of the editorial query.

Further, the digitalized library frees employers from the necessity of subsidizing the traditional news library's often inordinate need for room in urban facilities where the cost of space per square foot may be great. The physical storage of twenty, thirty, or one hundred years of clipping files requires an enormous area, often equal to or exceeding that allocated to the newswriters and editors. Even the practice of placing on microfilm early issues of a magazine or newspaper required the purchase of both specialized machines on which the files could be read and row upon row of cabinets in which that material could be stored. For reporters to access any of this material, the traditional news morgue required at minimum between two and five reference librarians, who would accept staff queries, go to banks of clipping files or microfilm cabinets, find the appropriate folder or film, and then bring back the sometimes voluminous folders for reporters to carry to their desk.

The traditional news library operates at an enormous cost, which becomes part of any publication's overhead. The savings in labor costs and plant space are a major selling point for companies, like Vu/Text or DataTimes, whose business is the digital storage of individual news libraries. Online technologies create extreme efficiencies in library use, not only in the flexibility and efficiency of staff librarians but in the elimination of these space requirements. At the computerized *Globe and Mail* in Toronto, for example, reporters seeking to access their newspaper's digitalized library simply key in the appropriate search phrase at desktop terminals. Files are stored digitally in the newspaper's computers, and can be searched not only more efficiently but more rapidly as well. For either general research or highly specific information retrieval, the electronic library allows reporters, researchers, or editors to retrieve information from their desktop terminal without the time-consuming, labor intensive, and sometimes expensive necessity of travel to libraries or official repositories of federal documents. Even if electronic databases resulted in a more efficient "old style news," the argument for adopting these technologies would be compelling on the basis of labor and plant costs alone.

New Markets: Old Product

The costs of introducing these new, electronic database systems are further offset by the ability of the newsletter, magazine, or newspaper to rent the use of its database to other, third-party users who may wish to access its published files in return for a user fee. In 1987, for example, approximately one-quarter of the *Richmond News Leader and Times-Dispatch*'s data-processing (and thus its library) costs was paid for through library royalties from Vu/Text.[3]

Digitalized libraries placed at system-wide disposal earn the library's owner a royalty each time they are accessed. As acceptance of this type of data resource grows, so do the revenues. The potential value of news files to reporters in distant geographic regions is dwarfed by the degree to which national newspaper files are used, at present, by bankers,[4] lawyers researching cases,[5] market analysts monitoring products and trends,[6] corporate officials seeking information on competitors, and public relations officials seeking to know how their clients are viewed in one or another region.[7]

The transformation of private, corporate library to marketable resource is clearest where publishers have made their news libraries the core of major and often specialized data services. Thus Dow Jones News Retrieval sells access to the company's newspaper, the *Wall Street Journal,* to both news and business customers. This electronic distribution system creates a new market for old stories, which, in the past, had little recurring value. Access to file information was traditionally limited to those with the time to visit and search microfilm or microfiche editions of the *Journal.* News indexes were general and often lacked the specificity such a search required. But online and through electronic search technologies, past stories are as accessible as those put on the Dow Jones News Service this morning, and the value of all information so stored increases as a function of its accessibility. In addition, DJNS sells access to a series of specialized financial databases, which are used extensively by the *Journal*'s editorial staff. Thus the electronic product becomes both news staff resource and, at the same time, a viable product on the open market, the greater public rental of which supports the newspaper's editorial research.

New Markets: New Products

Electronically stored newspapers and magazines thus create new markets for the products that have traditionally been sold only in print or, if broadcast, were as transient as last night's six o'clock news. Of perhaps most practical interest in this study has been the demonstrated potential for newswriters to seek across a broad geographic range for relevant information contained in the work of perhaps distant colleagues. Thus reporters in Vancouver may find in the reportage of fellow newspeople in New York, Akron, or San Francisco stories whose subjects are pertinent to the regional events they may be covering. Secondary but equally significant markets are found through similar searches by lawyers attempting to find background and precedent for cases in which they are involved, by market researchers exploring local trends, by public relations writers searching the work of their fellows, and by others with individual interest in the sometimes diverse work of writers around North America and the world.

While these markets are still relatively small for the majority of online publications—a matter of several thousand dollars a month—it must be remembered that both the technology and therefore the market are young. As data searching becomes increasingly common, it is likely to grow. The explosion in business-related databases and the competition, for example, to acquire distribution rights for documents filed with the Securities Exchange Commission (SEC) suggest that, as a product in its own right, electronically stored data will increase in profitability as a share of the total information market. In the 1700s, during the early part of the printing revolution, the commercial market for general publications (and thus for professional writers and allied print trades) was limited. Within one hundred years, however, the magazine and then the daily newspaper had become indispensable artifacts of the increasingly literate, English-speaking world and ubiquitous by the beginning of the twentieth century. To the degree that electronically stored information is, in fact, a new technology altering modes of both information production and exchange, its utilization as storage system and its marketing as a separate commodity will become an increasingly important segment of the news corporation's product line.

To my knowledge there has to date been no study by either economist or news executive that has attempted to assess the financial gains of the digitalized storage system. Clearly, new markets and new revenues are created when the potential readership of individual stories is increased from a specific market region on a single day to a national or global market over time. The potential for new products created by electronic databases (the electronic Dow Jones News Service, Knight-Ridder's Vu/Text, the Canadian InfoGlobe, etc.) also has an effect on newspaper economies. By creating a separate market for what, traditionally, was an individual newspaper's research tool (Dow Jones News Service's historic stock indexes, for example), not only does the new product gain an independent economic life, but it simultaneously subsidizes and thus decreases the general costs of production for the print medium. To date, studies of the relation between computerization and the news have focused on issues of pagination and economies resulting in traditionally defined modes of production. But it is clear from even this brief summary that the benefits accruing from electronic database use are more complex and relate as well to the value that can be assigned any single story as a function of market range and time.

Staff Economies and Flexibility

Other and equally significant savings accrue through the online technology's ability to decrease dramatically expenditures in labor or capital when reporters or editors need information that can only be acquired at a center physically distanced from their circulation or broadcast region. *Milwaukee Sentinel* business editor Avrum D. Lank, for example, told *Editor and Publisher* that keeping track of reports to the Securities and Exchange Commission by Wisconsin corporations cost his company thousands of dollars each year. Simply to pay an outside expert in Washington, D.C., to watch for filings by Wisconsin's ninety public companies cost his paper $900 a month and, when a SEC report was filed, an additional $10 each time the company called to inform him of that filing.

This price, he lamented, was the high price of receiving public information. In the 1980s, when mergers and takeovers abounded, Lank insisted it was also a necessary cost if his newspaper was to cover the circulation district's economic base. But even with costs of $900 a month and $10 whenever a report was filed with the SEC, it still took Lank's paper several days to receive the files secured by the contractor, who had to first make copies of the originals and then send those copies to Wisconsin. "If the Sentinel wants the information the day it is filed, [contractor] Bechtel[8] will provide it—at a watch cost of $50 per month per company, plus $10 a call, plus further charges for sending copies of the documents to the newspaper."[9]

Few news companies have been willing or able to pay for so expensive a monitoring service, despite the sometimes critical effect mergers, takeovers, corporate restructuring, or ownership changes may have on the community that a specific publication purports to serve. The option has been dependence on information provided by corporate officials, who, as we have seen, are by definition biased by their position and, perhaps, by private agendas in any corporate maneuver. Through the use of online databases, however, it is now possible and relatively inexpensive for a news agency or private interest group to monitor corporate submissions to the SEC by locally or regionally important corporate citizens. When merger, takeover, or buy-out situations develop, this electronic retrieval system makes it unnecessary for those reporters and editors anxious to receive pertinent filings to send a reporter to Washington or pay a federal expert to retrieve and mail or fax the documents back.

The savings thus achieved in both money and labor are substantial when compared to subcontracting or dispatching a reporter to the Securities and Exchange Commission headquarters in Washington. Steven Goldspiel, president of Disclosure, Inc., another SEC electronic information supplier, says that in the past his clients have been the banks, accounting firms, law firms, security brokers, and corporate libraries whose employers were involved in the critical business decisions that affect any single region.[10]

But news organizations have begun to access these same resources, which were, several years ago, the exclusive domain of the editorial subjects. For example, the Akron, Ohio, *Beacon Journal* used Disclosure, in conjunction with Vu/Text and other electronic information services, to track and analyze potential suitors for the Ohio-based Goodyear, a critical local employer. "We became quite good at checking the Disclosure [SEC] database for its company financial reports as we analyzed a potential buyer and its ability to put together the money to take over a company like Goodyear."[11]

Placing company names or symbols in CompuServe's Clipping Service or Dow Jones News's *Track* assures that any story on potential merger, takeover, or ownership changes in a company will be picked up by the automatic monitoring system. These services monitor specialized business news services, which, among other things, record filings affecting swings in company ownership (above 5 percent of the common stock) or the filing and announcement of official offers. Cost of these automatic retrieval facilities, when accessed twice daily, is limited to a minimal monthly fee and line usage costs of under $15 an hour to download all newly stored information. If a takeover or other corporate change does occur that might affect the corporate makeup and economic structure of a newspaper's circulation or TV station's broadcast region, the reporter—electronically alerted to the situation—can access relevant documents from the newsroom, without the expense of travel or the necessity of paying a D.C.-based consultant to search, locate, copy, and mail or fax documents to the medium's office.

One can argue that, just as electronic databases demonstrably increase the efficiency of news library staff members, they also increase the flexibility and efficiency of news reporters and editors. In the *Beacon Journal*'s case, financial reporters also functioned as library researchers, locating and analyzing federal documents. Statements and corporate promises in the context of bid and counterbid were examined by reporters in the light of the company's past economic and social performance. By searching the hometown newspapers of Goodyear suitors, *Journal* "business" reporters became their own stringers, seeking general information describing the quality and action of companies physically removed from their traditional circulation area. The result was that the newspaper's reporters wrote not simply as financial experts or as local "business" reporters but as reporters knowledgeable about both the general economic health of individual suitors and the position of those bidding companies in their respective home environments.

Newswriters were then able, editorially, to speculate on the effect a specific takeover attempt of Goodyear might have, based on a suitor's past performance in other markets or regions. They did not rely solely on the statements of

Goodyear executives, who individually might have a great deal to gain or lose through a bidding war. Nor did they accept on faith the assurances of corporate suitors who promised that, if successful, local jobs would be maintained and the community would benefit from the merger. The instrumental goal of objectivity and journalism's institutional goal of complete information were approached.

Credibility

Perhaps the greatest long-term economic benefit of the increasing use of these electronic resources may accrue from the transformation of news as an oral relay of official statements to the presentation of those statements in a critical and more balanced context. To the extent that this change creates a more complete, more "objective" system of public information, it may attract those who now choose not to read, watch, or listen to news products in their current form. In the United States, where the esteem of citizens for their newspeople and belief in the credibility of news publications (for all media) are low and still declining, increasing the perceived quality of the individual news story, program, or publication may be of crucial, long-term benefit for circulation. "In 1985, 53 percent questioned the independence of news organizations in covering the news; today, 62 percent do. Back then, 34 percent said that news reporting was often inaccurate; now it's 44 percent. Four years ago, 53 percent said news organizations 'tend to favor one side' in covering issues. Today that figure is 68 percent."[12]

This skepticism of viewer and reader is not simply directed at the local newspaper or television franchise. Between 1985 and 1989, a *Times Mirror* survey showed that only Cable News Network (CNN) increased in viewer esteem, with a "highly believable" rating of 38 percent in the earlier year and 43 percent at decade's end.[13] But CNN was the newest of stations during the late 1980s, and that relatively high rating may reflect an early affection for its all-news format by viewers totally disenchanted with traditional network formats and personnel. Only 34 percent of those polled rated NBC News as "highly believable"; ABC News was so rated by 33 percent of respondents, and only an abysmally low 31 percent of the CBS audience considered its news to be "highly believable." By way of comparison, in 1989 a "highly believable" rating of only 15 percent was given to Ronald Reagan, lower even than *USA Today*'s "highly believable" rating of 27 percent. The *Wall Street Journal* scored highest in this poll, with a 45 percent rating of "highly believable" in both 1985 and 1989.[14]

As Michael Robinson and Norman Ornstein noted wryly, "Likeability is nice but believability is vital."[15] For a newspaper or news station to sell a news product on the basis of its content, people must believe the information contained in its stories is accurate. Readers may "like" their local newspaper, appreciate complete box scores during the baseball season, or want, each morning, the complete listing of the previous day's stock trading. People may buy a newspaper for the Thursday food advertisements or for the weekend movie list. But the traditional product of newspapers and television news broadcasts is information, and, in that category, even the most trusted of them score under 50 percent.

One conclusion of this book has been to confirm the view of other critics (and the poll's respondents) who have argued that the news, as currently gathered and presented, is not very believable. At its best it may accurately reflect what the mayor, senator, city councilor, drug official, coroner, or president said an hour or eight hours previously. The relation between those statements and any reasonably complete, objective description of a specific event is neither assured nor likely. Officials have their own complex of interests, prejudices, ignorances, and needs. Even those who try for accuracy and objectivity will likely be biased in their statements, and that, apparently, is not lost on viewers and readers of the news. Polls have showed repeatedly that elected officials rarely score well in this type of opinion survey, and, if readers and viewers do not trust them, they will not trust and therefore not buy the vehicle whose primary function has been to translate officially sanctioned, oral speech into print or broadcast modes of production.

Thus a significant portion of the population may not buy newspapers or watch TV news programs in the belief that, to paraphrase Thomas Jefferson, a person who reads no newspaper is better informed than one who reads many because

he has fewer lies to unlearn. It may be that when news
accepts a more objective, more complex interpretation of
specific events, those disenfranchised viewers or readers
will decide it is again worth their time to tune in. Circulation
or viewer figures are the basis for the advertising rates set
by newspapers and broadcast news stations alike. If the
changes that electronic database technologies offer would
bring in more viewers and readers, then the resulting revenue increases would be another argument for their adoption.

REPORTERS AND EDITORS

For the news reporter, researcher, and editor, the benefits of electronic databases are even clearer. These advantages go far beyond greater ease in research or other prag-
matic boons of the digitalized database. Electronic databases and the changes their usage brings to the trade directly affect the institutional and instrumental myths or
goals in which newsmen and newswomen profess belief.
Appropriate use of electronic libraries thus will have a direct
bearing on the reporter or editor's professional and, perhaps,
personal self-esteem. That the primary role of the reporter
and editor is to function as a relay for the statements of
officialdom will come as no surprise to most professionals
with six months or more of experience in a radio, television,
or print-oriented newsroom anywhere in North America. I
have met few reporters and fewer editors who harbored for
long any illusion that the statements they presented as
"fact" bore any necessary resemblance to what they wit-
nessed on a daily basis. For many with whom I have talked,
their news career has been transformed from an ideal involving concepts of social service to a mundane way of making a
living. "I go in, write what they tell me and go home," a
Vancouver reporter said to me over beer. "I earn my pay by
being there."

Like their readers or viewers, many professionals are
dissatisfied with the format and the form that dictate the
news. For newswriters and editors, however, the frustration
is doubled because they are simultaneously consumers and

producers and thus even more aware of the deficiencies of the product the professional supposedly crafts with pride. Electronic information systems will not on their own transform the economic system that creates the context in which we work, but they can provide a new and exhilarating perspective within which news copy is prepared. It is intensely satisfying to face a physician involved in the unnecessary death of a child and have a wealth of information—from legal and medical sources—that contradicts absolutely the doctor's sworn and supposedly expert testimony that the death was "accidental." It is fulfilling to see a story based on that information published and disseminated across North America, and satisfying when the resulting debate leads to new and better health regulations. When a corporation trumpets the excellence of its product—a new light rail transit system, for example—and one researches its performance in other urban situations, the results may confirm those claims. One can then state with confidence that the whole has been tried and proved in other urban contexts. But if, in that survey of the literature, extraordinary problems—ranging from cost overruns to dangerous system failures—have shown the new transit system to be inadequate, it is with a sense of civic purpose that a reporter (and editor) can craft a piece saying, "This system is not for us."[16]

Jürgen Habermas argued that freedom comes from "self-reflection, [whereby] individuals can become aware of forces which have exerted a hitherto unacknowledged influence over them. Thus the act of knowing coincides with the goal of self-interest."[17] That freedom is supposed to be of primary benefit to the greater society, but it must begin with the news professionals who know forces are affecting them as citizens and are, at least in theory, individually charged with the public description of those powers. A system of information dissemination that empowers writer—hacks, flacks, or advocates—to critically examine the greater context of their subject's statements will be endorsed by all but the most cynical professional. Put baldly, adoption of these technologies will allow news professionals a greater measure of self-respect by providing at least the possibility of fulfilling their instrumental and institutional goals.

At present, journalistic objectivity is a confidence game, a torturous "hide-and-seek" of changing rules by which reporters try to gain a perspective from which they can, with some self-esteem intact, simultaneously face both subjects and readers. This situation has resulted in rather bizarre forms of behavior, which include voluntary refusal by some members of the Fourth Estate of their right to vote (so they will not be "involved" in elections they cover) and employer bans on participation in public demonstrations by all employees of their news organizations. These restrictions on constitutional duties and supposedly guaranteed rights of speech and congregation have been accepted by most news professionals as necessary in the name of journalistic objectivity. The result has not, of course, been objective news but simply the disenfranchisement of editorial workers from their nation's and region's democratic process.

Thus in 1989 a newspaper receptionist who had participated in a demonstration concerning the reproductive rights of women was fired by her employer because it was believed her actions compromised the newspaper's objectivity on the abortion issue. That the employee so dismissed worked not as an editor, writer, or reporter but rather as a telephone operator made no apparent difference. The principle of objectivity, which has come in news to mean "no personal involvement in the democratic process," was the order of the day. Eventually, that employee was reinstated, and the newspaper's rules were rewritten to limit the democratic freedoms only of those directly involved in newswriting and layout (reporters, photographers, researchers, editors). This decision was seen by many interested journalists around the nation as a fair and positive turn of events, and the amended rule was, most agreed, appropriate and necessary if the principle of objectivity was to be upheld.[18]

But as we have seen, objectivity is based on knowledge, on the verification of statements in the broadest possible context of prior occurrence and theory. Banning employee participation in the national debate on abortion, for example, will not make reporters more or less objective in their reportage of demonstrations or court cases. It simply removes their voices as citizens from the democratic process. Indeed, by forcing editorial workers to hide their convictions, we may find the end result is to introduce greater bias into the final editorial product because the reporters, editors, or researchers have no other outlet from which to argue or state their beliefs. The ideal of balance or fairness that objectivity supposedly describes does not require the removal of news professionals from the democratic process. Rather, it acknowledges that individuals (subject and writer alike) have specific perspectives and agendas. Objectivity by definition requires a system in which statements and actions can be tested and examined within the broader context of existing data and information. It is hoped that as the use of electronic databases creates a form by which objectivity becomes not only a myth but a realizable goal, reporters will no longer feel compelled to cede (in the name of objectivity) to their employers control of their individual, constitutionally protected rights.

Hacks, Flacks, and Advocates

One way of reviewing the issues of subjectivity, objectivity, and the reportorial function is to describe the various roles in the news process and their relation to the levels of information discussed in various chapters. These tensions and transformations can now be summarized with both brevity and some precision. In relation to any potential event there are, in general, four editorial postures that may affect the resulting story. These postures are those of "hacks," reporters assigned by a media organ; "subjects" who are authority figures (police officer, mayor, CEO, physician, etc.); flacks employed by a subject to promote their position; and "advocates" whose interest in an event is determined by its relation to their group's stated but limited goals (Mothers Against Drunk Driving, the National Rifle Association, Greenpeace, American Medical Association, etc.). These four different positions represent the public (the reporter as surrogate), the corporation (the flack), the nonprofit interest group (the advocate, and the interpretation of events by an official or officially sanctioned authority.

As Illustration 6.1 shows, the official, flack, and advocate have as their goal the acceptance by a newswriter of their interpretation of a journalistic event or occurrence (be it a shooting, a woman's desire to terminate a pregnancy, or release of monthly unemployment figures). Each of these roles—official, flack, and advocate—has a different and typically conflicting set of institutional, instrumental, and functional goals. But all require the media to perform for them a relay function, disseminating a specific perspective, and in that act bestowing a patina of truth ("it was in the newspaper") to their individual points of view. Whatever the sign—the datum of a single event—three of these four informational postures will interpret that information from their own perspective. What is signified by the observed increase in incidence of successful malpractice suits (a single datum) will be different for the official (Todd or Habash), for the advocate (for socialized medicine), and for the flack who crafts the press release issued by the American Medical Asociation, which may unilaterally and arbitrarily report a victory for Todd in the *Wall Street Journal* "debate."

Within this complex, reporters are faced with competing interpretations that they are supposed to relay through one or another medium. Newspeople operationally must translate (report) and summarize the oral statement of their subject(s) into a news story whose focus is that subject's, advocate's, or hack's specific statement delivered, typically, at a press conference or press "interview." Traditionally, reporters have had no basis from which to compare or contrast those views, no other resources to assist in their critique. That the interpretation may have little relation to the specific signifier, while perhaps clear to reporters, is a truth barred from their work by a lack of reference material. At best, reporters have been able to "balance" the official press conference statement with a file clip or paragraph giving a dissenting or qualifying quote issued by an opposing official or "advocate."

In theory, newspeople distinguish themselves from the flack and the advocate through instrumental and institutional goals that make of newswriting a public service. The goal of objectivity both distinguishes the reporter from the flack or advocate and, in theory, allows the newswriter to approximate institutional and instrumental goals of public service. But contemporary newswriters or researchers are constrained by the functional role of oral relay for the news

**Illustration 6.1
Roles and Relations**

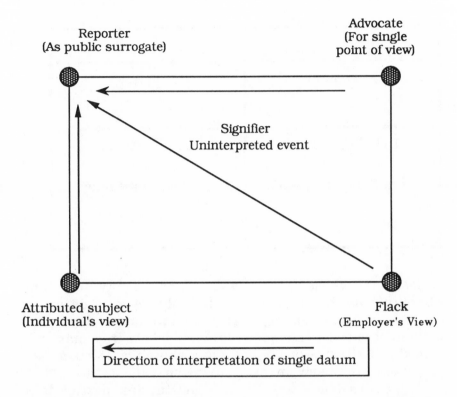

Reporter
(As public surrogate)

Advocate
(For single
point of view)

Signifier
Uninterpreted event

Attributed subject
(Individual's view)

Flack
(Employer's View)

Direction of interpretation of single datum

subject. They are limited by the narrative form, which insists that the journalistic subject is the official statement delivered at a narrowly defined time and place. Thus news professionals are constantly faced with a tension between, on the one hand, their self-perceived role as investigator and objective surrogate for the greater public and, on the other, the job of being a "reporter" who simply relays a subject's words (and position) into the public forum through print or broadcast news. As a "reporter," one can only summarize a subject's position, statement, or posture in the media. But this role in fact is similar to what "flacks" and "advocates" do for their respective clients.

Thus, as Illustration 6.2 attempts to show, the contemporary newswriters, researchers, editors, and reporters are constantly faced with two different and mutually exclusive postures. As an informed "investigator," the journalist is a

Illustration 6.2
Roles: Investigator versus Reporter

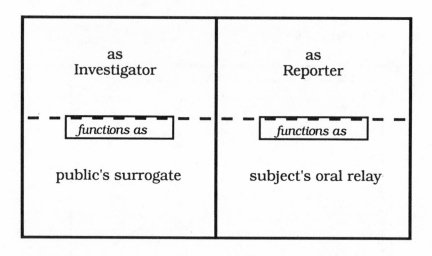

professional whose focus is the context of any story and whose information is based on relatively objective data. But the "reporter" is more typically an uninformed layperson without recourse to adequate data and whose information is gained only after the fact from the quotable official. Journalists are, at least in theory, investigators who stand as the public's surrogate in a democracy. For this institutional posture to be actualized, they need "objectivity" to be distinguished from the flack, subject, or advocate, whose job is to assign a meaning to any signifier. But this ideal cannot be met because the newswriter's traditional role is that of a "reporter" who relays without interpretation the statements of individuals whose posture, by definition, is biased.

There has been until now no way to resolve these opposing roles. Their very articulation has been dependent on the speed and specificity of electronic libraries, which allowed me to examine, within a broad context of technical writing, issues of medicine, law, the environment, and so on. Until the advent of electronic database technologies, this argument would have been virtually impossible to construct because the necessary data on which its analysis is based was not readily accessible to the general writer or reporter.

Illustration 6.3
Unary Transformation in the Ephemeral Story

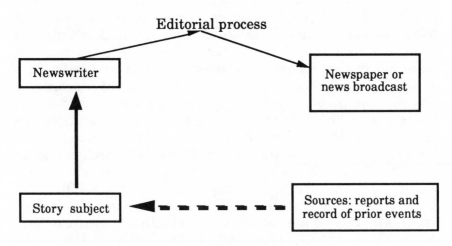

If the speed and specificity of electronic technologies have made this analysis possible, it similarly empowers the public information writer. Until recently there was no mechanism by which information could be brought to bear from a very broad technical base to test a statement, and thus "factuality" becomes "facticity" without regard to any exterior criterion. News reports were limited to the unary transformation by the nature of information available to the reporter or editor. The methodology of the news was geared to the oral datum, to "what" was said by "who" at a specific "where" and "when." Subjects (or flacks or advocates) were thus free to place any interpretation they wished on a boundary event, to define arbitrarily and to their own advantage what was signified by a prior occurrence. The reporter was forced to relay that interpretation without skepticism and without any objective investigation of its correctness.

But even minimal objectivity requires a greater context, a class of events or concepts in which the individual occurrence is to be assessed. The failure to find that greater context results in the biased and typically "unary" news story in which the editorial subject is the sole interpreter of all sources and the non-electronically aided news reporter functions as a relay, placing that interpretation before the public. As Illustration 6.3 makes clear, traditional reporters are constrained by form and context to accept the interpretation of the subject, the sole provider of editorial information. That official or expert may quote, summarize, or refer to other, prior reports, theories, research, or concepts, but these, as the broken arrow demonstrates, inform only the interview subject and are not accessible to the newswriter. He or she in turn summarizes information given orally, data which is then further mediated by the editorial process (for length, placement, illustration) before appearing as "news." Within this form there is no question of examining the conflicting instrumental, institutional, or functional goals of the speaker because the newswriter or researcher has no basis for that task. As Walter Lippmann said seventy years years ago: "the books and papers are in their offices."[19] Without them, there is no possibility of placing the boundary event, the antecedent occurrence, within any context that would question the statement, opinion, or position of the subject.

Electronic databases change these relations by placing the "books and papers" on the newswriter's or researcher's desk as well. As Illustration 6.4 shows, information from a variety of sources is no longer the exclusive prerogative of the subject. In treating any prior event, newspeople now have potential access to the same information as their subjects and can question the official's or "expert's" interpretation on the basis of that information. Statements made at a press conference or in a news release become, in this model, hypotheses to be examined in a broader context and with reference to impartial data chosen not solely by the subject but also by the newswriter or researcher. The reporter retains the function of oral relay, but that role is subsumed within the broader posture of investigator and public surrogate. "What was said" becomes a focus for the greater issues of "what it means," "how it happened," "why it occurred," and "who may be responsible."

Thus the news need not be limited by its data to purely unary transformations and a narrative form based on the function of oral relay. Journalists can choose to adopt in their work a perspective that insists on multiple transformation whose focus is the boundary event. Where the inci-

Illustration 6.4
Multiple Transformations:
Contextual or Structural Treatment

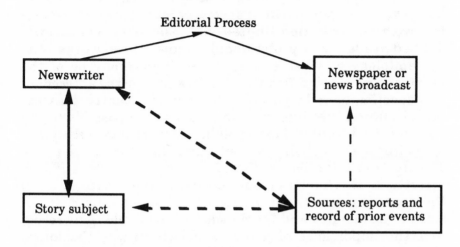

dence of leukemia among children is considered merely a
"statistical cluster," the similarity of that pattern of disease
with others reported elsewhere for a decade allows the
newsperson to question the comforting assurances of the
official Cancer Control Agency. On the basis of a wealth of
reports and sources (academic, federal, state or provincial,
and judicial), the newsperson examines and questions the
subject's conclusions, presented at a journalistic event (press
conference, press release, news interview), within the context of other, prior occurrences (children are also similarly
sick in Denver, Colorado; Stockton, California; Kamloops,
British Columbia, etce.) to fashion an "objective" and even a
"skeptical" description of not only "who," "what," "when,"
and "where" but, most importantly, "how" and "why."[20]
Newswriters remain bound by economic, social, and political considerations (as are their broadcast producers or print
editors), but within those restrictions they are free to craft
a story not only on the basis of "what the subject said" but,
more importantly, on the antecedent event itself.

One result of this complex of changes will be the greater
dissemination of information into the broad public forum by
what is at present a largely amateur class of scientific and

academic writer whose work, within the traditional print system of data storage, has received only narrow readership. There is currently a broad range of skilled and knowledgeable writers whose work, often extremely pertinent to local events, is published in specialty journals and newsletters with a distribution limited only to members of narrowly defined academic or professional groups. These works—the epidemiology of Wertheimer, for example—may be of the greatest possible significance in understanding the antecedent of a specific, boundary event. But, until recently, locating and obtaining that information has been impossible for all but the most skilled bibliographic researchers with enormous libraries at their disposal—and the time to use them. The electronic databases' digital soup puts this class of data directly in the hands of public information writers. Even those editors, like the *Province*'s Holden, who distrust the work of academics and "eggheads" on principle, will recognize the importance of a review article in anesthesiology that assigns absolute responsibility for patient deaths to physicians who do not adequately monitor their patients. When an engineering magazine discusses the collapse of building roofs as a result of the failure of contractors and subcontractors to review the strength of a structure during construction, the pertinence of those conclusions will be lost on neither editor nor reporter wishing to write intelligently about a local structural disaster in which no review process was used.

One can predict that the use of these technical resources will increase in part because such a change mirrors those that occurred during the printing revolution. In the eighteenth century, mercantalism and the new printing technologies brought a wide class of "amateur" writers into the public sphere and simultaneously made the act of writing a profession whose members were without allegiance to crown or lord. The newswriter worked for pay and at speed, translating the official's position into public statement. At the same time, specialized textbooks, journals, newsletters, and briefs were produced by an ever-growing number of literate and increasingly specialized experts—amateur writers, who, by this century, were contributing to literally thousands of publications whose readerships were defined by subject and not by narrow, geographic advertising. Just as the first printing revolution freed the writer from the crown's absolute control while creating a mass audience for the periodical, so this change in technology makes available a broad audience for technical and academic writers. It is perhaps fitting that newswriters, whose trade was born in the first revolution, should be early members of this new technical audience made possible by the electronic storage revolution.

From the *American Metallurgist* to *Zoologist Weekly*, the work in these technical journals has been available to all, if only one knew where to look. But that has been the problem. From the first experiment in modern journalism, when Samuel Johnson wrote of Britain's parliament in *Cave's Magazine*, to the mid-1980s when electronic database technology first became widely available, print created a system of public information limited only by the need to search physically through texts lined along miles of library shelves. But the limits of that information storage system were, in retrospect, rather extreme, and resulted in a type of public information that basically survived as a relay for the unexamined and typically oral statements of one or another official.

The efficiencies of electronic databases make information from specialized sources accessible to both the public surrogate and the sanctioned expert. Just as the printing revolution made possible both the popular journal and the scholarly text, so the new information revolution makes work from both amateur writer (but professional researcher) and periodical writer (but amateur researcher) widely available. Information from both spheres may now enter the broader forum through the reportorial relay, which is no longer necessarily limited to the oral.

Social Benefits

Not the least of the benefits that this new system of information storage and retrieval presents is, perhaps, the ability of journalists to begin to discuss and analyze their own goals and myths. Virtually alone among the social and information sciences, news as a branch of public information has been unable to rise from, at best, an ethnographic and descriptive style (and, at worst, a perspective of systematic distortion) to one allowing sustained analysis and the rudimentary elements of a descriptive theory. Despite the relatively recent promotion of journalism to the status of a discipline worthy of "schools" or "departments" in academe, it has had access to few of the tools by which other social sciences distinguish themselves from crafts.

Expository writing is a skill, but the study of English as a language and a literature is based on a series of paradigms and techniques that allow for the analysis of the meaning and biases of specific texts. Investment brokers learn the mechanics of their trade in short courses funded by employers, while economists study the general movement of capital within a clear paradigm of assumptions and theories. Journalists today are like the investment broker who tries to lecture a client on economics, or the advertising writer attempting an analysis of *Ulysses*. They are tradesmen seeking the overriding perspective of a discipline.

Electronic databases provide an objective foundation from which the underlying assumptions of the news business can be laid bare. They present a means by which those interested in the issues of public information can move from the "ethnographic" collection of story examples to the structural consideration of the narrative form and its relation to the broader social dynamic. Within the context of the perspective provided here, one made possible by new technologies, journalism has the potential to become self-reflective and self-critical. The perspective gained through the use of these resources, which makes existential events into members of a class of occurrence, allows for a level of analysis and abstraction that which has been previously inconceivable.[21]

Legitimacy

The popular myth of the Fourth Estate is that it stands as a watchdog for the citizenry against the excesses of its member estates. The myth has been, since the writing of the Fourth Amendment of the Bill of Rights, that a politically unaligned American press is a bulwark against unreasoned control of the citizenry. By prohibiting Congress from passing any law abridging the freedom or range of the press, the news profession was charged with assuring that an accurate and reasonably complete description of future events would be made available to the nascent republic, whatever the posture of the official or powerful individual might be.

One purpose of this book has been to demonstrate not only the failure of contemporary journalism, but, as importantly, to define the structural and systemic reasons for that failure. A second purpose has been to attempt to show how the use of these new technologies provides an opportunity for journalists to create a context in which "objective," "unbiased," and fundamentally "complete" information may enter the public forum on a regular basis. These technologies will not banish obtuse officials or corporate self-interest from the arena of public information. Nor can they naturally force information-based news conglomerates to place public service and the needs of society above the demand for continued and sustained high rates of profit. News is, after all, not apart from society but a force and factor in it, influenced by and simultaneously influencing the events it purports to cover.

Even so, the effect of technology on the diffusion and transformation of public information should not be considered as a minor or insignificant force for change. The change from an oral society in which the crown controlled public information to one in which commercially printed material was the rule occurred within the greater context of the mercantile and early industrial revolutions. The current transformation of a print-oriented to a digitalized information storage system—from an orally based, unary transformation to a textually based, multiple transformation—is similarly occurring within, influencing, and being influenced by a series of economic, social, and political changes whose end result may be no less revolutionary. The eighteenth-century printing revolution can be seen, in retrospect, as a crucial element in the broader context of change during that era. News, a subset of information, exists not alone but as a part of the whole and these changes will affect the totality.

For example, to the extent that news functions primarily as a vehicle for the "legitimation" of certain officials, officially entrenched positions, or general political systems, that function has depended on the continued use of news as a relay for officialdom's oral interpretations of complex signifiers. What the effect would be of a Fourth Estate freed by these technologies to research and question critically the statements of officials can only be guessed at. Certainly, some critics would argue that neither the owners nor the official overseers of the news world will welcome the enfranchisement of news producers and their clientele, the public. But it is a lesson of the printing revolution that officials find it difficult or impossible to prevent the resulting flow of information when technology and economies combine to make a new level of dissemination both possible and profitable.

NOTES

1. Edward S. Herman and Noam Chomsky, *Manufacturing Consent: The Political Economy of the Mass Media* (New York: Pantheon, 1988), chapter 1. Herman and Chomsky are used here as representatives of a larger body of analysis which they in turn refer to. The intention is not to suggest that they or their position are unique in the insistence that public information in a capitalist or post-capitalist society must be considered as an economic matter and not, as many newspeople and news academics would insist, a value-free phenomenon.

2. Andrew Ippolito, "Databases in Newspaper Libraries," *Editor and Publisher*, May 11, 1985, 60e.

3. Tim Miller, "Data Bases as a Source of Regional Information," *Editor and Publisher*, June 6, 1987, 78.

4. David Vine, "Banks Use News/Retrieval—and Often Profit," *Dowline*, Summer 1988, 18-20.

5. My acquaintance with online databases followed a Mississippi lawyer's request, in 1982, for copies of stories I had written two years earlier in Vancouver, B.C., on a local case of anesthesia-related death. Flattered at the request from one so distant, I asked the lawyer, Orma R. Smith, Jr., how he had learned of my stories. Smith said it was simply a matter of using electronic databases to search the popular

and technical literature. The combination of legal precedent and prior knowledge from various jurisdictions led, eventually, to a "satisfactory settlement" for the client. Orma R. Smith, Jr., personal communication, October 31, 1985.

6 . There is a substantial and specific industry literature in this area. For a brief, general view of how businesses track products and trends, see Donald B. Trivette, "News/Retrieval Data Satisfies an Ever-Growing Appetite for Information," *Dowline*, Summer 1989, 30-31.

7. See, for example, Deborah Burth, "Advertising and Marketing Pitches,"*Dowline*, Summer 1989, 28-29.

8. Bechtel Information Services is one of several companies compiling SEC filings electronically. Others include Disclosure, Inc., and Dow Jones Federal Filings, Inc.

9. "Government Information, at a Price," *Quill* 77:9 (October 1989), 17.

10. McMasters, "Government Information," 17.

11. Donna S. Willman, "Vu/Text's Online Databases Aid in Pulitzer Prize-Winning Coverage," Vu/Text news release, June 3, 1987. This release, carried electronically on the *PR Newswire*, emphasized the newspaper's use of Vu/Text newspaper databanks but acknowledged that Disclosure was also a critical feature for the *Beacon Journal*'s coverage.

12. Michael J. Robinson and Norman J. Ornstein, "Why Press Credibility is Going Down (and What to Do about It),"*Washington Journalism Review* 12:1 (January 1990), 34. Robinson and Ornstein's story is based on a Gallup organization survey of 1,507 adults for the Times Mirror Company.

13. Reports on the Times Mirror study can also be found summarized in the CompuServe Journalism Forum's library as document no. 76703, 3010.

14. Robinson and Ornstein, "Press Credibility," 36.

15. Robinson and Ornstein, "Press Credibility," 37.

16. In 1987 Honolulu, Hawaii, was considering buying a light rail transit system identical to that then in use in Vancouver, Canada. Members of the Honolulu City Council and reporters who went to Vancouver to see the system in operation returned full of praise for the rail line. For a magazine article, I searched the Vancouver newspaper libraries and wrote a story detailing a series of deficiencies in

the system that had resulted in a number of lawsuits and widespread dissatisfaction. See Tom Koch, "The Right Track?" *Honolulu Magazine*, March 1988, 122.

17. D. Held, *Introduction to Critical Theory* (London: Hutchinson, 1980), 318. Quoted in R.J. Johnston, *Philosophy and Human Geography: An Introduction to Contemporary Approaches*, 2d ed. (London: Edward Arnold, 1986), 116.

18. This case was discussed online by members of the CompuServe Journalism Forum (JFORUM) in December 1989 and January 1990. In the same vein, a Vero Beach, Florida, reporter was reportedly fired after she made and sent tiny wire coat hangers to Florida legislators to emphasize her belief that restrictions on legal abortion procedures would result in increased incidence of amateur "coat hanger" procedures. Again, the issue was objectivity. Doug Stanley, personal communication, CompuServe Journalism Forum, April 10, 1990, message no. 687720.

19. Walter Lippmann, *Public Opinion* (New York: Free Press, 1965), 157.

20. This "why" is not an existential question. Rather, it becomes "what was the specific and active agent causing the boundary event to occur?" If someone died, the question "why" asks is what were the factors that caused the heart to stop beating on that day and in that situation? The answer to this is always contextual and requeires reference to a more general body of knowledge.

21. For example, some of the methods employed here, which analyze relations between actors and their respective goals, are similar to structural anthropology's employment of group theory. From this perspective, as Jean Piaget noted, "It is neither the elements nor a whole that comes about in a manner one knows not how, but the relation among elements that counts." But without a perspective from which to view the elements of myth and goal, no such analysis has, in the past, been possible. For a brief statement of group theory and its use in anthropology, see Per Hage and Frank Harary, *Structural Models in Anthropology* (Cambridge: *Cambridge University Press*, 1983), 151-70. While Hage and Harary's examples come from anthropology and

primarily structural anthropologic studies of non-technological myths and cosmologies, the system could be applied, in theory, to news as a general belief system and individual stories as well.

Appendix

Databases and Vendors

BUSINESS AND FINANCIAL

Disclosure
Files from: Eighteen months
Supplier: Disclosure, Inc.
Provides: Detailed financial information contained in federally mandated filings to the Securities and Exchange Commission by public and private corporations.

ABI/Inform
Files from: January 1971
Supplier: Data Courier, Inc.
Provides: Lengthy abstracts from business and management magazines, stressing general business management and, secondarily, product information.

Business Periodicals Index
Files from: June 1982
Supplier: H.W. Wilson Company
Provides: An electronic version of the standard *Business Periodicals Index* with references from most major English-language business magazines concerned with marketing, economics, industry, and finance.

CACI Demographics
Files from: 1980 Census
Supplier: CACI Marketing Systems
Provides: A system of reporters, based on U.S. census materials, for every region of the United States by county, city, or zip code region. Easier to use (and more expensive) than the government CENDATA, the CACI reports focus on demographic characteristics, income levels, and shopping patterns for any targeted region. Also provide detailed employment information.

Dun's Market Identifiers
Files from: Yearly reports
Supplier: Dun's Marketing Services
Provides: Basic information from public records on virtually every U.S. business with more than ten employees. This service is one of a family of business-related databases from the same company. For example, *Dun's Financial Records* (DFR) provides credit reports on three-quarters of a million companies; *Dun's International Market Identifiers* provides credit reports on non-U.S. companies.

InfoGlobe
Files from: Varies by database
Supplier: The *Globe and Mail*
Provides: A series of online databases from Canada whose principal resource is the digitalized files of the *Globe and Mail*'s daily newspaper files. In addition, *InfoGlobe* provides comprehensive data on Canadian corporations based on audited financial statements from 1983 to the present and analysis of corporate performance on 1,800 companies from as early as 1984.

Fedfiles
Files from: Current data
Supplier: Federal Filings, Inc.
Provides: A complete and timely listing of all federally mandated corporate filings for public and private corporations. These include those required in merger and acquisition situations (14D-1, 14D-9), buybacks and leveraged buy-

outs (13E), ownership changes and 5 percent equity positions (13-D), quarterly and annual report details (10-Q and 10-K forms),and selected debt and equity security registrations (S-1 to S-4). Frankly, an unbelievable service.

PTS Databases
Files from: 1972
Supplier: Predicasts, Inc. In England, Predicasts, International.
Provides: A family of databases whose individual files index information on worldwide business literature. Individual databases include *PTS U.S. Forecast*; *PTS New Product Announcements*; *PTS Mars* (advertising and marketing); *PTS International Forecasts*; *PTS F&S Indexes* (company, product, and industry information including information on mergers and acquisitions worldwide).

Standard and Poor's
Files from: Depends on file accessed. Some go back to 1979.
Supplier: Standard and Poor's Corporation
Provides: Corporate reports based on annual and quarterly company reports, news releases, regulatory statements, etc.

GENERAL INFORMATION

DataTimes
Files from: Varies with publication accessed.
Supplier: DataTimes
Provides: Like Vu/Text, a purveyor of online regional newspapers with gateways to Australian news sources. Little overlap with Vu/Text's service.

Magazine Index
Files from: 1976
Supplier: Information Access Company
Provides: Files covering 370 magazines with a wide range of subject matter. Also see *Magazine ASAP*, a holding file for recent articles that will become part of *Magazine Index*.

National Newspaper Index
Files from: 1979
Supplier: Information Access Company
Provides: Full coverage of the *New York Times*, the *Wall Street Journal*, and the *Christian Science Monitor*.

NewsSearch
Files from: Updated monthly
Supplier: Information Access Company
Provides: A short-term index of stories, articles, and reviews from more than fifteen hundred magazines, journals, and newspapers. Holds on a temporary basis files that will be transferred, at the end of each month, to the *Legal Resource Index*, *Management Contents* and *Trade and Industry Index* databases. At the end of a month, files are placed on databases like *Magazine ASAP*.

PR Newswire
Files from: 1984
Supplier: PR Newswire Association, Inc.
Provides: The full text of corporate press releases to print and broadcast newsrooms and wire services. Updates added as needed to previously filed releases.

PTS MARS
Files from: 1980
Supplier: Predicasts, Inc.
Provides: The text of a whole series of advertising and product-specific journals—of most importance to the advertising industry. Searching is made possible on the basis of Standard Industrial Classification Codes.

Vu/Text
Files from: Varies with each newspaper.
Supplier: Vu/Text, Inc. a division of Knight-Ridder Co.
Provides: Full text of more than sixty-five U.S. newspapers. The premier U.S. purveyor of newspapers, whose stories can be searched with incredible specificity. As a supplier, Vu/Text allows clients to search all papers within the database globally with one search phrase. Through a distributor like IQuest, global searching is not allowed, and one must search

each paper individually. Offers a number of gateways including one to QL Search, a Canadian system with *Canadian Press* files beginning in 1981. Links to Dialog, owned by the same parent corporation, are promised.

GOVERNMENT

Cendata
Files from: 1980 census
Supplier: U.S. Census Bureau
Provides: Demographic and economic information from both the 1980 census and more recent intercensus surveys. Also included is the text of Census Bureau press releases. Compare with CACI.

American Statistics Index
Files from: Depends on statistics accessed.
Supplier: Congressional Information Service
Provides: A guide to all statistical publications of the U.S. government including periodicals and annual, biennial, and one-time reports.

Congressional Record Abstracts
Files from: 1976
Supplier: Capital Services International
Provides: Abstracts of the proceedings of the *Congressional Record*, which is the record of debates and actions by the U.S. Congress. Includes coverage of committee and subcommittee reports, laws, executive communications, speeches, floor debates (including inserted material), data on bills, roll-call votes, etc.

Federal Register Abstracts
Files from: 1977
Supplier: Capital Services International
Provides: Coverage of federal regulatory agency action published in the *Federal Register* and thus public information. Includes presidential proclamations, executive orders, proposed regulations, and compliance requirements and legal notices issued by federal agencies.

MEDICINE AND SCIENCE

Enviroline
Files from: 1971
Supplier: Environmental Information Center, Inc.
Provides: Digital version of the printed indexes, *Environmental Abstracts* and *Environmental Issues.* Provides abstracts of articles on environmental issues published in government documents, industry reports, conference reports, newspapers, and magazines.

Hazardline
Files from: Updated monthly
Supplier: Occupational Health Services
Provides: A directory of hazardous substances including the name, formula, properties, and dangers of each substance to humans. Includes appropriate responses to overexposure and spills.

Medline
Files from: 1966
Supplier: U.S. National Library of Medicine
Provides: Indexes articles in medical and biomedical sciences from three sources: *Index Medicus, Index to Dental Literature,* and *International Nursing Index.* Also offered in a simplified search version with some full-text services through PaperChase (Beth Israel Hospital).

SciSearch
Files from: 1970
Supplier: Institute for Scientific Information
Provides: A multidisciplinary database whose references are expanded from those in the print-based *Social Sciences Index.* It covers virtually every journal related to both pure and applied sciences.

SUPPLIERS, DISTRIBUTORS, PACKAGERS

Data Courier, Inc.   Supplier
6320 S. Fifth Street
Louisville, Ky. 40202

Bechtel Information Services   Supplier
15740 Shady Grove Road.
Gaithersburg, Md. 20877

BRS Information Technologies   Packager
1200 Route 7
Latham, N.Y. 12110

CACI Marketing Systems   Supplier
9302 Lee Highway, Suite 310
Fairfax, Va. 22031

CompuServe   Distributor
5000 Arlington Centre Boulevard
P.O. Box 20212
Columbus, Ohio 43220

Congressional Information Service   Supplier
4520 East-West Highway
Bethesda, Md. 20814

Cuadra Elsevier   Supplier
P.O. Box 1672
Grand Central Station
New York, N.Y. 10163-1672

Data User Services Division   Supplier
U.S. Bureau of the Census
Washington, D.C. 20233

DataTimes   Packager
818 N.W. Sixty-third Street
Oklahoma City, Okla. 73116

Dialog Information Services, Inc.   Packager/Dis-
3460 Hillview Avenue   tributor
Palo Alto, Cal. 94304

Disclosure, Inc.   Supplier
5161 River Road
Bethesda, Md. 20816

Dow Jones News Retrieval Service   Supplier/Pack-
P.O. Box 300   ager
Princeton, N.J. 08540

EasyNet   Packager/Dis-
Telebase Systems, Inc.   tributor
134 North Narbert Avenue
Narbeth, Pa. 19072

Federal Filings, Inc.   Supplier/Pack-
450 Fifth St. NW   ager
Washington, D.C.

InfoGlobe   Packager/Dis-
The *Globe and Mail*   tributor
444 Front Street West
Toronto, Ontario M5V 2S9
Canada

Information Access Company   Packager/Dis-
11 Davis Drive   tributor
Belmont, Cal. 94002

Institute for Scientific Information   Supplier
3501 Market Street
Philadelphia, Pa. 19104

Lexis/Nexis   Packager/Dis-
Mead Data Central   tributor
9393 Springboro Pike
P.O. Box 933
Dayton, Ohio 45401

NewsNet, Inc.   Packager
945 Haverford Road
Bryn Mawr, Pa. 19010

Occupational Health Services   Supplier
P.O. Box 1505
400 Plaza Drive
Seacaucus, N.J. 07094

PR Newswire Association, Inc.   Supplier
150 E. Fifty-eighth Street
New York, N.Y. 10155

Predicasts, Inc.   Supplier
11001 Cedar Avenue
Cleveland, Ohio 441106

Standard & Poor's Company   Supplier
25 Broadway
New York, N.Y. 10004

Vu/Text Information Services   Packager
325 Chestnut Street, Suite 1300
Philadelphia, Pa. 19106

Selected Bibliography

BOOKS

Altschull, Herbert, J. *From Milton to McLuhan: The Ideas Behind American Journalism*. White Plains, N.Y.: Longman, 1990.

Barthes, Roland. *The Eiffel Tower and Other Mythologies*. New York: Hill and Wang, 1979.

————*Camera Lucida*. Richard Howard, trans. New York: Hill and Wang, 1981.

Bate, W. Jackson. *Samuel Johnson*. New York: Harcourt, Brace, Jovanovich, 1975.

Brodeur, Paul. *Currents of Death: Power Lines, Computer Terminals and the Attempt to Cover Up Their Threat to Your Health*. New York: Simon and Schuster, 1989.

Brooks, Brian S., Kennedy; George, Moen; Daryl R., Ranly, Don; *News Reporting and Writing*, 3d ed. New York: St. Martin's Press, 1988.

Chomsky, Noam. *Necessary Illusions*. Toronto: CBC Enterprises, 1988.

Crosby, Harry H., and Bond, George R. *The McLuhan Explosion: A Casebook on Marshall McLuhan and Understanding Media*. New York: American Book Co., 1968.

Cuadra-Elser Staff. *Online Databases in the Medical and Life Sciences*. Santa Monica, Cal.: Cuadra Publications, 1987.

Darnton, Robert. *The Business of Enlightenment: A Publishing History of the "Encyclopedie" 1775-1800.* Cambridge, Mass.: Harvard University Press, 1979.

Davis, N.M., and Cohen, M.R. *Medication Errors: Cause and Prevention.* Philadelphia: George F. Stickley, 1981.

Diamond, Edwin. *The Last Days of Television.* Cambridge, Mass: MIT Press, 1982.

Eisenstein, Elizabeth. *The Printing Press as an Agent of Change.* 2 vols. Cambridge: Cambridge University Press, 1979.

Epstein, Edward J. *Between Fact and Fiction: The Problem of Journalism.* New York: Vintage Books, 1974.

Financial Sourcebooks Staff. *Online Sources: A Step-by-Step Guide to Access and Using Business and Financial Databases.* New York: Financial Sourcebooks, 1988.

Garfinkel, H. *Studies in Ethnomethodology.* Englewood Cliffs, N.J.: Prentice Hall, 1967.

Glossbrenner, Alfred. *The Complete Handbook of Personal Computer Communications.* New York: Brody, 1985.

————— *Alfred Glossbrenner's Master Guide to CompuServe.* New York: Brady, 1987.

————— *How to Look It Up Online.* New York: St. Martin's Press, 1987.

Hage, Per, and Harary, Frank. *Structural Models in Anthropology.* Cambridge: Cambridge University Press, 1983.

Herman, Edward S., and Chomsky, Noam. *Manufacturing Consent: The Political Economy of the Mass Media.* New York: Pantheon, 1988.

Hill, George Birkeck. *Boswell's Life of Johnson.* 6 vols. New York: Harper and Brothers, 1891.

Inlander, Charles B.; Levin, Lowell S.; and Weiner, E. *Medicine on Trial: The Appalling Story of Medical Ineptitude and the Arrogance That Overlooks It.* New York: Pantheon Books: 1988.

Jacobstein, Myron J. *Legal Research Illustrated.* Mineola, N.Y.: Foundation Press, 1987.

Johnston, R.J. *Philosophy and Human Geography: An Introduction to Contemporary Approaches.* 2d ed. London: Edward Arnold, 1986.

Keane, John. *Public Life and Late Capitalism*. New York: Cambridge University Press, 1984.

Kernan, Alvin. *Printing Technology, Letters, and Samuel Johnson*. Princeton: Princeton University Press, 1987.

Koch, Tom. *The News as Myth: Fact and Context in Journalism*. Westport, Conn.: Greenwood Press, 1990.

Lapham, Lewis P. *Money and Class in America*. New York: Ballantine Books, 1988.

Ley, David. *The Black Inner City as Frontier Outpost: Images and Behavior of a Philadelphia Neighborhood*, Washington, D.C.: American Association of Geographers, 1974.

Leighton, Joseph. *The Individual and the Social Order*. New York: Appleton, 1926.

Liebling, A.J. *The Press*. New York: Pantheon Books, 1981.

Lippmann, Walter. *Public Opinion*. New York: Free Press, 1965.

Lyons, Louis, ed. *Reporting the News*. Cambridge, Mass.: Belknap Press, 1965.

Manoff, Robert Karl, and Schudson, Michael, eds. *Reading the News*. New York: Pantheon, 1986.

McLuhan, Marshall. *The Gutenberg Galaxy: The Making of Typographic Man*. Toronto: University of Toronto Press, 1962.

——————*Understanding Media: The Extensions of Man*. New York: McGraw-Hill, 1964.

Prichard, Peter S. *The Making of McPaper: The Inside Story of USA Today*. New York: St. Martin's Press, 1987.

Rachline, Allan. *News as Hegemonic Reality*. New York: Praeger, 1988.

Ross, Steven S. *Construction Disasters: Design Failures, Causes, and Prevention*. New York: McGraw-Hill, 1984.

Sontag, Susan, ed. *A Barthes Reader*. New York: Hill and Wang, 1982.

Ullmann, John, and Honeyman, Steve, eds. *The Reporter's Handbook*. New York: St. Martin's Press, 1983.

Wain, John. *Samuel Johnson: A Biography*. New York: Viking Press, 1974.

White, Alan. *Truth*. New York: Anchor/Doubleday, 1970.

Wosik, John F. *The Electronic Business Information Sourcebook*. New York: John F. Wiley and Sons, 1987.

JOURNAL ARTICLES

Alexander, Bruce K.; Beyerstein, Barry L.; and Hadaway, Patricia F. "Effect of Early and Later Colony Housing on Oral Ingestion of Morphine in Rats." *Pharmacology and Biochemical Behavior* 154 (October 1981): 571-6.

Ambrosio, Joanne. "It's in the Journal. But This Is Reporting?" *Columbia Journalism Review* 2:2 (March 1980): 34.

Baily, Charles W. "A Century of Media Critics." *Washington Journalism Review* 11:7 (September 1989): 46.

Baird, Cathleen H. "Computerized Libraries Aid Newsrooms." *Presstime* 11:12 (December 1989): 28.

Bancroft, Raymond L. "The Demographic Beat." *American Demographics* (November 1982): 30.

Bennett, James R. "Newspaper Reporting of U.S. Business Crime in 1980." *Newspaper Research Journal* 3:1 (October 1981), 45-53.

Bennett, Richard. "Morphine Titration in Postoperative Laparotomy Patients using Patient-Controlled Analgesia." *Current Therapeutic Research* 32:1 (July 1982): 45-51.

Cole, R.D. "Negro Image in the Mass Media: A Case Study in Social Change." *Journalism Quarterly* 45 (1968): 55-60.

Cranberg, Gilbert. "A Flimsy Story and a Compliant Press." *Washington Journalism Review* 12:2 (March 1990): 48.

Daniel, Clifford, and Kristol, Irving. "The Times: An Exchange." *The Public Interest* 7 (Spring 1967): 119-23.

Donohue, L. "Newspaper Gate-Keepers and Forces in the News Channel." *Public Opinion Quarterly* 31 (1967): 61-68.

Eichorn, J.H. et al. "Standards for Patient Monitoring During Anesthesia at Harvard Medical School." *Journal of the American Medical Association* 256 (1986): 1017-20.

Endres, Fredric F. "Daily Newspaper Utilization of Computer Data Bases," *Newspaper Research Journal* 7:1 (Fall 1985): 29-34.

Feinstein, Richard Jay. Special Report. *The New England Journal of Medicine* 312:12 (March 21, 1985), 803-04.

Genovese, Margaret. "Sun-Times Gets Scoops at Press of Some Buttons." *Presstime* 3:3 (August 1981): 25-6.

Giordano, Al. "The War on Drugs: Who Drafted the Press?" *Washington Journalism Review* 12:1 (January 1990): 23.

Hadaway, Patricia F.; Alexander, Bruce K.; Coambs, R.B.; and Beyerstein, Barry L. "The Effect of Housing and Gender on Preference for Morphine-Sucrose Solutions in Rats." *Psychopharmacology* 66:1 (1979): 87-91.

Hadaway, Patricia F. and Alexander, Bruce F. "Rat Park Chronicle." *B.C. Medical Journal* 22:2 (February 1980): 54-56.

Hansen, Kathleen A.; Ward, Jean; and McLeod, Douglas M. "Role of the Newspaper Library in the Production of News." *Journalism Quarterly* 64:4 (1987): 717.

Haswell, Ken. "Extend Your Reach Electronically." *Quill* 76:2 (February 1988): 40.

Heeter, Carrie; Brown, Natalie; Soffin, Stan; Stanley, Cynthia; and Salwenet, Michael. "Agenda-Setting by Electronic Text News." *Journalism Research* (Summer 1989): 714-18.

Indra, Doreen M. "South Asian Stereotypes in the Vancouver Press." *Ethnic and Racial Studies* 2:2 (April 1979).

Ippolito, Andrew. "Databases in Newspaper Libraries." *Editor and Publisher*, 118:19 (May 11, 1985): 60-62e.

Jacobson, Thomas and Ullmann, John. "Commercial Databases and Reporting: Opinions of Newspaper Journalists and Librarians." *Newspaper Research Journal* 10:2 (Winter 1989): 16.

Judd, Robert P. "The Newspaper Reporter in a Suburban City." *Journalism Quarterly* 38 (Winter 1961): 38.

Kandel, D.B. and Raveis, V.H. "Cessation of Illicit Drug Use in Young Adulthood." *Archives of General Psychiatry* 46:2 (February 1989): 109-116.

Kerr, John and Niebauer, Walter E., Jr. "Use of Full Text, Database Retrieval Systems by Editorial Page Writers." *Newspaper Research Journal* 8:3 (Spring 1987): 21-31.

———— "A Baseline Study of the Use of Outsize Databases, Full Text Retrieval Systems by Newspaper Editorial Page Writers." Newspaper Division, Association for

Education in Journalism and Mass Communication, Norman, Oklahoma, ERIC no. Ed- 27765 (August 1986).

Leff, Mark S. "Phoning for Facts Doesn't Have to Mean Dialing for Dollars." *Quill* 78:2 (March 1990): 38-40.

Levin, Kurt. "Frontiers in Group Dynamics II." *Human Relations* 1 (1947): 143-53.

Martin, William P. and Singletary, Michael W. "Newspaper Treatment of State Government Releases." *Journalism Quarterly* 58 (Spring 1981): 93.

McCombs, Maxwell E. and Shaw, Donald L. "The Agenda Setting Function of the Mass Media." *Public Opinion Quarterly* 36 (1972): 177.

McMasters, Paul. "Government Information, at a Price." *Quill* 77:9 (October 1989): 17.

McNichol, Tom. "Databases: Reeling in Scoops with High Tech."*Washington Journalism Review* 9:6 (July 1987): 28.

Miller, Tim. "Information, Please, and Fast." *Washington Journalism Review* 5:7 (September 1983): 51-53.

————— "The Database as Reportorial Resource." *Editor and Publisher* 117:17 (April 28, 1984): 70.

————— "Data Bases as a Source of Regional Information." *Editor and Publisher* 120:23 (June 6, 1987): 78.

————— "The Data-Base Revolution." *Columbia Journalism Review* 27:3 (September 1988): 35-38.

————— "Databases: Finding Your World in the Electronic Newspaper." *Editor and Publisher* 121:37 (September 10, 1988): 78.

Nevas, Steve. "Coming Soon to a Screen Near You: The U.S. Supreme Court." *Quill* 78:2 (March 1990): 24-26.

Rambo, David C. "Database Searches."*Presstime* 9:3 (March 1987): 10.

Raveis, V.H. and Kanel, D.B. "Changes in Drug Behavior from the Middle to the Late Twenties: Initiation, Persistence, and Cessation of Use."*American Journal of Public Health* 77:5 (May 1987): 607-611.

Robins, Lee N. and Helzer, John E. "Drug Use Among Vietnam Veterans—Three Years Later." *Health World News* (October 27, 1975): 44-49.

Robinson, Clarence A., Jr. "U.S. Says Soviets Knew Korean Airlines 747 Was Commercial Flight." *Aviation Week and Space Technology* (September 19, 1983): 20.

Robinson, Michel J. and Ornstein, Norman J. "Why Press Credibility is Going Down (And What to Do About It)." *Washington Journalism Review* 12:1 (January 1990): 34.

Salmon, Charles T. "God Understands When the Cause is Noble." *Gannett Center Journal* 4:2 (Spring 1990): 22-34.

Scanlon, T. Joseph and Alldred, Suzanne. "Media Coverage of Disasters: The Same Old Story." *Emergency Planning Digest* (October 1982): 13-19.

Siglman, Lee. "Reporting the News: An Organizational Analysis." *American Journal of Sociology* 79:1 (July 1973): 133.

Soffin, Stan et al. "Online Databases and Newspapers: An Assessment of Utilization and Attitudes." Association for Education in Journalism and Mass Communication, San Antonio, Texas, ERIC no. ED-286178, August 1987.

Todd, Rusty. "Research: Media Watchers Gag Reporters." *IRE Journal* (Summer 1982): 6.

Toggerson, Steve K. "Media Coverage and Information-Seeking Behavior." *Journalism Quarterly* 58 (Spring 1981): 89.

Ward, Jean and Hansen, Kathleen A. "Commentary: Information Age Methods in a New Reporting Model." *Newspaper Research Journal* 7:3 (1986): 54

Whicher, C., and Ream, A. K. et al. "Anesthetic Mishaps and the Cost of Monitoring: A Proposed Standard for Monitoring Equipment." *Journal of Clinical Monitoring* 4 (January 1988): 15.

White, David M. "'The Gate-Keeper': A Case Study in the Selection of News." *Journalism Quarterly* 27 (1950): 383-90.

Wicklein, John, ed. *Public Broadcasting: A National Asset to Be Preserved, Promoted and Protected.* Ohio State University School of Journalism, Columbus, Ohio: Working Group for Public Broadcasting (Dec. 1988).

NEWSPAPERS AND POPULAR MAGAZINES

Alter, Jonathan. "The Art of the Profile." *Newsweek* (January 22, 1990): 54.

Alter, Jonathan and Star, Mark. "Race and Hype in a Divided City." *Newsweek* (January 22, 1990): 21-22.

Borrell, Jerry. "Is Your Computer Killing You?" *MacWorld* (July 1990): 23.

Bowen, Charles. "Forum Growth Creates Information Mecca." *Online Today* 8:7 (July 1989): 20.

Brinkley, Joel. "28,000 'Doctors' are Feared Unfit." *New York Times* (May 5 1986): 15.

Brodeur, Paul. "Annals of Radiation, The Hazards of Electronic Fields." *New Yorker* (June 12-29,1989).

———"The Magnetic-Field Menace." *MacWorld* (July 1990): 136.

Burth, Deborah. "Advertising and Marketing Pitches." *Dowline* (Summer 1989): 28-29

Cardinale, Anthony. "Mother Warns Not to Trust Officials on Dioxin." *Buffalo News* (April 26, 1990): A14.

Clark, Catherine. "CBC Evening News Report." Vancouver, B.C. (March 12, 1990).

Corn, David. "Fear and Obstruction on the K.A.L. Trail." *The Nation* 241 (August 17, 1985): 110-12.

Conroy, Cathryn. "News You Can Choose: Nonstop Global Coverage Delivered Online." *Online Today* 8:1 (January 1989): 16-21.

———This Is Not Your Father's Encyclopedia." *CompuServe Magazine* (January 1990): 56.

Cutler, B. J. "TV Drug-War Series Was Foreign Policy Disaster." *Honolulu Star-Bulletin* (January 23, 1990): B3.

Didion, Joan. "Letter from Los Angeles." *New Yorker* (February 26, 1990): 96.

Edell, Dean. "Doctors and Drugs." (Vancouver) *Province* (August 13, 1987).

Franken, Harry. "Suit in Coma Case Settled." *Columbus Dispatch* (September 19, 1987): 1B.

Glass, Andrew J. "Why Drug Crisis is Spinning Out of Control." *Honolulu Star-Bulletin* (March 10, 1988).

Greenfield, Jeff. "'Pack Journalism': Horde Copy." *Nightline* (September 27, 1989).

Greenfield, Meg. "I Didn't Tell You So." *Newsweek* (November 27, 1989): 104.

Grindlay, Lora. "Leukemia Study to Involve B.C. Kids." *Province* (June 26, 1990): 5.

Henry, William A., III, "The Right to Fake Quotes." *Time* (August 21, 1989): 49.

Higgins, Linda C. "Worry Over Power Lines Surges." *Medical World News* 30:17 (September 11, 1989): 22-24.

Horwood, Holly "Fatal Slip Unnoticed." *Province* (February 11, 1986): 4.

Hume, Mark. "Dead Man's Kin Urges Action Against Dentist." (Vancouver) *Sun* (March 25, 1986): A1.

Jorgensen, Bud. "A Company Should Be a Credit to Its Rating." *Globe and Mail* (November 9, 1990): B9.

Kim, Junu B. "How Dangerous is Electromagnetic Radiation?" *Bestways* 17:6 (June 1989): 13-15.

Koch, Tom. "The Right Track?" *Honolulu Magazine* (March 1988): 122.

Lapham, Lewis P. "A Political Opiate." *Harper's* (December 1989): 43-47.

Larson, Erik. "A New Science Can Diagnose Sick Buildings—Before They Collapse." *Smithsonian* (May 1988): 116-29.

Lerner, Michael A. "The Fire of 'Ice'." *Newsweek* (November 27, 1989): 37.

McQuade, Walter. "Why All Those Buildings Are Collapsing." *Fortune* (November 19, 1979).

Margulius, David L. "Your Right to What Uncle Sam Knows." *PC/Computing* (October 1989): 79-85.

Markoff, John. "Fast Modems: All Dressed Up, With Only a Slow Way to Go." *New York Times* (February 25, 1990): F10.

Masnerus, L. and Roberts, K. "AMA Takes On Inept Doctors." *New York Times* (July 6, 1986): E7.

Mayer, Jane. "Street Urchins: In the War on Drugs, Toughest Foe May Be The Alienated Youth." *Wall Street Journal* (September 18, 1989): 1.

Miller, Mark Crispin. "TV's Anti-Liberal Bias." *New York Times* (November 17, 1988).

Mittelstaedt, Martin. "Is It Really All the News That's Fit to Print?" *Globe and Mail* (October 8, 1988): D3.

Pearson, David. "007: What the U.S. Knew and When We Knew It." *The Nation* 239 (August 18, 1984): 105-24.

——— "007: Questions that Won't Go Away." *The Nation* 245 (September. 5, 1987): 181-87.

Pearson, David and Keppel, John. "New Pieces in the Puzzle of Flight 007: Journey into Doubt." *The Nation* 241 (August 17, 1985): 104-09.

Schmidt, Susan. "Review of Complaint Delayed Despite Court Request." *Washington Post* (January 12, 1988): 17.

Schulman, Susan. "Ex-Manager Says Plant Dumped PCBs at Site." *Buffalo News* (April 26, 1990): A1.

Simon, Roger. "Simon Says Ad-Pulling Is a Form of Censorship." *Ka Leo O Hawai'i* (September 20, 1989): 4.

Shear, Jeff. "Knight Ridder's Data Base Blitz." *Insight* (October 31, 1988): 44-45.

Sherman, Stratford P. "Smart Ways To Handle the Press." *Fortune* (June 19, 1989): 69.

Trivette, Donald B. "What's Different About DowQuest?" *Dowline* (Summer 1989): 20-26.

Vine, David. "Banks Use News/Retrieval—and Often Profit." *Dowline* (Summer, 1988): 18-20.

Waldholz, Michael. "Malpractice Liability: Can the Law Serve Both Doctors and Patients?" *Wall Street Journal* (April 4, 1986): 23.

Willmann, Donna S. "VuText's Online Databases Aid in Pulitzer Prize-Winning Coverage." Vu/Text Information Services Press Release (June 3, 1987).

UNSIGNED ARTICLES

"American Notes: Commending The Vincennes." *Time* (May 7, 1990): 37.

"Aviation Writer Scores Scoop by Using On-Line Data Base." *National Association of Science Writers* (Summer 1988).

"Court Allows $250,000 Limit For Pain, Suffering: Ceiling on Malpractice Award Upheld." *Los Angeles Times* (November 30, 1987): 2.

"Death Sets Off Alarm." *Province* (February 3, 1987): 9.

"Drugs Thwart Justice, Lawyers Find." *Columbus Dispatch* (December 1, 1988).

"Electric Furnace Dust Is Still a Problem." *American Metal Market* (September 19, 1988): 15a.

"Jury Awards Man $28 M in HHC Suit." *Newsday* (May 13, 1988).

"Move to Save Lives in Operating Room: Researchers Urge Anesthesia Standards." *Sacramento Bee* (August 22, 1986): A24.

"Poverty/Drugs Factor Ignored, Jackson Says." *Honolulu Star-Bulletin* (September 16, 1988): C1.

"Protopappas Loses Bid for Hearing in Multiple Murders." *Los Angeles Times* (July 21, 1988): 3.

"Raymie Zahn, Coma Victim Dies." (Florida) *News Sun Sentinel* (January 4, 1987).

"Re-Examining the 36-Hour Day." *Time* (August 31, 1987): 54.

"Report Sees Greater Nurses' Shortage." *Buffalo News* (May 18, 1990): A4.

"Three Lawsuits in 5 Years Result in Investigation of Texas Physicians." *Houston Post* (May 15, 1988): 1B.

"Unite and Conquer." *Newsweek* (February. 5, 1990): 50-55.

"US Turns Screw On Hazmat." *Chemical Marketing Reporter* (August 15, 1988): 749.

"Woman Sues after Son Dies during Surgery" *Lexington Herald-Leader* (July 13, 1987): B1.

Index

About the Author

TOM KOCH is a writer, journalist, and information consultant. He is the author of *The News as Myth* (Greenwood Press, 1990), *Six Islands on Two Wheels,* and *Mirrored Lives* (Praeger, 1990).